LECTURES ON THE MATHEMATICAL METHOD
IN ANALYTICAL ECONOMICS

Mathematics and its Applications

A Series of Monographs and Texts Edited by
Jacob T. Schwartz, Institute of Mathematical Sciences,
New York University

Volume 1

Jacob T. Schwartz, LECTURES ON THE MATHEMATICAL METHOD IN ANALYTICAL ECONOMICS

Additional volumes in preparation

Lectures on the Mathematical Method in Analytical Economics

By JACOB T. SCHWARTZ
Institute of Mathematical Sciences
New York University

G|
|B

GORDON AND BREACH
SCIENCE PUBLISHERS · NEW YORK

To My Father

Preface

Mathematical economics has made immense technical progress in the last twenty years. Unfortunately, it has to a too large extent remained isolated within the larger historical context of economic debate, somehow ignoring rather than clarifying the great issues around which this debate has raged; like a delicate precision clockwork which the economist admires, as in a jeweler's window, before setting back to serious work with pick and shovel. For this reason I have tried, in the lectures from which the present volume is taken, to direct attention particularly to these issues, and have attempted to put economics in the foreground and mathematics together with mathematical rigor in the background—although, alas, mathematics in doing its good services has a way of calling attention to itself. Where perfect generality has meant relative vagueness of results, while reasonable assumptions have led to suggestive conclusions, I have, in consequence, preferred to make rather than to omit these assumptions.

Our treatment begins with the Leontief input-output model, which develops as a general framework for all that is to follow. After an introductory treatment of price theory in the Leontief model, we pass to a consideration of business-cycle theory, following the ideas pioneered by Lloyd Metzler and attempting their extension. This, in turn, leads us into the realm of notions associated with the name of Keynes; the "input-output" path along which we approach these ideas emphasizes, besides their dynamic foundations, the fact that they are less necessarily purely aggregative than is commonly suggested. Finally, we turn what we have learned into a critique of the "general equilibrium" approach which Walras built up as the final form of the theory of supply and demand, attempting to bring the notions of Walras and the notions of Keynes to an unbiased confrontation. With this we conclude.

He who reads the preface of a mathematical work is apt to have in mind the troublesome question of mathematical prerequisites to the reading of the text. These are as follows. "Matrices and vectors" is a subject which is more and more a standard elementary tool for the economist. The reader of the present work is expected to be familiar with the basic theory of matrices and linear transformations as it is set forth in Finkbeiner's *Introduction to Matrices and Linear Transformations* (Freeman, 1960), in Halmos' *Finite Dimensional Vector Spaces* (Van Nostrand, 1958), in Appendix A to the first volume of Karlin's *Mathematical Methods and Theory in Games, Programming, and Economics* (Addison-Wesley, 1959) or, for that matter, in any one of a number of quite satisfactory recent texts on this subject. A reasonable working knowledge of elementary calculus is also assumed. From time to time we use some more abstruse mathematical theorem; perhaps a fixed point theorem, perhaps some other. In these cases, a careful statement of the theorem, and a reference to its proof, will be given.

In order to keep our feet on the ground, we have made frequent reference to statistical and empirical data, intending that the approximate size of the quantities which our theoretical analysis reveals as significant should be estimated. The econometrically oriented economist is apt to be horrified by our rude reductions of his careful and accurate econometric headings. I wish to plead three circumstances in extenuation of the statistical sins which are to be committed in what follows. In the first place, as has already been said, only approximate estimates are aimed at. In the second, the empirically evolved headings in econometric tables and time-series are rarely exactly those of which our theoretical analysis makes us wish to be informed, so that a process of interpolation and surmise is inevitable in any case. Desiring rough estimates, we have carried through this process of estimation and surmise ruthlessly. Finally, in view of the two reasons already given, it seemed less reasonable to hunt at length through a vast and often uncertain statistical literature for data that might improve our accuracy, than to rest content with less accurate estimates made from readily available data.

I have tried in the final exposition to preserve the somewhat colloquial style of a lecture series, rather than transforming this into the cold polish of ordinary scientific exposition.

I should like to thank Mr. A. C. Williams of the research division of the Socony-Mobil Oil Company for his patient and deeply thoughtful work in elaborating the lecture notes from which the present work has developed, and Dr. John Muth of the Carnegie Institute of Technology and Mr. Arnold Faden of Columbia University for their very instructive suggestions and criticisms. The errors that remain in the present work are, of course, my own invention. I should like to thank Mr. Ralph Knopf for assistance with proof-reading, and Miss Ursula Burger for her quite exceptional intelligence, speed, and devotion in typing the manuscript. Acknowledgment is also made to the authors and publishers of the works cited: to the Yale University Press for permission to quote from L. Von Mises' *Human Action;* to the D. Van Nostrand Company for permission to quote Henry Hazlitt's *The Failure of the New Economics;* to Ruth Mack and the National Bureau of Economic Research for permission to quote Miss Mack's *Consumption and Business Fluctuations;* to Harcourt, Brace & World, Inc. for permission to quote J. M. Keynes' *General Theory of Employment, Interest, and Money;* and to the *Encyclopædia Britannica* for permission to quote remarks of Prof. F. H. Knight. Finally, I should like to thank the Alfred P. Sloan Foundation for its support during the period in which this book was written.

JACOB T. SCHWARTZ

Paris, August 1961

Contents

The Leontief Model and the
Technological Basis of Production

Introduction and Outline

1. What Will and What Will Not Be Treated.

Mathematical economics currently includes, and perhaps is even dominated by, a number of branches with which we will have little to do. Thus, in order to define the subject of the present lectures, it is well to say something about these excluded branches. One topic that we shall not discuss to any great length is the subject that might be called *efficiency economics* in general, and is often called by the several names of its principal techniques—*linear programming, operations research*, perhaps also *theory of games*. In these subjects, the aim is to find the optimal adjustment, in one or another sense, to a given situation; they refer with greatest cogency and success to the profit-making possibilities of a single firm. As an omnibus reference to this area of thought let me cite Vajda's *Linear Programming and the Theory of Games*, and also von Neumann and Morgenstern's sparkling *Theory of Games and Economic Behavior*. Nor will we deal with *econometrics*, i.e. applied and theoretical economic statistics, except incidentally. Instead, we shall take economics as the cognitive study of a given object, the economy, and ask in the sense of natural science: what is this object like, how does it behave, and why? For this reason, we find the term *analytical* prefacing *economics* in our title. In spirit, our economics will be theoretical or speculative rather than directly empirical, and thus close in its basic approach to what has been called classical economics. In form, however, we will be more systematically mathematical. The branch of mathematics of which we will make greatest use will be the theory of matrices; let me here make reference to D. T. Finkbeiner's *Intro-*

3

duction to Matrices and Linear Transformations, to Paul Halmos'
Finite Dimensional Vector Spaces, Gantmacher's *Theory of Matrices,*
and note the existence of numerous other introductory works on this
subject. From time to time we will use a bit of calculus.

We will begin with a discussion of the theory of equilibrium prices—
what has been traditionally called value theory—and go on to a
discussion of business cycle theory, beginning with a model like that
introduced by Lloyd Metzler, and developing the connection between this cycle theory and the equilibrium analysis that is more
commonly called Keynesian. In the economic literature let me cite,
in the first place, the famous *General Theory* of Keynes, which, as a
pioneering work of science, is worth studying in spite of its numerous
pedagogical and even theoretical mare's nests. A stimulating com-
panion volume for the admirer of Keynes is Henry Hazlitt's *The
Failure of the New Economics. An Analysis of the Keynesian Falla-
cies.* A superior mathematical exposition of the Keynesian theories is K. Kurihara's *Introduction to Keynesian Dynamics;* another,
particularly fine, work of a similar sort is H. J. Brems's *Output,
Employment, Investment.* Much of what we have to say will make
reference to the "input-output" model of W. Leontief, on which there
exists a vast literature. A good sample of this literature, full of
references, is *Activity Analysis of Production and Allocation,* T. C.
Koopmans, ed. Our attempts to compare speculative results with
economic reality will be enormously facilitated by the extensive and
painstaking work of the *National Bureau of Economic Research,*
published in the form of a great many separate studies. A very fresh
and stimulating empirical account of business cycles is the easily
available *Business Cycles and their Causes* by W. C. Mitchell.

2. A Bouquet of Warnings

Mathematics may perhaps have a valuable role to play in economics—but its application brings several dangers. Mathematics
necessarily works with exact models. In the course of investigating
such a model, it is easy to forget that the mathematical exactness of
one's reasoning has nothing to do with the exactness with which the
model reflects economic reality. For this reason, a few dampening
admonitions are in order. I quote the first and most severe from
Ludwig von Mises' *Human Action:*

The problems of prices and costs have been treated also with mathematical methods. There have even been economists who held that the only appropriate method of dealing with economic problems is the mathematical method and who derided the logical economists as "literary" economists.

If this antagonism between the logical and the mathematical economists were merely a disagreement concerning the most adequate procedure to be applied in the study of economics, it would be superfluous to pay attention to it. The better method would prove its preeminence by bringing about better results. It may also be that different varieties of procedure are necessary for the solution of different problems and that for some of them one method is more useful than the other.

However, this is not a dispute about heuristic questions, but a controversy concerning the foundations of economics. The mathematical method must be rejected not only on account of its barrenness. It is an entirely vicious method, starting from false assumptions and leading to fallacious inferences. Its syllogisms are not only sterile; they divert the mind from the study of the real problems and distort the relations between the various phenomena.

The deliberations which result in the formulation of an equation are necessarily of a nonmathematical character. The formulation of the equation is the consummation of our knowledge; it does not directly enlarge our knowledge. Yet, in mechanics the equation can render very important practical services. As there exist constant relations between various mechanical elements and as these relations can be ascertained by experiments, it becomes possible to use equations for the solution of definite technological problems. Our modern industrial civilization is mainly an accomplishment of this utilization of the differential equations of physics. No such constant relations exist, however, between economic elements. The equations formulated by mathematical economics remain a useless piece of mental gynnastics and would remain so even if they were to express much more than they really do.

A corresponding sentiment is voiced by Keynes in his *General Theory*:

It is a great fault of symbolic pseudo-mathematical methods of formalizing a system of economic analysis, such as we shall set down in section VI of this chapter, that they expressly assume strict independence between the factors involved and lose all their cogency and authority if this hypothesis is disallowed; whereas, in ordinary discourse, where we are not blindly manipulating but know all the time what we are doing and what the words mean, we can keep "at the back of our heads" the necessary reserves and qualifications and the adjustments which we shall have to make later on, in a way in which we cannot keep complicated partial differentials "at the back" of several pages of algebra which assume that they all vanish. Too large a proportion of recent "mathematical" economics are mere concoctions, as imprecise as the initial assumptions they rest on, which allow the author to lose sight of the complexities and interdependencies of the real world in a maze of pretentions and unhelpful symbols.

A more optimistic if still cautious opinion is stated by Professor F. H. Knight in the 1954 *Britannica*.

Any brief statement of principles is bound to make economic theories appear thinner and more remote from the concrete facts of economic life than they are. There is a place and a need for all degrees of generality. In recent decades this need has found increasing expression in the developing and spreading study of mathematical economics, in which exposition is made accurate and compact by the use of graphs and of algebraic formulae.

Only by the use of mathematics is it possible to bring together into a single comprehensible picture the variety, the complexity, and most of all the interdependence of the numerous factors which determine prices, costs, output and demand and the wages or hire of productive agents. . . . The principal value of such elaborate and abstract systems lies in forcibly reminding the enquirer that a change in practically any economic variable has direct or indirect effects on innumerable other magnitudes, and so preventing him from fatally oversimplifying conceptions of economic cause and effect. . . .

The more theoretical parts of economics cannot be taken to be a complete and adequate account of the mechanism of modern economic life. They afford serviceable approximations to partial, but important aspects of the truth.

The most striking and possibly the most important characteristic of recent work in economics, as contrasted with the older, is its greater realism. It does not attempt to do without abstract conceptions, but it does attempt to take these from the world of affairs, or bring them into line with facts.

Hoping to approach Professor Knight's high goal, we may begin our investigations.

3. Introduction of a Model (Single Labor Sector)

By an economy we shall mean a complex of activities in which various commodities are produced and subsequently either consumed or utilized in the production of further commodities. If the economy absorbs commodities from outside itself, or if it supplies commodities to the outside, it is called *open*. On the other hand, if the economy is completely self-contained it is called *closed*. We wish to describe a model of an economy. Our model will in the first instance be open, in that labor must be supplied to the system by a "household sector" and products must be supplied to the household sector by the system. The model will then be "closed" by introducing labor as an additional commodity which is "used up" in the production of various other commodities, and for the production of which these various other commodities are required.

After formulating our model, we shall first indicate the manner in which it gives rise to a simple but interesting theory of prices; next give a brief discussion of the extent to which the model is a faithful reflection of the real economy; and subsequently pass to an extended mathematical analysis of the model, and to an investigation of the question of what additional and useful relationships among the various parameters of an economy can be elucidated by using the model.

We begin by establishing, in some definite but entirely arbitrary way, a certain standard physical unit for each commodity, as, e.g. 1 car, 1 ton of coal, 1 bushel of wheat, etc., hereinafter called one unit of the commodity. The process of production of any commodity requires appropriate amounts both of *circulating* and of *fixed capital*. Thus, for instance, to produce one ton of pig iron it is required, in the first place, that certain amounts of coal—say, half a ton, and certain amounts of iron ore—say, one and a half tons, be used up; but, in addition it is required that a blast furnace be tied up, for a certain period, say for half a day. The blast furnace is *tied up* but not *used up*, and hence reckons only as fixed, but not as circulating capital.

These two aspects of production will be described in our general model as follows. Let the economy involve a total of n commodities, i.e. let $C_1, \cdots, C_n$ be a total list of the commodities produced in an economy; cars, cigarettes, typewriters, etc. To produce one unit of any given commodity C_i, it is (technologically) required that various amounts π_{ij} of other commodities C_j be used up; in addition, it is (technologically) required that ϕ_{ij} units of C_j be tied up (and thus not available for the manufacture of some other product) for a standard production period, say one day, even though these ϕ_{ij} units of C_j are not necessarily used up. Note that if the standard unit of C_1 is, say, a bushel, and that of C_2 is, say, one ton, π_{12} has the dimensions tons per bushel, and ϕ_{12} the dimensions ton-days per bushel.

ϕ_{ij} is said to be the amount of C_j *utilized* in the production of one unit of C_i, while π_{ij} is said to be the amount of C_j *consumed* in the production of one unit of C_i. When a commodity is *consumed* it is also *utilized* and therefore we shall assume

(1.1)   If $\pi_{ij} > 0$ then $\phi_{ij} > 0$ $i,j = 1, \cdots, n$.

The model as we have thus far defined it is called the *open Leontief model;* the matrix π_{ij} is often called the *input-output matrix*, and analysis of such a model is often called *input-output analysis*. The matrix ϕ_{ij} may be called the *fixed capital matrix*. It is clear upon a moment's reflection that this open model, as it has been defined, permits us to deduce, from a given "final demand" for a certain "bill of goods," what inputs are required; and thus, for instance, by considering the desired output of military goods in a wartime situation, to predict where "bottle-necks" are apt to develop. This sort of application has often been stressed; reference may be made to the work *Activity Analysis of Production and Allocation* cited above. Matrices π_{ij} for the American economy divided into fifty and into two hundred sectors have been computed by the Bureau of Labor Statistics. Our interest, however, will not be in this direct sort of "bottleneck analysis," but in the use of the input-output model as a framework for more abstract economic analysis. For this reason, we proceed at once to a description of a corresponding closed model.

To close our model, we must introduce labor as an input and as an output. Let π_{jo} denote the amount of labor (measured say, in man-hours) required for the production of C_j, and let π_{oj} be the amount of C_j which is "consumed in order to produce a man-hour of labor," i.e., the average real wages paid out per hour of labor. By the introduction of these matrix elements the model economy is rendered closed, i.e. the set of commodities produced is the same as the set of commodities utilized in production.

In our simple linear economic model (often called the closed Leontief model) we may readily set up a theory of prices. Let $p_0, p_1, \cdots, p_n$ be the prices of the various products produced; then $p_0, p_1, \cdots, p_n$ are also the prices of the commodities utilized and/or consumed in production.

We formulate the conditions that must be satisfied by the p_i.

The price of a commodity C_i is made up of the sum of two terms.

The first is the sum of the values of all of the products consumed in the manufacture of C_i, i.e.

$$(1.2) \qquad \sum_{j=0}^{n} \pi_{ij} p_j.$$

The second is the "return to capital," "markup," or "profit" proportional to the sum of the values of the products which are utilized but not necessarily consumed in the manufacture of C_i, i.e.

$$(1.3) \qquad \rho \sum_{j=0}^{n} \phi_{ij} p_j.$$

(We take $\phi_{io} = 0$).

We have here taken an essential step in assuming the rate of profit, ρ, to be the same for all types of production. This corresponds to the ordinary assumption, in the theory of prices, of "free competition"; it can be justified in the usual way by arguing that a situation in which the production of different commodities yields different rates of profit cannot be stable, since investments would be made only in the industry yielding the highest rate of profit to the exclusion of other commodities yielding lower rates of profit. Long-term equilibrium, of which our simple theory is alone descriptive, would be reached only when all such rates of profit became equal. The proportionality constant ρ has the dimensions per cent per day (or year).

Forming the price of C_i additively out of the two expressions (1.2) and (1.3), we have the set of equations

$$(1.4) \qquad p_i = \sum_{j=0}^{n} \pi_{ij} p_j + \rho \sum_{j=0}^{n} \phi_{ij} p_j, \quad i = 1, \cdots, n.$$

Thus far we have only an "open" system of equations for the prices p_i. We can obtain a closed system by recalling that π_{oj} denotes the collection of commodities which form real wages for an hour's labor; thus the price p_0 of an hour's labor must be given by the equation

$$(1.5) \qquad p_0 = \sum_{i=0}^{n} \pi_{oi} p_i.$$

If we introduce additional matrix elements ϕ_{oj} by putting $\phi_{oj} = 0$, we may write (1.5) in the same form as the equation (1.4), and hence may write (1.5) and (1.4) together in the simple form

$$(1.6) \qquad p_i = \sum_{j=0}^{n} \pi_{ij} p_j + \rho \sum_{j=0}^{n} \phi_{ij} p_j, \quad i = 0, \cdots, n.$$

This set of $n+1$ equations is homogeneous in the $n+1$ variables p_j, but contains the additional unknown ρ. Thus, we would expect that the system (1.6) determines the quantity ρ and the set of n ratios of the $n+1$ quantities p_i. We will show in the next lecture that this is rigorously correct. Before going over to the necessary detailed and general mathematical investigation, however, let us examine some simple transformations and special cases of the system (1.6).

In the first place, we may make use of the particularly simple form of equation (1.5) to eliminate p_0 from the system (1.6). This gives

$$(1.7) \qquad p_i = \sum_{j=1}^{n} [\pi_{ij} + (1 - \pi_{oo})^{-1} \pi_{io} \pi_{oj}] p_j + \rho \sum_{j=1}^{n} \phi_{ij} p_j, \quad i = 1, \cdots, n.$$

If we define a modified input-output and fixed capital matrix by

$$(1.8) \quad \tilde{\pi}_{ij} = \pi_{ij} + (1 - \pi_{oo})^{-1} \pi_{io} \pi_{oj}; \quad \tilde{\phi}_{ij} = \phi_{ij}, \quad i,j = 1, \cdots, n,$$

the system (1.7) takes on the form

$$(1.9) \qquad p_i = \sum_{j=1}^{n} \tilde{\pi}_{ij} p_j + \rho \sum_{j=1}^{n} \tilde{\phi}_{ij} p_j,$$

i.e. takes on a form exactly analogous to that of the system (1.6) but with the price p_0 eliminated. The system (1.9) may in consequence be called the *labor-eliminated* form of our price equations, and the matrices $\tilde{\pi}_{ij}$ and $\tilde{\phi}_{ij}$ the *labor-eliminated input-output matrix* and the *labor-eliminated fixed capital matrix* respectively. The transformation which leads from (1.6) to (1.9) may be given the following heuristic interpretation. If each time labor appears as an input in production we replace this input by the corresponding real wage bill, we come to a hypothetical situation in which the only inputs required for the production of commodities are other (non-labor) commodities. Thus we may, if it is convenient for one or another theoretical purpose, consider our model to refer to a self-enclosed world of material commodities, produced out of each other with no additional input. We will make use of this modified description of our model economy (which is, of course, entirely equivalent to our initial description) at a number of points in what follows.

It is instructive to study the system (1.9) in its most trivial special case, the case $n = 1$, i.e. the case in which there is only one commodity. If there is but one commodity equations (1.9) become

$$(1.10) \qquad\qquad p = \tilde{\pi}_{,,} p + \rho \tilde{\phi}_{,,} p$$

with the solution

$$(1.11) \qquad\qquad \rho = (1 - \tilde{\pi}_{,,})/\tilde{\phi}_{,,}.$$

The "price" in this case has, of course, no significance, since our theory is one of relative prices, i.e. price ratios, only, the "absolute price level" being meaningless in a theory like the one before us. The rate of profit, however, is given by (1.11). The most significant observation we can make about this equation is that *the rate of profit, ρ, is positive if and only if $\tilde{\pi}_{,,} < 1$*, i.e. if and only if we are able to produce one unit of commodity without consuming an equivalent or larger amount of commodity. It is clear that only in this case is production capable of yielding a physical surplus. The case $\tilde{\pi}_{,,} > 1$ describes an economy inevitably fated to extinction through starvation, and may be typified by the unenviable situation of an invalid on a desert island, who to gain strength to gather one coconut must eat two. It is clear that in such a situation any initial supply of commodity will diminish to zero as time progresses; this situation may then be described as a "starvation economy." The phenomenon which we meet here in its most primitive form can occur also for economies in which there are many commodities; the present paragraph may serve as forewarning of this fact.

Equation (1.11) also shows that ρ is inversely proportional to the amount of capital which must be tied up to produce a unit of the single commodity occurring in our model. Thus equation (1.11) shows that, in this simple case, the rate ρ of profit behaves in an entirely reasonable manner.

4. Critical Discussion of the Model

We have assumed a model in which all relationships are linear and homogeneous, that is, we have assumed "constant returns to scale."

Thus we have neglected all possible economies and diseconomies of scale, and have as well neglected the fact that significant pieces of equipment are not continuously divisible: one cannot build 0.78 of a blast furnace. The force of these objections, however, should be substantially diminished by the prevalence of mass-production, which, by taking systematic advantage of economies of scale, will tend to operate largely in the linear range of production. Many processes may still deviate to a considerable degree from linearity; even so, we remember that calculus tells us that more general functional relationships can often be represented by linear approximations, useful at least over small intervals.

A more substantial difficulty of the above sort arises in those situations in which production makes use of unique natural resources without duplicates; the circumstances in which *economic rents* arise. These resources might be mines, oil wells, agricultural land especially well adapted (as, e.g. by climate) for the production of one or another commodity, etc. These phenomena also are ignored by our model, which implicitly assumes that no producer can have a clear technological advantage over any other producer.

We have also assumed, in writing production coefficients π_{ij} and ϕ_{ij}, that both input and fixed capital costs can be assigned unambiguously to a given output; so that we neglect the common fact that many costs are joint costs rather than costs assignable to a particular output, and that many commodities are produced jointly, some being "by-products" of the production of others. Administrative and auxiliary costs, in particular, would fit only grudgingly into a model like the one before us. Generally speaking, our input-output model portrays the conditions of industrial production rather better than the economic circumstances either of the trade or the service sectors. Since industry amounts only to some 30% of total economic effort, we must be on guard against distortions which may arise from the overly "industrial" view of the economy as a whole which the use of a strict input-output model imposes on us.

We have, of course, neglected all indication of the role of taxes; something will be said on this score later on, however.

Our model is certainly not very explicit as to how transportation costs shall enter, though such costs can be fitted into our model by distinguishing as separate commodities the same physical object in different locations—"ingots f.o.b. mill," and "ingots delivered," and taking "trucking" or "rail transport" as an input required to transform "ingots f.o.b. mill" into "ingots delivered." The same remark might in principle apply to other categories of auxiliary costs, so that one might in principle distinguish between "ingots delivered" and "ingots checked, counted, and recorded," for instance.

A more serious objection is the following. Our model does not take into account the fact that the same commodity can very often be produced by any one of a number of schemes, each requiring the consumption and utilization as fixed capital of different amounts of the "input" commodities, or of the same commodities in differing proportions. On this score, we shall adopt the following point of view. The objective of "efficiency economics" (theory of games, linear programming, and the extensions of these doctrines) is that of determining, according to some given criterion, methods for selecting the "best" production plan, i.e. the plan best according to a criterion of profitability. The efficiency economists usually confine their attention to parts of an economy that are so small that the price structure of the total economy cannot sensibly be affected by the choice of the production scheme within the portion of the economy under study, and under such conditions, the choice of maximum profit under the existing (invariant) prices seems a reasonable one as the criterion for "best." The point of view taken here is that the production coefficients are to be thought of as those obtained by such "local" optimizations, which then becomes the "given" production coefficients in our model. This, of course, neglects the mutual interaction of the "local optimizations" through the price mechanism; nevertheless, we may hope that these neglected interactions cannot affect the general configuration of prices so severely as to introduce grave errors into our more approximate procedure. A more elaborate analysis of this point is reserved for a later lecture (cf. Lecture 17).

In assuming a homogeneous "labor" as input to all sorts of production we are, of course, ignoring the existence of a variety of distinct labor specialties and skills, convertible into each other only with some difficulty, and paid at different rates. We will see subsequently that by generalizing our model to include several labor sectors some of the force of this objection can be removed. A more serious objection along the same lines comes from our inclusion of the real wage bill as the row π_{oj} in the input matrix, as if input to labor was also technologically determined. In the first place, we have ignored the fact that different people will choose to spend their money in different ways. Some of the force of this objection may be met by remarking that the elements π_{oj} may be regarded as statistically average consumption indices. But what is more to the point, the total wage rate is determined not technologically but socially; thus, say, it is presumably possible technologically if not socially to reduce the American wage-rate to wage-rate which supports the urban population of China, i.e., by a factor of twenty. The elements π_{oj} cannot be regarded as technological inputs necessary for the minimal sustenance of labor, but as a socially determined "living wage." Machines will never quarrel with their employers about what inputs they require, but labor may! On the other hand, if the elements π_{oj} are taken to represent "household demand" for the various commodities C_j, their legitimacy as elements of an input-output matrix seems doubtful, since these demands depend upon price, income distribution, etc. We will unravel these difficulties as we go along; one method is to study price theory in an open rather than in a closed model. Neoclassical "Walrasian" economics has had something to say on this score; we shall examine its contributions when we come to study Walras' notion of general equilibrium.

The elements π_{io} are themselves dubious, if not as dubious as the elements π_{oj}. To know these necessary labor inputs we must distinguish the boundary between necessary labor input and "feather-bedding"; a boundary which is in continuing dispute. (At the moment these lines are written, a number of railroads are shut down in consequence of a dispute over the question of whether the operation of tugs requires a "float man" in addition to a "deck man.")

A number of criticisms may be directed against the manner in which a uniform rate ρ of profit has been introduced into our model. In the first place, the rate of profit is dependent on the rate of industrial turnover, and will rise, for example, if two shifts rather than one shift are worked with given capital equipment. Thus the number of days for which capital equipment must be tied up in the production of a given output is determined as much socially as technologically. In assuming a rate of profit invariant from industry to industry, and in basing this assumption on an argument involving considerations of long-term equilibrium, we are open to criticism on the grounds that the time required for an economy to come to equilibrium is not short compared with the effect of the perturbing factors, e.g. technological advances which affect the production coefficients π_{ij} and ϕ_{ij}, nor, for that matter, short relative to the apparent frequency of social disturbances and disasters.   Nor is the actual economy entirely free of monopoly!   But, before involving ourselves with any of these complications, let us study the mathematical features of the model at hand.

Basic Mathematics of the Input-Output Model

1. Some Mathematical Notations and Definitions

Capital letters, both Roman and Greek, will be used to denote matrices. Boldface letters will denote column vectors. The individual elements of a matrix A will be denoted by a_{ij}, while the individual elements of a vector $\mathbf{a}$ will be denoted by a_i. The transpose of a matrix will be denoted by a prime, i.e. $B = A'$ means $b_{ij} = a_{ji}$. A row vector will be written as the transpose of a column vector, i.e. $\mathbf{a}'$. The "scalar product" of a row vector $\mathbf{x}'$ by a column vector $\mathbf{y}$ is written $\mathbf{x}' \cdot \mathbf{y}$, by which is meant $\Sigma_i x_i y_i$. This same product may on occasion be written as $\mathbf{y} \cdot \mathbf{x}'$, or, where no confusion can arise, as $\mathbf{x}'\mathbf{y}$ or $\mathbf{y}\mathbf{x}'$. If A is a matrix, the scalar product of $\mathbf{x}'$ with the vector $A\mathbf{y}$ may be written $\mathbf{x}'A\mathbf{y}$, $\mathbf{x}' \cdot A\mathbf{y}$, or $\mathbf{x}'A \cdot \mathbf{y}$. If $\mathbf{a}$ and $\mathbf{b}$ are n-dimensional vectors with components a_i and b_i $(i = 1, \cdots, n)$, then

$\mathbf{a} = \mathbf{b}$ means $a_i = b_i$ $(i = 1, \cdots, n)$;

$\mathbf{a} \geqq \mathbf{b}$ means $a_i \geqq b_i$ $(i = 1, \cdots, n)$;

$\mathbf{a} \geq \mathbf{b}$ means $a_i \geqq b_i$ $(i = 1. \cdots, n)$ and for some component s, $a_s > b_s$;

$\mathbf{a} > \mathbf{b}$ means $a_i > b_i$ $(i = 1, \cdots, n)$.

For matrices A and B, the expressions $A = B$, $A \geqq B$, $A \geq B$, $A > B$, have the similar meanings $a_{ij} = b_{ij}$ (all i,j), $a_{ij} \geqq b_{ij}$ (all i,j), $a_{ij} \geqq b_{ij}$ (all i,j), and for some r,s $a_{rs} > b_{rs}$.

We note that, using this notation, $\mathbf{a} > \mathbf{b}$ implies $\mathbf{a} \geq \mathbf{b}$ implies

17

$\mathbf{a} \geq \mathbf{b}$ so that $\mathbf{a} \geq \mathbf{b}$ is the weakest statement. Also $\mathbf{a} \leq \mathbf{b}$ means $\mathbf{b} \geq \mathbf{a}$, etc.

A vector $\mathbf{a}$ such that $\mathbf{a} > 0$ will be called a *positive vector*, and the set of all n-dimensional positive vectors is called the *positive orthant*. A vector $\mathbf{a}$ such that $\mathbf{a} \geq 0$ will be called a semi-positive vector, and the set of all n-dimensional semi-positive vectors is called the *semi-positive orthant*. A vector $\mathbf{a}$ such that $\mathbf{a} \geq 0$ will be called a non-negative vector, and the set of all n-dimensional nonnegative vectors is called the *nonnegative orthant*.

Matrices A such that $A > 0$, $A \geq 0$, and $A \geq 0$ are called *positive*, *semi-positive* and *nonnegative* matrices respectively.

We will also make frequent use of a number of other standard mathematical terms and notations. The set of all elements (of a sort to be understood from context) having the properties P and Q, and belonging to a set S, will be written

$$\{x \mid x \, \epsilon \, S; \; x \text{ has property } P; \; x \text{ has property } Q\}.$$

A set S contained in Euclidean space will be called *closed* if it contains the limit of every convergent sequence of its own points; it will be called *convex* if the three statements $\mathbf{p} \, \epsilon \, S$, $\mathbf{q} \, \epsilon \, S$, $0 \leq t \leq 1$ imply that $t\mathbf{p} + (l - t)\mathbf{q} \, \epsilon \, S$, that is, if S contains the full line-segment between any two of its points. For a discussion of these notions the reader is referred to the work of Karlin cited in the Preface.

2. Theorems on Connected Nonnegative Matrices

Written in terms of vectors, equations (1.6) become

(2.1) $$\mathbf{p} = \Pi\mathbf{p} + \rho\Phi\mathbf{p}$$

where the matrices Π and Φ have the elements π_{ij} and ϕ_{ij} respectively, and have the properties

(2.2) $$\Pi \geq 0, \Phi \geq 0 \quad \text{respectively.}$$

We intend to show that, under suitable conditions on the matrices Π, Φ, equation (2.1) has a unique solution, $\mathbf{p}, \rho$. There is, however, a case in which this assertion is patently false, which must be excluded. Suppose that our economy E divides into two unconnected subeconomies E_1, and E_2, the commodities in E_1 never being used for the production of commodities in E_2, and vice versa. It is then clear that E_1 and E_2 may be totally unrelated, so that E_1 might have a certain natural rate of profit ρ_1, and E_2 a certain natural rate of profit ρ_2 which, by the assertion we wish to make, would both be unique. Then plainly the equation (2.1) for the whole economy E would have no *unique* solution. To rule out this sort of phenomenon, we shall make the plausible hypothesis that every commodity in our economy is ultimately required for the production of every other commodity. More formally, we make the following definitions.

DEFINITION 2.1. C_j *is* directly required *in the production of* C_i *if* $\pi_{ij} > 0$.

DEFINITION 2.2. C_j *is* ultimately required *in the production of* C_i *if there is a sequence* $C_j, C_{j_1}, C_{j_2}, \cdots, C_{j_l}, C_i$ *such that each member of the sequence is directly required in the production of the next member.*

We shall then restrict our study to the case of an economy for which every commodity is ultimately required in the production of every other. Since we have already assumed a homogeneous labor force, the condition would be met if each commodity either ultimately requires labor in its production or is ultimately consumed by laborers as their "input."

Physically separated economies, i.e. several societies with no interactions, could not, of course, be considered as having a homogeneous labor force, and if such a system were considered in a single model like (2.1) the condition would not be met. In this case there would not, in general, be a solution to the system of equations (2.1). In order that such a model have a solution we would have to allow the rate of profit to take on different values for each of the separate economies.

The matrix Π, if it is to describe an economy in which every commodity is ultimately required in the production of every other one, must have the following properties.

(i) $\pi_{ij} \geq 0$.

(ii)   For each pair of indices (i,j) there must exist a set of indices $j_1, j_2, \cdots, j_l$ such that

(2.3) $\pi_{ij_1} \pi_{j_1 j_2} \cdots \pi_{j_l j} > 0$.

DEFINITION 2.3. *A matrix with the properties* (i) *and* (ii) *is called* a connected matrix.

We note in passing that a connected matrix is characterized by the property that no permutation of the columns (or rows) can put the matrix in the form

$$\left[\begin{array}{c|c} X & Z \\ \hline 0 & Y \end{array}\right];$$

here, X and Y are square matrices.

We now turn to the mathematical study of connected matrices. Throughout the following development it is assumed that the matrix A is connected.

THEOREM 2.1. *Let A be a connected nonnegative matrix. There exists a vector $\mathbf{x}$ and a number λ such that $\mathbf{x} \geq 0$ and such that the vector equation*

$$(2.4) \qquad\qquad A\mathbf{x} = \lambda\mathbf{x}$$

is satisfied. The vector $\mathbf{x}$ is unique to within a multiplicative constant; the number λ is unique and positive. The vector $\mathbf{x}$ has the additional property $\mathbf{x} > 0$.

Such a vector $\mathbf{x}$ is called a positive eigenvector belonging to A, while λ is called the eigenvalue belonging to $\mathbf{x}$.

The proof of our theorem will be broken up into a sequence of lemmas.

LEMMA 2.1 *If $\mathbf{x} \geqq 0$ and $A\mathbf{x} = 0$, then $\mathbf{x} = 0$.*

Proof: $A\mathbf{x} = 0$ plainly implies $A^2\mathbf{x} = 0$ and hence implies $A^l\,\mathbf{x} = 0$ for $l \geq 1$. Thus

$$(2.5) \qquad \sum_{i}\sum_{j_1}\cdots\sum_{j_l}\sum_{k} a_{ij_1}a_{j_1j_2}\cdots a_{j_lk}x_k = 0.$$

Since $x_k \geq 0$, each term in this sum is zero. Thus

$$(2.6) \qquad\qquad a_{ij_1}a_{j_1j_2}\cdots a_{j_lk}x_k = 0$$

for all values of the indices $i, j_1, j_2 \cdots j_l$. The connectedness of A requires that one of these coefficients be positive, and therefore $x_k = 0$ for all k. Q.E.D.

LEMMA 2.2. *There exists a positive number λ such that $A\mathbf{x} = \lambda\mathbf{x}$ has a solution with $\mathbf{x} \geq 0$.*

Proof: Pick some fixed $n - 1$ dimensional hyperplane in n-dimensional space intersecting each of the n coordinate axes at a positive value. (The hyperplane

(2.7) $$\sum_i x_i = 1$$

will do.)   Each vector $\mathbf{x} \geq 0$ on the hyperplane (e.g. each solution of (2.7) which lies in the semi-positive orthant) is mapped by A into some point $\mathbf{x}^{(1)}$ in the semi-positive orthant; this follows at once from the fact $A \geq 0$, and from Lemma 2.1.   Multiplication by a proper scaling factor depending on $\mathbf{x}^{(1)}$ will send $\mathbf{x}^{(1)}$ into a vector $\mathbf{x}^{(2)}$ lying on the original hyperplane (i.e., take $\sigma = \sum_i x_i^{(1)}$, then $x_i^{(2)} = (1/\sigma)x_i^{(1)}$).   Put $\mathbf{x}^{(2)} = \phi(\mathbf{x})$.   We have then defined, in these two steps, a continuous mapping ϕ of the closed, bounded convex subset

$$\{\mathbf{x} \mid \mathbf{x} \geq 0, \ \textstyle\sum_{i=1}^n x_i = 1\}$$

of a Euclidean space into itself.

Here we may make use of the famous *fixed point theorem* of Brouwer, whose statement is as follows.

THEOREM.   *Let S be a closed bounded convex set in n-dimensional Euclidean space, and let ϕ be an arbitrary continuous mapping of S into itself.   Then there exists at least one point $p \, \epsilon \, S$ such that $\phi(p) = p$, i.e., at least one point $p \, \epsilon \, S$ which remains fixed under the mapping ϕ.*

This is merely the first of many occasions on which we will make use of this remarkable result.   A proof may be found in Dunford-Schwartz, *Linear Operators*, Vol. I, p. 468.

Applying Brouwer's theorem, it follows that there exists a vector $\mathbf{x}$ such that $\left(\sum_{i=1}^n x_j^{(1)}\right)\mathbf{x} = A\mathbf{x}$.   If we put $\lambda = \sum_{i=1}^n x_i^{(1)}$, it is clear that we have

$$A\mathbf{x} = \lambda \mathbf{x}$$

and

$$\lambda > 0, \ \mathbf{x} \geq 0. \quad \text{Q.E.D.}$$

LEMMA 2.3.   *If $\lambda > 0$, $A\mathbf{x} = \lambda \mathbf{x}$, and $\mathbf{x} \geq 0$, but $\mathbf{x} > 0$ is false, then $\mathbf{x} = 0$ (i.e. if $\mathbf{x}$ is a nonnegative solution of $A\mathbf{x} = \lambda\mathbf{x}$, and if some component of $\mathbf{x}$ is zero, then all components of $\mathbf{x}$ are zero).*

The proof is similar to that of Lemma 2.1, and will be left to the reader.

Lemmas 2.2 and 2.3 establish the existence of solutions $\mathbf{x}$, λ of the equation $A\mathbf{x} = \lambda \mathbf{x}$ which have the required properties $\mathbf{x} > 0$, $\lambda > 0$.   It only remains to establish the uniqueness of this vector and number. Let $B = A'$, i.e. let B denote the transpose of A. Then B is plainly a nonnegative connected matrix. Thus, by what we have already proved, there must exist a vector $\mathbf{y} > 0$ and a number $\mu > 0$ such that

$$By = \mu y,$$

i.e., a vector and a number such that

$$y'A = \mu y'.$$

Forming the scalar product of each side of the last vector equation with any nonnegative eigenvector $\mathbf{x}$ of A corresponding to the eigenvalue λ, we obtain

$$\lambda y' \cdot \mathbf{x} = y'A\mathbf{x} = \mu y' \cdot \mathbf{x}, \quad \text{i.e.,}$$
$$\lambda y' \cdot \mathbf{x} = \mu y' \cdot \mathbf{x}.$$

Thus, since $\mathbf{x} \cdot y' > 0$, we have

(2.8) $$\lambda = \mu.$$

Now, since $\mathbf{x}$ was any eigenvector of A satisfying $\mathbf{x} \geq 0$, with λ the corresponding eigenvalue, (2.8) implies that all eigenvalues of A be equal to μ, i.e. (2.8) shows that the eigenvalue λ is unique.

Next, we must show that the positive eigenvector $\mathbf{x}$, whose existence we have established, is unique up to a scalar factor. To this end, let $\mathbf{x}^{(1)}$ be an eigenvector, i.e. let

$$A\mathbf{x}^{(1)} = \lambda \mathbf{x}^{(1)}.$$

We define

$$t = \min_j (x_j^{(1)}/x_j),$$

and suppose in addition that the index j for which the indicated ratio assumes its minimum is the index $j = s$. Then plainly

$$\mathbf{x}^{(1)} - t\mathbf{x} \geq 0$$

while

$$x_s^{(1)} - tx_s = 0.$$

Since

$$A(\mathbf{x}^{(1)} - t\mathbf{x}) = \lambda(\mathbf{x}^{(1)} - t\mathbf{x})$$

it follows by Lemma 2.3 that

$$\mathbf{x}^{(1)} - t\mathbf{x} = 0,$$

thus establishing that the eigenvector is unique to within a multiplicative constant. This completes the proof of Theorem 2.1. Q.E.D.

COROLLARY. *Let B be the transpose of A, and let* **x** *and* **y** *be vectors such that*

(i) $\mathbf{x} \geq 0$ *and* $A\mathbf{x} = \lambda\mathbf{x}$
(ii) $\mathbf{y} \geq 0$ *and* $B\mathbf{y} = \mu\mathbf{y}$.

Then

$$\lambda = \mu.$$

According to Theorem 2.1, the (unique) value λ such that $A\mathbf{x} = \lambda\mathbf{x}$ has a positive solution depends only on A. This number λ will henceforward be called the *dominant of A* and denoted by dom (A). Let us list this as a formal definition.

DEFINITION 2.4. *If A is a connected nonnegative matrix, the unique quantity λ of Theorem 2.1 will be called the* dominant *of A, and written* dom (A), *while the vector* **x** *of Theorem 2.1 (unique up to a positive numerical factor) will be called the* dominant eigenvector *of A.*

We may now reformulate the preceding corollary as follows.

COROLLARY. *Let A be a connected nonnegative matrix, and B be the transpose of A. Then B is a connected nonnegative matrix, and* dom $(B) =$ dom (A).

We now establish some useful facts about the quantity dom (A).

LEMMA 2.4. *Let $k > 0$ be given.*

(i)   *If for some vector $\mathbf{z} \geq 0$ the inequality*

$$A\mathbf{z} \geq k\mathbf{z}$$

   is satisfied, then dom $(A) > k$.
(ii) *If for some vector $\mathbf{z} \geq 0$, the inequality*

$$A\mathbf{z} \leq k\mathbf{z}$$

   is satisfied, then dom $(A) < k$.
(i') *If for some vector $\mathbf{z} \geq 0$ the inequality*

$$A\mathbf{z} \geq k\mathbf{z}$$

   is satisfied, then dom $(A) \geq k$.

(ii′) *If for some vector $\mathbf{z} \geq 0$ the inequality*

$$A\mathbf{z} \leq k\mathbf{z}$$

is satisfied, then dom $(A) \leq k$.

Proof of (i): Let B be the transpose of A, and let $\mathbf{y}$ be a positive eigenvector of B; let $\lambda = \mathrm{dom}\,(A) = \mathrm{dom}\,(B)$. Then since every component of $\mathbf{y}$ is positive it follows from the hypothesis

$$A\mathbf{z} \geq k\mathbf{z}$$

that

$$\mathbf{y}' \cdot A\mathbf{z} > k(\mathbf{y}' \cdot \mathbf{z}).$$

Hence

$$\mathbf{z}'B \cdot \mathbf{y} > k(\mathbf{z}' \cdot \mathbf{y})$$

so that

$$\lambda(\mathbf{z}' \cdot \mathbf{y}) > k(\mathbf{z}' \cdot \mathbf{y})$$

and

$$\lambda > k.$$

This proves (i). Statements (ii), (i′), and (ii′) may be proved similarly. Q.E.D.

THEOREM 2.2. dom (A) *is a strictly increasing function of the connected nonnegative matrix* A, *i.e., if* $A^+ \geq A$, *then* dom (A^+) $>$ dom (A).

Proof: Let $A^+ \geq A$.
Then, if $\lambda^+ = \mathrm{dom}\,(A^+)$, there exists a vector $\mathbf{x}^+ > 0$ such that

$$A^+\mathbf{x}^+ = \lambda^+\mathbf{x}^+.$$

Hence

$$A\mathbf{x}^+ \leq \lambda^+\mathbf{x}^+$$

and by Lemma 2.4, $\lambda^+ >$ dom (A).   Q.E.D.

The following theorem can be proved in the same way.

THEOREM 2.3. dom (A) *depends continuously on the connected nonnegative matrix* A.

Elaboration of the detailed proof of this theorem is left to the reader.

We are now able to prove the result on prices and rate of profit at which we have aimed.

THEOREM 2.4. *Let Π be a connected nonnegative matrix. The equation*

$$(2.9) \qquad\qquad \mathbf{p} = \Pi\mathbf{p} + \rho\Phi\mathbf{p}$$

has a positive solution $\mathbf{p}$ with $\rho \geq 0$ if and only if dom $(\Pi) \leq 1$. *In this case ρ is unique and $\mathbf{p}$ is unique to within a multiplicative constant.*

Proof: If (2.9) has a positive solution $\mathbf{p}$, then by definition, dom $(\Pi + \rho\Phi) = 1$, and conversely. Since, by Theorem 2.2, dom (A) is an increasing function of A, $\rho \geq 0$ implies dom $(\Pi) \leq 1$. Moreover, by Theorem 2.3 and the definition of dom (Φ),

$$\text{dom } (\Pi + \rho\Phi) \geq \text{dom } (\rho\Phi)$$
$$\geq \rho \text{ dom } (\Phi)$$

i.e. dom $(\Pi + \rho\Phi) \to \infty$ as $\rho \to \infty$. Since dom $(\Pi + \rho\Phi)$ has a value ≤ 1 for $\rho = 0$, tends to ∞ as $\rho \to \infty$, and is a strictly increasing continuous function of ρ, we conclude that dom $(\Pi + \rho\Phi) = 1$ has exactly one solution for $\rho \geq 0$.

On the other hand, if dom $(\Pi) > 1$, then by Theorem 2.2 dom $(\Pi + \rho\Phi) > 1$ and there is no positive solution $\mathbf{p}$ of the equation (2.9). Q.E.D.

COROLLARY. *The quantity ρ of the preceding theorem is strictly positive if and only if* dom $(\Pi) < 1$.

The economic interpretation of Theorem 2.4 is immediate. Positive profit is possible only if dom $(\Pi) < 1$. By Lemma 2.4 and the corollary of Theorem 2.1, this condition is equivalent to the condition that there exists a vector $\mathbf{a}' \geq 0$ such that $\mathbf{a}'\Pi \leq \mathbf{a}'$, i.e., to the condition that there exists some scheme of production capable of yielding a physical surplus. The dichotomy dom $(\Pi) < 1$ vs. dom $(\Pi) > 1$ is then evidently a direct generalization of the dichotomy $\tilde{\pi}_{,,} < 1$ vs. $\tilde{\pi}_{,,} > 1$ whose significance was elaborated at the end of Section 3 of the preceding lecture. Only the case dom $(\Pi) < 1$ is of interest; the case dom $(\Pi) > 1$ describes, in the sense ex-

plained in the previous lecture, a "starvation economy." If a positive rate of profit is possible, the rate of profit is unique and the prices
are positive and unique too within a multiplicative constant. That
is, the rate of profit and the ratios of the prices depend only upon the
production coefficients π_{ij} and ϕ_{ij}. Moreover, all prices are strictly
positive, i.e. nothing is "free."

Thus we are led to conclude that price-ratios are determined by
the technological conditions of production; in particular, no considerable role seems to be left for the "supply and demand" considerations which are so central to the customary economic theory of
price. This conclusion, of course, is less compelling than it might
be owing to the fact that the elements π_{oj} of the input-output matrix
are descriptive of consumer preferences. To put our conclusion on a
sounder basis, we must study the theory of prices in an open Leontief
model. This will be done in the next lecture.

We may add the following interesting argument to what has been
said above. Let $q_1, \cdots, q_n$ be the total stocks of commodities
$C_1, \cdots, C_n$ available at the beginning of some definite production
period. If amounts $a_1, \cdots, a_n$ are to be produced, then $\mathbf{q}$ and $\mathbf{a}$
must be related by the inequality

$$(2.10) \qquad q_j \geq \sum_{i=1}^{n} a_i \phi_{ij}, \quad j = 1, \cdots, N.^{[1]}$$

Let a_0 be the smallest amount of labor necessary as input for the
production of the commodities $C_1, \cdots, C_N$ in the amounts $a_1, \cdots, a_N$,
as determined by the formula

$$(2.11) \qquad a_0 = \sum_{i=0}^{N} a_i \pi_{io}.$$

We now inquire as to the conditions under which a proportional
increase of at least ρ^* in each stock-total is possible in one production
period. During the production period an amount a_j of C_j is produced, but an amount $\Sigma_i a_i \pi_{ij}$ is consumed. The condition that the
proportional increase in the level of stocks be at least ρ^* is then
evidently

$$a_j - \sum_{i=0}^{n} \pi_{ij} a_i + q_j \geq (1 + \rho^*) q_j.$$

[1] We recall that $\varphi_{oi} = \varphi_{jo} = 0$.

If we use the inequality (2.10) we have

$$a_j - \sum_{i=0}^{N} \pi_{ij} a_i - \rho^* \sum_{i=1}^{N} a_i \phi_{ij} \geq 0, \quad j = 1, \cdots, N.$$

Replacing a_0 by its value as given by (2.11), this may be written as

$$a_j - \sum_{i=1}^{N} (\pi_{ij} + (1 - \pi_{oo})^{-1} \pi_{io} \pi_{oj}) a_i - \rho^* \sum_{i=1}^{N} a_i \phi_{ij} \geq 0, \quad j = 1, \cdots, N.$$

Putting $\pi_{ij} + (1 - \pi_{oo})^{-1} \pi_{io} \pi_{oj} = \tilde{\pi}_{ij}$ and $\tilde{\phi}_{ij} = \phi_{ij}$ for $i,j = 1, \cdots, N$; and writing also $\mathbf{a}'$ for the N-dimensional vector whose components are $a_1, \cdots, a_N$, we may write this last equation as

$$\mathbf{a}' \geq \mathbf{a}' \tilde{\Pi} + \rho^* \mathbf{a}' \tilde{\Phi}.$$

It follows by Lemma 2.4 and the corollary of Theorem 2.1 that dom $(\tilde{\Pi} + \rho^* \tilde{\Phi}) \leq 1$. Now, we saw in the preceding lecture that the quantity ρ was determined by the condition that the equation

$$\mathbf{p}' = \tilde{\Pi} \mathbf{p}' + \rho \tilde{\Phi} \mathbf{p}'$$

have a positive vector solution $\mathbf{p}'$. Thus, by Definition 2.4, ρ is determined by the condition that dom $(\tilde{\Pi} + \rho \tilde{\Phi}) = 1$. It follows at once by Theorem 2.2 that our hypothetical rate ρ^* of stock increase satisfies the inequality

$$\rho^* \leq \rho.$$

Heuristic interpretation of this inequality yields a statement to which economics has been so devoted that it may be called the Main Theorem of Economics: no planned scheme of production can (without lowering wages, which is painful, or improving efficiency, which is doubtful) yield a greater annual increase in stocks than the normal rate of profit of free competition. More flamboyantly, free enterprise is the best of all possible systems! Our subsequent analysis will not fail to find flies in this ointment. Nevertheless, our assertion has a decidedly nontrivial force.

Theory of Prices in the
Open Leontief Model.   Some Statistics

1. Determination of Prices by ρ

We were only able to extend the open system (1.4) of equations for prices to the closed system (1.6) by making use of the coefficients π_{oj} representing the components of the real wage bill, and writing the additional equation

$$(3.1) \qquad p_0 = \sum_{j=0}^{n} \pi_{oj} p_j.$$

Since, as has already been pointed out, these particular coefficients are hardly determined as much by technology as are the other production coefficients (including the coefficients π_{jo} which denote the amount of labor required for the production of a unit of C_j) it is of interest to study the theory of prices in a corresponding model in which equation (3.1) is suppressed, i.e., to study the theory of prices in an open Leontief model.

Suppressing equation (3.1), we are left with the homogeneous equations

$$(3.2) \qquad p_i = \pi_{io} p_o + \sum_{j=1}^{n} \pi_{ij} p_j + \rho \sum_{j=1}^{n} \phi_{ij} p_j, \quad i = 1, \cdots, n.$$

This is a set of n equations for the set of $n+1$ unknowns consisting of ρ and the n ratios of the prices $p_0, p_1, \cdots, p_n$. We may consequently surmise that these equations determine all but one of the

$n + 1$ unknowns. To see that this is in fact the case, let us first pass to an inhomogeneous system by introducing the variables $\tilde{p}_1 = p_1/p_0$, $\tilde{p}_2 = p_n/p_0, \cdots, \tilde{p}_n = p_n/p_0$. In terms of these variables we may write

$$(3.3) \qquad \tilde{p}_i - \sum_{j=1}^{n} \pi_{ij}\tilde{p}_j - \rho \sum_{j=1}^{n} \phi_{ij}\tilde{p}_j = \pi_{io}, \quad i = 1, \cdots, n.$$

This is a nonhomogeneous set of n equations in the $n + 1$ unknowns $\tilde{p}_1, \cdots, \tilde{p}_n$ and ρ. Guided by the expectation that the specification of any one of the unknowns will make the solution of the system determinate, we shall begin by studying this system as a system of equations determining the unknowns $\tilde{p}_1, \cdots, \tilde{p}_n$ in terms of the parameter ρ.

Let $\overset{\circ}{\Pi}$ be the matrix whose elements are π_{ij} $(i,j = 1, \cdots, n)$, i.e. $\overset{\circ}{\Pi}$ is the matrix obtained by deleting the zero row and the zero column from Π. We shall assume in the rest of the present lecture, for convenience' sake and in order to be able to make ready reference to the results of the preceding lecture, that $\overset{\circ}{\Pi}$ is connected. It would not be hard to generalize our analysis to cover cases in which this assumption is not satisfied. Let $\overset{\circ}{\Phi}$ be similarly defined as the matrix whose elements are ϕ_{ij} $(i,j = 1, \cdots, n)$, i.e. $\overset{\circ}{\Phi}$ is the matrix obtained by deleting the zero row and the zero column from Φ. Let $\mathbf{v}$ be the vector whose components v_i are π_{io}. The vector whose elements are $\tilde{p}_i$ $(i = 1, \cdots, n)$ we shall denote simply by $\tilde{\mathbf{p}}$. Equations (3.3) then become

$$\tilde{\mathbf{p}} - \overset{\circ}{\Pi}\tilde{\mathbf{p}} - \rho\overset{\circ}{\Phi}\tilde{\mathbf{p}} = \mathbf{v}$$

or

$$(3.4) \qquad (I - \overset{\circ}{\Pi} - \rho\overset{\circ}{\Phi})\tilde{\mathbf{p}} = \mathbf{v}.$$

We now ask under what circumstances the matrix $(I - \overset{\circ}{\Pi} - \rho\overset{\circ}{\Phi})$ has an inverse for, when the inverse exists, we obtain the explicit solution

$$(3.5) \qquad \tilde{\mathbf{p}}(\rho) = (I - \overset{\circ}{\Pi} - \rho\overset{\circ}{\Phi})^{-1}\mathbf{v}$$

for the prices $\tilde{p}_i$ as a function of the parameter ρ. (We note again that no assumption as to the detailed nature of consumer demand enters into our considerations.) A suitable answer to this question may be obtained from the following theorem.

THEOREM. *Let A be an arbitrary matrix. Let μ (possibly complex) denote any number for which there exists a nonzero solution $\mathbf{z}$ (again possibly complex) to*

$$A\mathbf{z} = \mu\mathbf{z}.$$

(Even in the complex case, such a number is called an eigenvalue of the matrix A.) If every such μ satisfies $|\mu| < 1$, then the sum $\sum_{k=0}^{\infty} A^k$ converges and is equal to the inverse of $I - A$; that is

$$(I - A)^{-1} = \sum_{k=0}^{\infty} A^k.$$

This theorem is the matrix-theoretic generalization of the scalar formula:

$$1/(1 - x) = \sum_{k=0}^{\infty} x^k \quad \text{for} \quad x < 1.$$

Proof of this theorem would involve us in an unprofitably extensive discussion of the theory of matrices. The reader interested in examining such a proof should consult Dunford-Schwartz, *Linear Operators*, Vol. 1, p. 559.

We now prove a number of lemmas which permit us to apply the preceding theorem to the problem at hand.

LEMMA 3.1. *If M is a connected nonnegative matrix, and $M\mathbf{z} = \mu\mathbf{z}$ for some nonzero vector $\mathbf{z}$, then $|\mu| \leq \mathrm{dom}\,(M)$.*

Proof: Let

$$M\mathbf{z} = \mu\mathbf{z}.$$

Then

$$\left| \sum_j m_{ij}z_j \right| = |\mu|\,|z_i|$$

so that

$$\sum_j m_{ij}\,|z_j| \geq |\mu|\,|z_i|.$$

Let $y_j = |z_j|$ so that $\mathbf{y}$ is a real nonnegative vector. Then

$$\sum_j m_{ij}y_j \geq |\mu|\,y_i.$$

Hence, by Lemma 2.4, $\mathrm{dom}\,(M) \geq |\mu|$.   Q.E.D.

We omit the very similar proof of the following slightly stronger statement.

COROLLARY 3.2.   *Under the hypotheses of Lemma 3.1 we have either*

$$\mu = \text{dom } (M)$$

or

$$|\mu| < \text{dom } (M).$$

LEMMA 3.3.   *If M is a connected nonnegative matrix, and if $\text{dom } (M) < 1$, then the inverse $(I - M)^{-1}$ exists and is the sum of the series $\sum_{k=0}^{\infty} M^k$.*

Proof: This follows at once from Lemma 3.1 and the theorem which precedes it.   Q.E.D.

LEMMA 3.4.   *If M is a nonnegative matrix, so are all its powers.*

Proof: Immediate by induction.   Q.E.D.

LEMMA 3.5.   *If M is a connected nonnegative matrix, and $\text{dom } (M) < 1$, the inverse $(I - M)^{-1}$ is a nonnegative matrix.*

Proof: This follows at once from Lemmas 3.3 and 3.4.   Q.E.D.

LEMMA 3.6.   *If M and M' are nonnegative matrices, M being connected, while $\text{dom } (M) < 1$, $\text{dom } (M') < 1$, and $M \leq M'$, it follows that*

$$(I - M)^{-1} < (I - M')^{-1}.$$

Proof: It is plain that the connectedness of M and the relationship $M \leq M'$ implies the connectedness of M'. We may show by induction that $M^k \leq (M')^k$; thus it follows from Lemma 3.3 that $(I - M)^{-1} \leq (I - M')^{-1}$. On the other hand, let i and i' be any two indices of the matrix M. Since $M \leq M'$, there is (by definition of the relationship) at least one element $m_{jj'}$ of M which is *strictly smaller* than the corresponding element $m'_{jj'}$ of M'. Since M is connected, there exists a sequence $i, i_1, \cdots, i_l, j$ and a sequence $i_{l+1}, \cdots, i_q, i'$ such that the product

$$m_{ii_1} m_{i_1 i_2} \cdots m_{i_l j} m_{j' i_{l+1}} \cdots m_{i_q i'}$$

is nonzero.   Hence

$$(3.6) \quad m_{ii_1} m_{i_1 i_2} \cdots m_{i_l j} m_{jj'} m_{j' i_{l+1}} \cdots m_{i_q i'} < m'_{ii_1} m'_{i_1 i_2} \cdots m'_{i_l j} m'_{jj'} m'_{j' i_{l+1}} \cdots m'_{i_q i'}.$$

It follows at once from this inequality, and from the inequality $m_{st} \leq m'_{st}$ valid for all indices s and t, that the i,i' element of the matrix M^{q+3} is strictly smaller than the corresponding element of the matrix $(M')^{q+3}$. Our conclusion now follows immediately from the formulae for $(I - M)^{-1}$ and $(I - M')^{-1}$ given by Lemma 3.3. Q.E.D.

COROLLARY. *If M is a connected nonnegative matrix, and $M \leq M'$, M' is also a connected nonnegative matrix.*

It follows from Lemma 3.3 that a sufficient condition that $I - \overset{\circ}{\Pi} - \rho\overset{\circ}{\Phi}$ have an inverse, is the condition dom $(\overset{\circ}{\Pi} + \rho\overset{\circ}{\Phi}) < 1$. Let ρ_{max} be the least upper bound of the set of ρ such that dom $(\overset{\circ}{\Pi} + \rho\overset{\circ}{\Phi}) < 1$. Since by Theorems 2.2 and 2.4 dom $(\overset{\circ}{\Pi} + \rho\overset{\circ}{\Phi})$ is a strictly increasing continuous function of ρ, it follows at once that ρ_{max} may equivalently be defined as the unique solution of the equation dom $(\overset{\circ}{\Pi} + \rho_{max} \overset{\circ}{\Phi}) = 1$. That is, ρ_{max} is the unique number for which there exists a positive solution x_{max} to the system

$$(3.7) \qquad (\overset{\circ}{\Pi} + \rho_{max} \overset{\circ}{\Phi})x_{max} = x_{max}.$$

This system may be written

$$(3.8) \quad (x_{max})_i = \sum_{j=1}^{n} \pi_{ij}(x_{max})_j + \rho_{max} \sum_{j=1}^{n} \phi_{ij}(x_{max})_j, \quad i = 1, \cdots, n.$$

Comparing the system (3.8) with the system (3.2), we see that ρ_{max} is the rate of profit which obtains when p_0, the wage rate, is zero, and that x_{max} is the corresponding vector of commodity prices. By Theorem 3.2 and its corollary, $\rho_{max} > 0$ if and only if dom $(\overset{\circ}{\Pi}) < 1$, i.e., if and only if, with the wage rate at zero, the physical machine of production is capable of producing a surplus. (Compare the corresponding discussion in the preceding lecture; since an economy violating this condition is not worth considering, we will make the assumption dom $(\overset{\circ}{\Pi}) < 1$ in all that follows.)

Clearly, ρ_{max} is the rate of profit which is obtained by taking $v = 0$ in (3.3), i.e., the rate of profit which would obtain if no wages at all are paid. Then for $\rho < \rho_{max}$, i.e., for rates of profit such that positive wages are paid, dom $(\overset{\circ}{\Pi} + \rho\overset{\circ}{\Phi}) < 1$, and $(I - \overset{\circ}{\Pi} - \rho\overset{\circ}{\Phi})$ has an inverse. Thus, referring once more to the fundamental equation (3.4), determining prices, we now conclude that not only are the prices $\tilde{\mathbf{p}}(\rho)$ uniquely determined independently of demand once a rate of profit $0 < \rho < \rho_{\max}$ is specified, but also, using Lemma 3.6, that the prices so determined are, as they must be, strictly positive.

Lemma 3.6, applied to the solution (3.5) of the system (3.2), yields the following theorem immediately.

THEOREM 3.7. *All components of* $\tilde{\mathbf{p}}(\rho)$ *are strictly increasing with* ρ *for* $0 \leq \rho < \rho_{\max}$.

Thus, as ρ increases, the relative price of every single commodity, as measured by the hourly wage rate, increases. It follows that not only ρ but in fact any one of the price-ratios $\tilde{p}_i$ may be taken as a parameter determining a unique solution to the system (3.3). If we know the price of any commodity in terms of the hourly wage rate, it follows that ρ, and hence all the price ratios, are determined by our system of equations (3.2).

We emphasize once more for the benefit of the reader familiar with the conventional "neoclassical" or "marginal utility" analysis that, considering the almost vanishing role played by consumer preference in the above analysis, we have before us very strong presumptive evidence against the marginal utility theory (or more precisely, against its special significance). More detailed comparison of the input-output and marginal utility theory will be made in subsequent lectures.

2. Generalization to Several Labor Sectors

All our arguments up to the present point were based upon the assumption of a single, homogeneous, labor sector. We shall now consider briefly the modifications which would arise if we took the inhomogeneity of the labor force into account, introducing several kinds of labor as commodities C_0, C_{-1}, C_{-2}, etc., with corresponding production coefficients $\pi_{i,0}, \pi_{i,-1}, \pi_{i,-2}$, where $\pi_{i,-k}$ is the amount of labor of type k required for the production of one unit of C_i. Let the ratios of the wages paid to the different kinds of labor be $1, x_{-1}, x_{-2}, \cdots$. Then equations (3.3) become

$$(3.9) \qquad \tilde{p}_i - \sum_{j=1}^n \pi_{ij}\tilde{p}_j - \rho \sum_{j=1}^n \phi_{ij}\tilde{p}_j = \pi_{io} + \sum_k \pi_{i,-k}x_{-k}$$

which shows that by a simple substitution for π_{io} of

(3.10) $\pi_{io} + \sum_k \pi_{i,-k} x_{-k}$

the preceding analysis may be brought to include the case in which
there is a nonhomogeneous labor force for which the ratios of the
wages are known. The prices are then determined by ρ and by the
ratios of the wage levels for each of the several kinds of labor.

3. Relation of the Leontief Model with Standard Economic Statistics

To relate the present model to statistics taken from one or another
actual national economy, we must exhibit the definition, in terms of
the present model, of the various conventional statistical headings
in terms of which a national economy is ordinarily described. The
quantities whose significance appears most immediately are the totals
$a_1, \cdots, a_n$ of production, in a given period, of the commodities
$C_1, \cdots, C_n$ of the economy. Such totals will ordinarily be available
as series titled "annual production of coke" or "annual generation
of electric power," etc. The vector a' whose components are
$a_1, \cdots, a_n$ may be called the *total national product vector* (for the
given period) *in real terms*. It is a list of the total amounts of all
commodities produced, irrespective of whether or not the commodity
is subsequently consumed in the production of further commodities.

Even here, where our concept is apparently clear-cut, and hence
to a yet more significant extent in dealing with less straightforward
theoretical notions, we run up against annoying problems of practical
and statistical definition. Is "total production of vegetables" to
include products grown for immediate consumption in farm gardens?
We might wish that it did: but the statistician may legitimately
object that to gather reliable figures on such production is extremely
difficult. Hence one settles for data describing vegetable production
as it appears on the commercial market, thereby becoming statistically
accessible. This problem, which may appear mild when one thinks
of material commodities, becomes pressing when we pass to the consideration of services. In the first place, let us remark that unless
services are included among the commodities $C_1, \cdots, C_n$, our list
$a_1, \cdots, a_n$ of total production figures may constitute an entirely in-
adequate description of economic activity. But to include services
raises statistical problems. Consider, as an exceptionally definite

service category, "haircuts." Should totals for this service include
only the activity of the professional barber, or should it include the
widespread efforts of amateurs as well? What then about "shaves,"
commonly a self-performed service, or "preparation of cooked food"
in which the restauranteur stands side-by-side with a larger group
of housewives? Or consider the situation to be dealt with in treating
a varied service category like medical care. It hardly be either
feasible or instructive to present a complete breakdown of this general
activity into its components; one rather expects a summary total
heading. To obtain such a heading, one has hardly any choice but
to weight individual terms according to prices actually charged.
This is made all the more necessary by the fact that in attempting
to compile useful general totals of economic activity, which may
with some legitimacy be called by such imposing titles as *national
income, gross national product*, etc., the statistician sorely needs the
check which is provided by definitions which make "total valuation
of goods and services produced" equal to "total income expended"
upon these same goods and services. But this means valuing things
at their actual prices, even though, for instance, this may lead, implicitly if not explicitly, to the "services" provided by an extortionist
appearing in a national income account as if these services were justly
describable as "extortions, x in number, to the total value of y
dollars." The proper treatment of taxes, of course, provides similar
problems.

Another serious problem is the treatment of house rents. On the
expenditure side, these sum to a significant total; on the product
side, we are somewhat perplexed to find the hypothetical commodity
"shelter" altogether immaterial in form, its "production" following
immediately from the presence of certain fixed capital equipment. In
order that the purchase of housing for personal use should not lead
to excessively large subtractions from such a heading as "gross
national product," it is then necessary to include an item covering
imputed rental income of householders, as little as such a practice
seems to conform to the assumption implicit in our input-output
model.

Even the assignment of production or expenditure to a given
period may be questionable, as significant items may be "carried
over" or "carried forward" in statistics as well as on corporate
books. And how, for instance, shall additions to inventory and

inventories be measured, amidst constantly changing price levels and technology? We find, as usual in science, that the clear-cut distinctions of a theoretical model apply to the complex empirical situation only approximately. With all these reservations in mind, we may continue to describe the significance, in terms of our model, of the main headings of national income accounting.

The components of the vector $a' - a'\overset{\circ}{\Pi}$ are the total amounts of the various commodities produced net of commercial, agricultural, and industrial consumption; i.e., the total amounts of commodities produced but not subsequently consumed in the production of other commodities. This then is the total bill of goods available as income for individual consumption, increase of stocks or fixed capital investment, national defense purposes, etc. To estimate the size of this vector by a single number it is appropriate to multiply each production figure by the unit price of the commodity involved and to sum. Taking actual prices in this calculation, we arrive at the total commonly called *net national product* (NNP). It is appropriate, however, to make a correction for the distortion of prices by sales, property, and excise taxes, and various indirect business liabilities of this sort. Without such a correction, an increase in the sales tax rate or the property tax rate appears as an increase of apparent product. The correction is ordinarily made by subtracting the total of business indirect tax liability from the NNP (and by making a small additional correction for the effects of corporate pension plans and a few other items listed as "business transfer payments"); this yields the total commonly called *national income* (NI). It is then the heading national income which most closely approximates our theoretical expression $(a' - a'\overset{\circ}{\Pi}) \cdot \bar{p}(\rho)$ (cf. (3.3) and the following paragraph). The given definition of net national product has the advantage that it is equal to the sum of personal consumption expenses (including property and sales tax payments), net investment, net exports, and government purchases of goods and services; this equality provides a useful statistical check.

If we add to the net national product the total estimated depreciation of fixed capital for the period under consideration, we obtain the *gross national product*. This somewhat hybrid heading gains significance from the fact that it is hard to make a firm distinction between capital depreciation in the sense of actual loss of usefulness through wear and capital depreciation as investment in plant modernization. Wear of fixed capital should be included, in accordance with our model, on a suitable prorated basis, in the elements of the circulating capital matrix π_{ij} and subtracted as is indicated by the formula $\mathbf{a}' - \mathbf{a}'\mathring{\Pi}$; equipment depreciated through obsolescence and to clear the way for modernization might perhaps be regarded as a form of final output, even though it may not be a very useful form of output.

The difference between national income and the total wage bill, deflated by the average rate of hourly wages, is given in our model by the formula

$$(3.11) \qquad \mathbf{a}'(I - \mathring{\Pi}) \cdot \tilde{\mathbf{p}}(\rho) - \mathbf{a}' \cdot \mathbf{v}.$$

(Compare (3.3) and the paragraph following for definition of these quantities.) This is a measure of the total value of commodities remaining for investment, special luxury consumption, military purposes, or other use, after wages are paid (and before saving out of wages). It may be called the *national dividend*, and may, of course, be stated either in deflated dollar or current-dollar terms.

The ratio of the national dividend to the national income is called the *retention fraction*. Explicitly, the retention fraction $r(\rho)$ is given by

$$(3.12) \quad r(\rho) = [\mathbf{a}' \cdot (I - \mathring{\Pi})\tilde{\mathbf{p}}(\rho) - \mathbf{a}' \cdot \mathbf{v}]/[\mathbf{a}' \cdot (I - \mathring{\Pi})\tilde{\mathbf{p}}(\rho)].$$

In order to make the order of magnitude of the various quantities described in the present section apparent, we now present some statistical information.

Our figures are based on data given by the Department of Commerce, modified by the following rough procedures so as to conform more closely to our theoretical headings:

(a) Proprietors' income is separated into a "salary" and a "profit" part, the separation being based on the assumption that unincorporated business is approximately as profitable as incorporated business.

(b) Debits are then made for personal income tax and for indirect tax payments, the stated totals for each of these taxes being debited on a proportional basis against each liable form of income.

(c) The relevant headings in the resultant partition of Gross National Product are then summed to give an estimate of National Dividend.

TABLE Ia

U. S. 1957 Approximate Salaries Before and After Taxes, Showing
Estimated Deductions for Income, Excise, and Property Taxes
(Billions of Dollars)

	Est. before taxes	Est. personal tax correction	Est. indirect tax correction	Est. after taxes
Wages and salaries of employees	247	32	28	187
Net pension, social security, unemployment insurance, and other public and private social transfer payments	15	0	2	13
Farm proprietors' income	12	2	1	9
Professional and business self-employment income	21	3	3	15
Rental income of persons	12	1	1	10
Total wages and salaries	307	38	35	234

TABLE Ib

U. S. 1957 Approximate Profits and Interest Before and After
Personal and Indirect Taxes, Showing Estimated Deductions
for Taxes (Billions of Dollars) [a]

	Est. before taxes	Est. personal tax correction	Est. indirect tax correction	Est. after taxes
*Noncorporate profits	10	1	1	8
*Corporate dividends	12	2	1	9
*Corporate retained profits	9	0	0	9
*Net private interest	13	2	1	10
*Government interest payments	6	0	0	6
Total profits and interest	50	5	3	42

[a] Items marked * to be included in national dividend.

TABLE Ic

U. S. 1957 Government Expenditures on Goods and Services
(Billions of Dollars) [a]

*State and local government net investment	4
Additional state and local government expenditures	32
Federal nonmilitary expenditures	6
*Federal military expenditures	44
Total government expenditures on goods and services	86

[a] Items marked * to be included in national dividend

TABLE Id

Relation of Tables Ia–c to Gross National Product Account
(Billions of Dollars)

Total wages and salaries after taxes	234
Private dividends and interest after taxes	42
Total government expenditures on goods and services	86
Government surplus and foreign transfers	3
Subtotal (NI estimate)	365
Actual national income	367
Depreciation	38
Excise, property, and miscellaneous indirect taxes	38
Total (GNP estimate)	441
Actual Gross National Product	440

TABLE Ie

U. S. 1957 Estimated National Dividend
(Billions of Dollars)

Private profits and interest (Table Ib)	42
Federal military expenditures	44
Net state and local government investment	4
National Dividend	90

From the approximate figures in the tables, we may estimate the
retention fraction as $\frac{90}{365}$, or 25%.

The rate of profit ρ, as it would appear in our input-output model, is the ratio of national dividend to total capital plant value.

We take the statistics in Tables IIa and IIb from a study of capital wealth by Lampman (*Review of Economics and Statistics*, (1959)); c.f. also the extensive study by Goldsmith: *A Study of Saving in the United States*, 3 Vols., Princeton University Press (1956).

Using Tables Ie and IIb, we may estimate the rate ρ of profit, as it would appear in our model, as the quotient of national dividend

TABLE IIa

Approximate Capital Account of United States, 1953
(Billions of Dollars) (after Lampman)

Residences	295	Individual
Consumer durables	123	property or use
Public improvements	100	
Commercial buildings and structures	160	
Industrial equipment	135	
Industrial and trade inventories	107	
Gold and silver	27	
Total	947	
Land valuations	209	
	1156	

TABLE IIb

Estimated U. S. 1957 Productive Capital Account
(Billions of Dollars)

Commercial buildings and structures	160
Industrial equipment	135
Inventory	107
Public improvements	100
Total productive capital acct.	502

over total productive capital, thus $\frac{90}{502}$ or 18%. We may illustrate the significance of this figure by stating that the productive capital of the United States could be used to duplicate itself in something more than five years.

This profit rate ρ which describes the physical economy is to be reconciled with the rather different average rate of yield on stocks and bonds as follows. Somewhat more than $\frac{1}{4}$ of the national dividend of 90 billion never appears on corporate books as profit at all, appearing instead as withholding tax from wages and salaries; another $\frac{1}{4}$ or so does not appear as disposable profit because of corporate taxes. These two factors would alone reduce the apparent profit rate to something like 8.5%. About $\frac{1}{4}$ of the remaining profit is retained by corporations for internal expansion further reducing the apparent profit rate to 6.5%. Finally, the practice of the Federal and State governments of imposing taxes and paying part of these taxes as interest to government bond holders, coupled with the circumstance that the institution of land rent means that land-values enter into the computation of profit rates, means that instead of dividing by the total value 502 billion of capital improvements, we must rather divide by the sum of private capital improvements, government bond values, and commercial land values, approximately $400 + 300 + 150 = 850$ rather than 500. This larger denominator would reduce the apparent profit rate to approximately 3.8%, which is to be compared to the current (1960) average bond yield of 3.5% on tax-free municipal bonds, 4.8% on taxable corporate bonds, and average stock yield of 3.6% on corporate stocks.

4. A Rough Statistical Test

The model used here for the study of prices is based on the assumption of constant return to scale, or, in other words, it is based on the assumption that the π_{ij} and ϕ_{ij} are constants and not functions of the total amounts a_i of production of the various commodities. The fundamental result indicated by our study of the model is that the relative prices depend only upon the production coefficients (if labor is included as a commodity) or, more cautiously (when labor is not included) that the relative prices depend only upon the production coefficients and the rate of profit ρ. From this we must conclude that if we assume a constant ρ, the relative prices should be independent of the production level. We may use the fluctuation of production levels over the course of the business cycle to obtain a rough empirical check on this theoretical conclusion. Over periods of time short enough to consider the Π and Φ constant the present theory then indicates that the relative prices should be much the same in a boom period and in a period of recession. Let us compare this conclusion with the empirical data on the business cycle as precisely elucidated by W. C. Mitchell.

TABLE IIIa

Average Peak and Trough Production Levels for 4 Cycles 1919–1938
(after Mitchell)

	Peak	Trough	Variation, %
Industrial production	120	87	33
Auto production	130	70	60
Cotton	120	90	30
Housing contracts	130	90	40
Factory pay	125	85	40

TABLE IIIb

Average Relative Prices for the 1919–1938 Peak and Trough Production
Level Years (after Mitchell) Deflated by Wholesale Price Level

	Peak	Trough	Variation, %
Wholesale prices of finished goods	100	100	0
Wholesale prices for semi-manufactured goods	104	97	7
Raw materials	105	96	9
Wholesale foods	100	98	2
Retail foods	101	97	4
Pig iron	106	94	12
Farm prices	106	96	10

Table IIIa shows the production levels of various key U. S. industries averaged over four peak years and over four trough years in the period 1919–1938, indicating production level fluctuations of 30% to 60%. Table IIIb then shows the prices of various commodities (adjusted to the wholesale prices of finished goods) averaged over the same four peak years and over the same four trough years. The differences in prices are certainly much smaller than the differences in production levels, perhaps small enough to indicate a certain relevance of the present model, and to justify its further study.

Our model suggests that the larger relative variations in raw materials prices (as compared to prices of manufactured goods) ought to be associated with a smaller validity of the assumption of constant returns to scale. We will cite some evidence supporting this suggestion, as it applies in the particular case of hide production, in a subsequent lecture. Of course, many other circumstances give rise to price variations over the course of the business cycle. Speculation, that is, adjustment to anticipated future conditions rather than present conditions, must be taken into account; as well as differences in the storability of goods of various types. The phases of the business cycle are not static equilibrium situations.

Concluding Discussion
of the Leontief Model

1. Some Comparative Statistics

It is of interest to compare the United States gross national product account presented in the last lecture with the corresponding account for other national economies.

Of course, all international comparisons of income accounts are dubious to a certain extent. Thus, for instance, definitions of wages and of salaries vary; price ratios and foreign exchange rates vary, so that dollar equivalents are hard to establish; the extent to which a given economy is properly represented by commercial data making no allowance for subsistence economy varies also.

The British account for 1957 is as shown in Table IV below.

From the approximate figures below, we may estimate the retention fraction r as 3.1/17.0, or 18%, compared to the U. S. figure of 25%.

We shall not attempt to make an estimate of the capital resources of Britain, and hence will not calculate the rate of return on productive capital for Britain.

Let us note that the input-output model must be applied even more cautiously to Britain than to the U. S., since the British import-export business amounts to 4 billion pounds sterling or over 20% of the value of Britain's gross national product, while the corresponding figure for the U. S. is some 20 billion dollars or less than 5% of the value of the gross national product.

We may compare the two above sets of figures with data for an

TABLE IV

Britain 1957 Approximate Gross National Product Account,
in Billions of Pounds Sterling [a,b]

Wages and salaries of employees	9.6
Pension, social security, unemployment benefits, and national health	1.6
Proprietors self-employment income	1.2
Total wages and salaries after all taxes	12.4
*Rent, dividends, and interest	1.3
*Retained public and private corporate net profit	0.2
Total private sector income after all taxes	13.9
*Military expenditure	1.6
Nonmilitary central government expenditure, goods and services	0.4
Local governmental expenditure	1.1
Total real national income	17.0
Government surplus	0.6
National income	17.6
Excises less subsidies	2.5
Net national product	20.1
Capital consumption allowance	1.8
Gross national product	21.9

[a] Based on data from the *National Income and Expenditure* volume of the Central Statistical Office of Great Britain, figures reduced to U. S. Department of Commerce basis.

[b] Items marked * are to be included in national dividend.

ambitious underdeveloped country by examining the national accounts of China; here, of course, we are limited by the paucity of reliable data. The following figures are taken from the careful analysis by Li: *Industrial Development of Communist China*. The account of production is shown first in Table V. From Tables V and VI we may estimate the retention fraction r as $\frac{23}{110}$, or 21%.

Estimates for the gross product of the U. S. S. R. are also rather sparse. We give, in Table VII, estimates prepared by H. Block, and published in *Trends in Economic Growth. A Comparison of the Western Powers and the Soviet Bloc. A Study Prepared for the Joint Committee on the Economic Report by the Legislative Reference Service of the Library of Congress*, United States Government Printing Office, Washington, 1955.

The retention fraction r here is at the exceptionally high level of

TABLE V

China 1957 Estimated National Income
Account (Billions of Yuan) [a]

Agriculture	45
Industry and mining	24
Construction	5
Transport	4
Trade	14
Service	18
Total national income	110

[a] The official exchange rate is 1 Yuan = $0.43 U. S.

TABLE VI

China 1957 Estimated Net Investment and National Dividend Account
(Billions of Yuan) [a]

*Producers' equipment	3
*Commercial and government construction	4
Housing construction	1
*Construction for agriculture, flood control, and forestry	2
*Commercial and industrial inventory investment	0.5
*Agricultural inventory investment	1
*Net investment outside state plan	1
*Additional miscellaneous investment and military procurement	11.5
Total national dividend	23.0

[a] Items marked * to be included in national dividend.

TABLE VII

Estimated U. S. S. R. 1953 Gross National Product,
Corrected for Excise Taxes (after II. Block) [a]

Consumption	51
Social services	9
Administration	4
Defense	18
Net investment	25
National income	107
Depreciation	3
Gross national product	110

[a] Prices of physical components estimated in billions of U. S. 1953
Dollars.

40%, compared to 18% for the United Kingdom, 22% for China, and 25% for the U. S.

2. The Leontief Model and Labor Productivity

The retention fraction is not an indicator of the standard of living, as is evident from the fact that the retention fractions for the U. S., Britain, and China, are quite comparable, but the standards of living are quite different. The standard of living depends also, and more significantly, upon the values of the production coefficients, and in particular upon the coefficients π_{jo} describing the amount of labor required for the production of various commodities, i.e., upon "labor productivity." Table VIII below allows a rough comparison of the amount of labor required for the production of some typical basic commodities in Britain and in the United States, thus explaining the higher standard of living in the U. S. Of course, factors such as quality of product, hours of labor expended, etc., are neglected in our crudely quantitative comparison, but it is hardly likely that they could affect the comparison to any considerable degree.

TABLE VIII

Rough Estimates of Comparative Labor Productivity in the U. S. and the United Kingdom, 1957 [a]

	U. S.		United Kingdom		Approx. ratio to U. S.
	Millions employed	Production	Millions employed	Production	
Vehicles	2		1.2		3
mill. cars		5.5		0.9	
mill. trucks		1.2		0.3	
Textiles, bill. yds.	1	12	0.9	2.5	5
Coal mining, mill. tons	0.25	500	0.75	220	7
Agriculture, forestry, and fishing	6		1		2
mill. doz. eggs		5		1	
mill. acres of grain		150		7	
mill. tons potatoes		24		6	
mill. tons fish		2.5		29	

[a] The data for this table are from the *Europa Yearbook*, 1960.

TABLE IX

Ratios of Labor Productivity in Selected Industries, U. S./Britain (1948)

Tin Containers	4.96	Grain milling	1.86
Cardboard containers	4.24	Bicycles	1.88
Pig iron	4.91	Rubber tires	2.03
Wool yarn	4.53	Jute yarn	1.77
Radio receiving tubes	3.74	Beet sugar	0.85
Cigarettes	3.63	Building bricks	1.77
Wool carpets and rugs	3.28	Paint brushes	1.74
Glass containers	3.06	Cotton piece goods	1.78
Soap	2.89	Boots and shoes	1.67
Paper sacks	2.77	Rope and twine	1.61
Watches	2.59	Margarine	1.23
Ice cream	2.14	Cement	1.39
Animal feeds	2.06	Razor blades	1.12
Biscuits	2.18	Canned fish	1.20
Malt liquors	1.08	Ice	0.69

TABLE X

Rough Comparative Estimates of Agricultural Labor Productivity for
various Countries, Mid-1950's [a]

	Total pop. (mill.)	Employed (mill.)	Agriculture employed (mill.)	Production (mill. tons)		Ratio to U. S.
				Grain	Potatoes	
U. S.	180	60	8	150	12	1
Great Britain	50	24	1	7	6	2
W. Germany	52	24	4	12½	26	2
Czechoslovakia	13	6	2	4½	9	3
Poland	29	17	8	12	35	4
U. S. S. R.	210	105	45	141	86	4
Japan	90	43	15	15	10	12
Turkey	24	14	9½	14	1½ (rice)	12
Mexico	33	10	6	6	—	20
China	600	300	260	175	23	27
Indo-China	12	7	5	—	3½ (rice)	28
U. S. (1910)	—	—	—	—	—	3

[a] The data for this table is from the *Europa Yearbook*, 1960.

More precise ratios of labor productivity in the year 1948 have been given by M. Frankel, *American Economic Review* (1955), v. 45, p. 94. We have reproduced some of Frankel's data in Table IX above.

Table X gives crude estimates of labor productivity in agriculture (computed on a grain and potatoes basis) for a number of economies. The close relation between this one parameter and the general socio-economic state of a nation is striking.

3. Some Power Series Expansions

Since according to Theorem 3.7 the price vector $\tilde{\mathbf{p}}(\rho)$ is a strictly increasing function of ρ, it follows from the definition (3.12) of the retention fraction $r(\rho)$ that the retention fraction is a strictly increasing function of ρ.[1] It is plain from the definition (3.12) that $r(\rho)$ has the value zero for $\rho = 0$, in which case the national dividend is zero, and has the value one for $\rho = \rho_{\max}$, which case, as we saw in our preceding lecture, is defined by the hypothetical circumstance that the wage rate sinks to zero. Thus we may regard ρ as a function of r. Figure 1 illustrates the relationship between ρ and r.

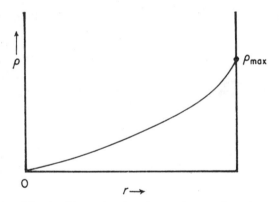

Fig. 1.   Retention fraction and rate of profit.

[1] The monotonicity of this relationship corresponds to the popular adage "you can't have your cake and eat it too." This rueful fact apparently constitutes a dialectical contradiction. I quote from Li: "The inverse relationship between the rate of accumulation and the rate of consumption is considered as one of the 'internal contradictions' to be resolved." See Mao Tse-Tung "Concerning the Correct Disposition of the Problem of the People's Internal Contradictions," *Jen-min jih-pao*, June 19, 1957.

It is interesting to express the rate of profit ρ as a function of r by evaluating the coefficients in the expansion:

$$(4.1) \qquad \rho(\gamma) = \sum_{k=1}^{\infty} \gamma_k r^k,$$

making use of (3.11) and (3.12), i.e. by solving (3.12) for ρ, obtaining a solution in the form of a power series expansion. To do this let us first define

$$(4.2) \qquad f(\rho) = \mathbf{a}'(I - \overset{\circ}{\Pi})\tilde{\mathbf{p}}(\rho)$$

so that, from (3.12), it follows that

$$r = (f(\rho) - f(o))/f(\rho)$$

and hence

$$f(\rho) = f(o)/(1 - r).$$

Thus

$$f(\rho) = f(o)(1 + r + r^2 + \cdots)$$

i.e.

$$f(\rho) - f(o) = f(o) \sum_{k=1}^{\infty} r^k$$

or

$$(\rho f_\rho(o) + \tfrac{1}{2}\rho^2 f_{\rho\rho}(o) + \cdots) = f(o) \sum_{k=1}^{\infty} r^k$$

which may be written as

$$(4.3) \qquad \left(f_\rho(o) \sum_{k=1}^{\infty} \gamma_k r^k + \tfrac{1}{2} f_{\rho\rho}(o) \left(\sum_{k=1}^{\infty} \gamma_k r^k \right)^2 + \cdots \right) = f(o) \sum_{k=1}^{\infty} r^k.$$

The coefficients γ_k may now be evaluated by setting equal the coefficients of like powers of r from both sides of the equation; we obtain the equations

$$(4.4a) \qquad f_\rho(o)\gamma_1 = f(o)$$
$$(4.4b) \qquad f_\rho(o)\gamma_2 + \tfrac{1}{2}\gamma_1^2 f_{\rho\rho}(o) = f(o) \quad \text{etc.}$$

Thus, to first order in r,

$$(4.5) \qquad \rho = (f(o)/f_\rho(o))r + 0(r^2)$$

To evaluate the coefficients $f(o)$, $f_\rho(o)$, etc. in terms of the production coefficients, thereby obtaining a more explicit expression for the ratio $f(o)/f_\rho(o)$, we use equation (3.5):

$$\tilde{\mathbf{p}}(\rho) = (I - \mathring{\Pi} - \rho\mathring{\Phi})^{-1}\mathbf{v}.$$

This formula must now be expanded as a power series in ρ. The desired expansion may be carried out by a procedure which is quite standard in the theory of matrices. First, we use the formula $A^{-1} = B^{-1}(AB^{-1})^{-1}$ to separate the factor $(I - \mathring{\Pi})^{-1}$ out of the expression $(I - \mathring{\Pi} - \rho\mathring{\Phi})^{-1}$. This gives

$$\tilde{\mathbf{p}}(\rho) = (I - \mathring{\Pi})^{-1}(I - \rho\mathring{\Phi}(I - \mathring{\Pi}))^{-1}\mathbf{v}.$$

Next we expand the expression $(I - \rho\mathring{\Phi}(I - \mathring{\Pi})^{-1})^{-1}$ in a geometric series, making use of the theorem whose statement follows formula (3.5) (which theorem is surely applicable for sufficiently small ρ). This gives

$$\tilde{\mathbf{p}}(\rho) = (I - \mathring{\Pi})^{-1}\mathbf{v} + \rho(I - \mathring{\Pi})^{-1}\mathring{\Phi}(I - \mathring{\Pi})^{-1}\mathbf{v}$$
$$+ \rho^2(I - \mathring{\Pi})^{-1}\mathring{\Phi}(I - \mathring{\Pi})^{-1}\mathring{\Phi}(I - \mathring{\Pi})^{-1}\mathbf{v}$$
$$+ \cdots$$

which gives an explicit power-series expansion for the price-vector in terms of ρ. Thus

$$(\partial/\partial\rho)\,\tilde{\mathbf{p}}(o) = (I - \mathring{\Pi})^{-1}\mathring{\Phi}(I - \mathring{\Pi})^{-1}\mathbf{v}$$

or

(4.6) $$(\partial/\partial\rho)\,\ddot{\mathbf{p}}(o) = (I - \mathring{\Pi})^{-1}\mathring{\Phi}\tilde{\mathbf{p}}(o);$$

from (4.1), we then obtain

$$f_\rho(o) = \mathbf{a}'(I - \mathring{\Pi})(\partial/\partial\rho)\,\tilde{\mathbf{p}}(o) = \mathbf{a}'\mathring{\Phi}\tilde{\mathbf{p}}(o).$$

We may consequently write

(4.7) $$f(o)/f_\rho(o) = [\mathbf{a}'(I - \mathring{\Pi})\tilde{\mathbf{p}}(o)/\mathbf{a}'\mathring{\Phi}\tilde{\mathbf{p}}(o)].$$

Hence, finally, an expression for ρ as a function of r valid to second order in r is given by

(4.8) $$\rho(r) = [\mathbf{a}'(I - \mathring{\Pi})\tilde{\mathbf{p}}(o)/\mathbf{a}'\mathring{\Phi}\tilde{\mathbf{p}}(o)]r + 0(r^2.)$$

In this connection we note also the equation

(4.9) $$\tilde{\mathbf{p}}(\rho) = (I - \mathring{\Pi})^{-1}\mathbf{v} + 0(\rho)$$

valid to first order.

Equations (4.8) and (4.9) together express two well-known forms of the classical "labor theory" of prices and profit.

The first-order equation (4.8) expresses a theory of prices with the following heuristic significance: let the "labor content" of a commodity be defined as the actual labor consumed in its production, plus the labor content of all the commodities consumed in its production. Letting L_i denote the labor content of a unit of C_i, the following equation is an immediate consequence of the definition:

$$(4.10) \qquad L_i = \pi_{io} + \sum_{j=1}^{n} \pi_{ij} L_j$$

$$= v_i + \sum_{j=1}^{n} \pi_{ij} L_j.$$

Thus $(I - \mathring{\Pi})\mathbf{L} = \mathbf{v}$. Comparing this equation with (4.9), we see at once that $\mathbf{L} = \tilde{\mathbf{p}}(o)$. Thus, taking $\tilde{\mathbf{p}}(\rho) = \mathbf{L}$ corresponds to expanding about $\rho = 0$ (i.e., $r = 0$) and omitting all higher terms. Similarly, the second order equation (4.8) for ρ is that which is obtained by expanding the function $\rho(r)$ about $r = 0$, and by subsequent omission of all terms of higher order than the first.

4. Excise Taxes

It is quite easy to apply the price theory which has been developed to the situation in which excise taxes are imposed on some or all of the commodities in our model economy. Let τ_i, $1 \le i \le n$, be the excise-rate on commodity C_i (figured as a percentage of basic price). Then the reasoning which led us to the equation (1.5) leads us, if we take these taxes into account, to the equation

$$(4.11) \qquad p_i = \pi_{io} p_o + \sum_{j=1}^{n} \pi_{ij}(1 + \tau_j) p_j + \rho \sum_{j=1}^{n} \phi_{ij}(1 + \tau_j) p_j.$$

Denoting p_i/p_o by $\tilde{p}_i$ and setting $v_i = \pi_{io}$ as before, we have

$$(4.12) \qquad \tilde{p}_i - \sum_{j=1}^{n} \pi_{ij}(1 + \tau_j) \tilde{p}_j - \rho \sum_{j=1}^{n} \phi_{ij}(1 + \tau_j) \tilde{p}_j = \mathbf{v}_i.$$

If we write $\mathring{\Pi}_\tau$ and $\mathring{\Phi}_\tau$ for the matrices whose elements are $\pi_{ij}(1 + \tau_j)$ and $\phi_{ij}(1 + \tau_j)$ respectively, we may write the equations (4.12) in vector form as

(4.13) $(I - \mathring{\Pi}_\tau - \rho\mathring{\Phi}_\tau)\tilde{\mathbf{p}}(\rho,\tau) = \mathbf{v},$

with the solution

(4.14) $\tilde{\mathbf{p}}(\rho,\tau) = (I - \mathring{\Pi}_\tau - \rho\mathring{\Phi}_\tau)^{-1}\mathbf{v}.$

If the tax rates τ are small, we may use the techniques of the preceding section to make a power series expansion of the price-vector $\tilde{\mathbf{p}}(\rho,\tau)$ in the quantities τ_i. To first order in the tax rates τ_i we would have

(4.15) $\tilde{\mathbf{p}}(\tau,\rho) = (I - \mathring{\Pi} - \rho\mathring{\Phi})^{-1}\mathbf{v}$
$$+ (I - \mathring{\Pi} - \rho\mathring{\Phi})^{-1}(\hat{\mathring{\Pi}}_\tau + \hat{\mathring{\Phi}}_\tau)(I - \mathring{\Pi} - \rho\mathring{\Phi})^{-1}\mathbf{v} + 0(\tau^2),$$

where $\hat{\mathring{\Pi}}_\tau$ and $\hat{\mathring{\Phi}}_\tau$ denote the matrices whose elements are $\pi_{ij}\,\tau_j$ and $\phi_{ij}\tau_j$ respectively. Equation (4.15) may be written in terms of the vector $\tilde{\mathbf{p}}(\tau)$ of prices before the imposition of taxes as

(4.16) $\tilde{\mathbf{p}}(\tau,\rho) = \tilde{\mathbf{p}}(\rho) + (I - \mathring{\Pi} - \rho\mathring{\Phi})^{-1}(\hat{\mathring{\Pi}}_\tau + \hat{\mathring{\Phi}}_\tau)\tilde{\mathbf{p}}(\rho).$

The question which is traditional in the theory of excise taxes, to wit, the question "to where are excise taxes shifted" is thus answered by our theory (cf. especially (4.13)) as follows. Excise taxes are shifted unrestrictedly through the economy, finally resting upon the individual consumer, unless these taxes are absorbed in whole or part by a fall in the profit rate ρ. Does ρ fall? About this question the theory tells us nothing.

In the theory of excise taxes our input-output model then gives us the same ready if somewhat approximate answer that it gives us in the simple theory of prices.

5. Concluding Remarks

Our discussion of the theory of prices in the Leontief input-output model may now be (at least temporarily) concluded. As we have seen, this price theory is simple, definite in its point of view, and unambiguous in its conclusions. Since our model omits so many of the factors affecting prices in the real economy, however, we would be ill-advised to take this theory as more than an elaboration of important principles. We may take the prime significance of our discussion of the Leontief model to lie less in the price-theory which has been elaborated than in the circumstance that the model provides a reasonably realistic framework within which the material functioning of a real economy may be described. Writing an input-output matrix gives us a bird's eye view of the overall flow of commodities in an economy, i.e. the process whereby the growth of certain stocks proceeds via subtraction from other stocks. We shall now make use of this framework to give a theory, like that of Metzler, of the business cycle.

PART **B**

Theory of Business Cycles

Business Cycles. Introductory Considerations

1. Some Notions from the Theory of Games

As an illuminating introduction to the mathematical theory of business cycles, we shall present a very brief discussion of some aspects of game theory especially as applied to a particular idealized game, which will be called "majority." Certain phenomena which will be seen to play a role in this game are suggestive of the "Crisis of Confidence" phenomenon which most economists agree is a major factor in the business cycle. We present this tid-bit of game theory not out of an intent to make serious use of the theory, but simply to fix attention upon a basic phenomenon by making some sharp definitions.

Let us begin with a heuristic definition of the notion of a "game." The word "game" refers to any activity in which several persons or teams must choose, from a finite list of possible alternatives defined by specific rules, a particular alternative, i.e. a *"move"* must be made, following which further choices must be made in sequence from (in general) a new list of alternatives, which list depends, according to specific rules, upon the previous moves of all the players or teams. There is also a rule whereby play terminates after a finite number of such "moves," a rule specifying the amount of information about the previous moves and the situation of other players which any given player is to have at any given stage of play, and, finally, a rule whereby after the termination of play there is a certain payoff to each of the players. This *"payoff function"* is a function of the

59

moves selected by each player at each stage of the completed play. More generally, the payoff to each player may be a stochastic function of the moves made, i.e. it may assign an "expected payoff" rather than a "definite payoff" to each completed series of moves after termination of play. A particular realization of the rules is called a "play" of the game. Thus, while we might say, in ordinary usage, "Last night I played three games of chess," we should express this idea in the present terminology by "Last night I played three plays of the game chess."

Consideration of the class of all games from the point of view of the above very general definition makes it evident that an important simplification can be made. It is sufficient to consider games in which each player has only one move. Indeed, given any game in which each player has a sequence of moves to make in the course of play, we can consider instead a certain logically if not practically equivalent game in which each player has only one move to make; we may specify the new game in terms of the old game as follows. Each player, instead of making his moves in sequence according to the sequentially varying situation in which he finds himself, is to decide in advance what choice he will make in every situation which can possibly arise; submission of this "strategy" (perhaps in the form of a thick bound volume) to an umpire is to be the player's (single) move. (Think of chess by post card, where (partial) strategies of this sort, rather than single moves, are regularly exchanged.) Once all players hand such a set of instructions to an umpire, the umpire can then determine the result of the play without further consultation with the players. The payoff is, of course, to be the same as if the game were played in its original form. The set of all permissible strategies is then the set of permissible moves, in the new game, for the various players. We shall take it as heuristically plain without any additional formal discussion that in a certain appropriate sense the modified game is logically equivalent to the game in its original form. This has the great advantage of allowing us to assume in all that follows, without loss of generality, that all games are such that each player makes only one move during the play.

Then for any particular play of a game each of the players must select one and only one particular alternative, or move, from a finite list of moves defined by the rules of the game. Game theory shows, however, that for certain games it may be advantageous for one or another player to "randomize" his move, i.e. to assign a probability to each of the permissible moves, with the understanding that the player's choice of a move in any particular play of the game is to be determined stochastically according to those probabilities. This sort of strategy is what we shall call a *random strategy*. If a random strategy reduces to a nonrandom strategy, i.e. if there exists some particular permissible move for which the associated probability is 1, we call the strategy "pure," otherwise the strategy is called "mixed." The space of all assignments of probability numbers (or probability density functions) to the possible moves open to the jth player is called the "*strategy space*" for the jth player.

We summarize the above discussion in the three following formal definitions.

DEFINITION. *An n-person game is a set of n functions $f_1(k_1, \cdots, k_n)$, $f_2(k_1, \cdots, k_n), \cdots, f_n(k_1, \cdots, k_n)$ of n integer-valued variables $k_1 \cdots k_n$, the jth integer k_j being restricted to lie in an interval $1 \leq k_j \leq K_j$. The integer K_j is called the* number of moves *open to the jth player; the function f_j is called the* payoff *function to the jth player.*

DEFINITION. *A set of* randomized strategies *for the n-person game of the preceding definition is a set of vectors $\alpha_1, \cdots, \alpha_n$ having the properties*

(a) $\alpha_j = [\alpha_j{}^{(1)} \cdots \alpha_j{}^{(K_j)}]$ *is a vector in K_j-dimensional space, $j = 1, \cdots, n$.*

(b) *The components of α_j are nonnegative and satisfy the equation*

$$\sum_{k=1}^{K_j} \alpha_j{}^{(k)} = 1, \quad j = 1, \cdots, n.$$

DEFINITION. *Let $\alpha_1, \cdots, \alpha_n$ be a set of randomized strategies for the n-person game of the two preceding definitions. Then the randomized-strategy payoff function $F_j(\alpha_1, \cdots, \alpha_n)$ to the jth player is the function*

$$F_j(\alpha_1, \cdots, \alpha_n) = \sum_{k_1=1}^{K_1} \sum_{k_2=2}^{K_2} \cdots \sum_{k_n=1}^{K_n} \alpha_1{}^{(k_1)} \alpha_2{}^{(k_2)} \cdots \alpha_n{}^{(k_n)} f_j(k_1, k_2, \cdots, k_n).$$

The three preceding definitions are basic. We shall now make a more theoretical statement by giving the definition of the important notion of equilibrium point.

DEFINITION.   Let $\alpha_1, \cdots, \alpha_n$ be a set of (randomized) strategies for the n-person game of the preceding definitions.   Then this set of strategies is called an equilibrium point for the n-person game if

$$F_j(\alpha_1, \cdots, \alpha_n) \geqq F_j(\alpha_1, \cdots, \alpha_{s-1}, \alpha, \alpha_{s+1}, \cdots, \alpha_n),$$

for each vector α in the strategy space for the jth player.

Thus an equilibrium point is a set of strategies such that if *any player j* ALONE *deviates from his "equilibrium" strategy he can do himself no good*, that is, he cannot receive a larger payoff than what he would get by choosing the equilibrium strategy α_j.

Nash, to whom this interesting notion of equilibrium point is due, has established the following reassuring theorem.

THEOREM (J. Nash).   *Every game has an equilibrium point.*

The proof makes use of the Brouwer fixed point theorem; since our interest in game theory is merely tangential, it would constitute an excessive digression if we gave its details.   We refer the reader interested in the details of this proof to Nash's original paper in the *Annals of Mathematics*, v. 54 (1951), pp. 286–295.

We may supplement the above definition of the notion of equilibrium point with the following additional definition:

DEFINITION.   Let $\alpha_1, \cdots, \alpha_n$ be an equilibrium point for an n-person game, as in the preceding definition.   Then $\alpha_1, \cdots, \alpha_n$ is said to be a stable equilibrium point if we have

$$F_j(\alpha_1, \cdots, \alpha_n) > F_j(\alpha_1, \cdots, \alpha_{s-1}, \alpha, \alpha_{s+1}, \cdots, \alpha_n)$$

for each vector α in the strategy space for the jth player.   An equilibrium point which is not stable is called unstable.

Thus a stable equilibrium point is one at which each individual player finds that he has a unique best strategy determined by the strategies of the other players.   If, at such a stable equilibrium point, any player deviates from his equilibrium strategy while all the other players adhere to theirs, he must surely suffer some nonzero penalty.

2. The Game of "Majority"

The game "majority" is defined for an odd number $n \geq 3$ of players.   Each player has two possible moves, "stay" and "go"; the payoff function is as follows.   If a player chooses "stay" his payoff is zero, regardless of the actions of the other players. If a player chooses "go," and a majority of all players has chosen "go," his payoff is $P > 0$, but if a majority of all players has chosen "stay" his payoff his $-Q < 0$.

Let p_j be the probability assigned to the move "stay" by the jth player. Then the strategy spaces A_j are $\{p_j \mid 0 \leq p_j \leq 1\}$ respectively. It is nearly evident heuristically that this game has exactly two stable equilibrium points, namely $p_1 = p_2 = \cdots p_n = 0$ and $p_1 = p_2 = \cdots = p_n = 1$. An exact analysis which we omit as an unnecessarily extensive digression from the main course of our interest, confirms this and reveals the existence of exactly one additional (unstable) equilibrium point, that in which each p_j is equal to the constant β defined as the unique root of the equation

$$\sum_{k \leq n+1} \binom{2n}{k} \beta^k (-\beta)^{2n-k} = P/P + Q$$

which lies between zero and 1. The heuristic irrelevance of this additional equilibrium point relates directly to its instability, manifested in the fact that at this unstable equilibrium any individual player is free to change his strategy without suffering any loss, and that once he has done so, all the other players are forced to follow suit. Only the two stable equilibria, that in which all players play "stay," and that in which all players play "go," are relevant to our heuristic discussion. Note that if all players are playing the pure strategy "stay" or the pure strategy "go" no one of them can improve his payoff by deviating from this strategy.

We may profitably supplement our static description of the equilibrium points with a heuristic account of the dynamic trend toward these equilibrium points, as it might take place in repeated plays of the game. In repeated plays of the game, each player might adopt a policy somewhat as follows: "If on the last play a majority has chosen 'go' then I shall 'go' during the present play, but if a majority has chosen last time to 'stay' then I shall 'stay' during the present play." If this policy is generally followed it is not difficult to see that the set of strategies actually played must rapidly converge to one or another of the two equilibrium points mentioned above. All further play will merely confirm the equilibrium attained: i.e., all the players will choose the strategy which confirms the equilibrium into which they have jointly fallen. Note that it is not even necessary that any of the individual players know explicitly what the other players are doing, or even be explicitly conscious of the connection between individual payoff and majority action. All that is necessary is that an umpire or some other neutral objective mechanism repeatedly announce the payoffs accruing to the individual players, thereby giving them a chance to learn empirically the difference between a profitable and an unprofitable course of action.

Suppose next that each player modifies his policy on repeated plays to be as follows: "If on the previous play a majority has chosen to 'go' then I shall choose 'go' on this play with probability $1 - \nu$, while if a majority has chosen to 'stay' I shall choose to 'stay' on this play with probability $1 - \nu$." If ν is taken to be zero we have the former situation; if ν is taken to be positive even though small, the situation will be somewhat different. Successive plays will see the majority "jump" from "stay" to "go," remain at the "go" situation for a time inversely proportional to a power of ν, and then jump back again.

Let us define ad hoc the *level of activity* for a particular play of the game to be the total payoff if a majority "goes," or the total losses if a majority "stays," so that if k players choose "go" the level of activity is kP or $-kQ$ depending on whether or not k is a majority. The above description then shows that the levels of activity will jump from levels close to zero to levels close to nP, and back again.

Now consider one last form of policy that the players might adopt. Suppose that the probability ν is chosen not as a constant but rather as some increasing function of the actual number of players who deviated from the majority on the last play. The players could justify such a policy as follows. Even though the majority is still choosing to "stay," the existence of quite a few players who have deviated from the majority makes it appear that things may be "picking up."

If the players adopt such a policy, the existence of a few dissenters from the majority might lead on the next play to even more dissenters (or to be more precise to a higher probability of there being more). While the previous case of fixed ν led to jumps from the one level of activity to the other, the dynamic here is better described as a wandering from the one level of activity to the other, and back again.

It is surprising how many features of the "psychological" side of the business cycle, as remarked upon by empirical students of business affairs, are recaptured in this rather trivial model. It might even be claimed that the model reflects a basic property of a wide class of sociological situations. An amusing example is furnished by the familiar situation in which a group of four or five persons regularly lunch together. When the group gathers to start out for lunch, the following situation arises. Those who go will, if they are in the majority, obtain lunch as a premium, while those who stay will obtain nothing. On the other hand, those who go, if they are in the minority, will suffer a loss either through embarrassment at their own presumed slight rudeness, through having to return and fetch the laggards or wait on a windy corner, etc. The reality and relevance of the stagnant equilibrium in "majority" is quite apparent in the familiar situation in which the lunchers stand around, often for considerable periods, each wondering why it is so hard to get started.

There is, of course, something highly paradoxical about the stagnant equilibrium in the game of "majority." Each player deplores the situation which he himself helps to create. Alas! individual optimization and collective optimization have here diverged.

It is also to be noted that, in the "majority" game with $2n + 1$ players, at least $n + 1$ players must cooperate to free themselves from the stagnant equilibrium. We may then say that this equilibrium point is *stable of order n*. The generalization of this notion to the equilibrium points of arbitrary games is evident.

3. Some Economic Facts

The game-theory of the preceding section makes it plain that in a situation in which persons suffer penalties or losses for not following the majority, a situation of general stagnation quite out of accord with the wishes of any individual or small group of individuals is possible. To be able to apply this general remark to economics we must show how these "penalties" arise in economics. I shall make a number of general comments on this point, elucidating them in a very specific way by reference to the highly illuminating study of the shoe-leather-hide industry which we owe to Ruth P. Mack.

The basic distinction which must be made is that between *staple* and *nonstaple* goods. Many industrial processes transform staple into nonstaple goods. Consider, e.g. an automobile plant making very specific cars and trucks (specific as to body design, upholstery, paint) out of staple metal sheets and steel bars, etc.; a clothing or shoe manufacturer cutting staple lengths of cloth into the forms demanded by specific patterns; for a most extreme case, a manufacturer of personalized stationery imprinting his customers' names on blank sheets of paper. Such a process can only be economically rewarding if it is carried out for immediate sale to a guaranteed market, or, as the common phrase has it, if the specific product is made "to order." That is, the manufacturer of a specific product can safely proceed with his economic operations only if the economic machine as a whole is moving, so that, in particular, his market holds up. To continue production during a falling off of the market is in such circumstances pure folly, since the random variations of demand-style from one item to another closely similar but distinguishable item can well mean that production "for inventory" is in reality production of trash (in the economic sense), to be sold at a substantial discount or at a loss, or, even in the best case, to clog inventories, tying up much-needed capital and driving profits to an unpleasantly low level.

Thus the manufacturer must, like the player in "majority," follow the actions of others; and industrial fluctuations show the oft remarked phenomenon of "crises of confidence" which appear in their most elementary form upon consideration of that model game. The caution which all these circumstances impose upon the manufacturer is well described by Mack. Mack remarks:

Periodic planning of the amount, style, color, and price of shoes to be produced during the ensuing months (very typically six months) is common among shoe manufacturers. The sales forecasts on the basis of which plans are laid are prepared with great care. Ordinarily, plans for the fall line are formulated around April or May, and for the spring line around October. In planning a line, a great deal is taken for granted and typically not subjected to review each season—the general sort of shoe to be manufactured, the type of customer to whom it is meant to appeal, the price line at which it will be expected to retail, the marketing channels to be used, the process of manufacture, the capacity of the factory, and even detailed cost figures for many of the pieces or operations involved in the manufacture of the various classes of products. Moreover, many individual models, at least for manufacturers of staple shoes, will be carried over from the previous year. But more typically, styles will change from season to season, though change itself may follow a discernible trend. For women's high-style shoes, many new models will be introduced not only at the planning period, but frequently during the season.

The sales forecasts will be made for each line of shoes—that is, for each group of models falling into some broader category such as a given retail price line, technique of manufacture, or use designation. For a large company, the forecasts may be built by reconciling the summed estimates of individual salesmen and district managers with estimates made by the heads of the company or various branches of the company. In a small company, the guess as to future sales may be done scientifically or by ear. Generally, the core of the estimating process is the record of last year's sales or of sales for the past several years. This figure is then modified by adding the amount that the business may be "going ahead" and by judgments on the condition of retailers' stocks and on general business conditions in the coming season. The prognosis of the business climate will affect not only the estimate of total sales but also its composition. If, for example, the forecast of economic weather is gloomy, lower price lines may be emphasized; or shoes made for stock may gain in importance relative to those made to order.

The sales forecasts are often used as the basis for financing plans, marketing plans, personnel plans, or for the integration of various branches of the business. They may also become the basis of leather buying. But as far as I can determine, they do not typically provide the basis for day-to-day production schedules.

The reason for this is clear enough: the specificity of the product is too great to permit extensive manufacture of anything except the particular style, color, material, size, and width of shoe that someone has ordered. Shoe manufacturers testify to this, claiming that most shoes in this country are made to order. Of course some anticipation of peak requirements takes place; also, an in-stock department is carried by many manufacturers. But even in in-stock departments, though a particular shoe is not manufactured in response to a particular order, information conveyed by the incoming order on what shoes are being bought and in what quantities is closely audited before shoes are ticketed for production.

It is most illuminating to observe the difference between the situation respecting manufacture of specific items as portrayed above, and that which prevails in the manufacture of staples, as also the characteristic differences between the manufacturer's attitude toward staples and semi-staples. Mack remarks on the production of leather:

The vegetable tanning of sole leather—and this ancient art is still the one commonly used for the production of leather soles—requires two or three months. This means that, even were it possible to obtain hides from packers or dealers almost immediately, it would typically not be feasible for a tanner to wait until orders for sole leather are on his books before he acquires the hides to be used in filling them. Almost of necessity, sole-leather orders are filled from finished or in-process inventories. These inventories were large in the interwar period—almost an eight-month supply; a little over half were in the form of finished leather or cutstock. Viewed the other way around, finished sole leather is so durable and staple a product that it is possible for trade customs that imply large finished stocks to take root— customs affecting ordering and production.

As it is, production can follow a far smoother course through time than would be possible if a closer link to orders had to be maintained. This is important because it is expensive for a sole-leather plant to operate at a level very different from its planned capacity, since the size of the packs and the time in each process is not readily adjusted. I am told that the preferred method of reducing output is to close down the plant for a day or more a week. Large inventories also mean that buying can be smoother and more sensitively adjusted to seasonal and other patterns in the availability of hides of a desired quality than could otherwise be the case. This is important in view of the basic by-product character of hides and the consequent limited flexibility of supply.

The tanning of upper leather, on the other hand, is a relatively swift operation in which the use of chemicals, notably chrome salts, makes it possible to complete tanning and finishing in a few weeks, though a month or more is often required for the convenient routing of the successive preparatory, tanning, and finishing operations. Orders are often written with a delivery date six weeks or more away, consequently it is physically possible to buy hides to be made up into specific lots of side upper leather for which orders are on hand. Also, side leather is required in all sorts of colors, qualities, and surface finishes, so that large stocks of finished leather are a far riskier property than equal quantities of sole. But since hides are in large measure a by-product, with the associated elements of inflexibility in their supply, it would be advantageous to free hide buying (under stable market prospects) of the need to duplicate all the ups and downs of leather selling. The solution is to split the manufacturing operation in the middle. After the basic tanning processes have been completed, leather can be dried and stored in the crust awaiting specification of color and finish.

All this suggests that stocks of in-process and finished upper leather will not be as large as those of sole leather; they averaged three and three-quarters monthly supply for the interwar period, less than half the supply of sole leather. It suggests, too, that stocks in process (including the semi-finished dried leathers awaiting finishing operations) will be somewhat larger relative to production and to finished stocks than for sole. And indeed they are; in spite of the far shorter production period, in-process stocks of upper leather constituted a somewhat larger proportion of all stocks than was the case for sole leather. They were 54 per cent of the total upper leather stocks of tanners—an average of about two months' supply over the interwar period.

The same business necessities which we have observed in the basic field of manufacture, and the same sensitivity toward variations in the position of a commodity along the staple–nonstaple scale, also govern the operations of the retailer. We quote again from Mack:

Next, a retailer must offer a selection of types and styles of shoes for most of the price lines stocked. For women's shoes there is the oxford, the low-heeled slipper, the high-heeled slipper, the open toe or open heel or both, the conservative types, and the high-mode types. Most styles need to be carried in several colors and leathers. In the popular-priced field, the number of styles offered in a single store will, other things the same, be far fewer than in a store appealing to wealthier customers, where several hundred style numbers of women's shoes may be carried. But, at best, it is difficult to limit selection for women's shoes to less than several dozen numbers. The problem is, of course, still more complicated for a family shoe store.

In these problems the shoe retailer shares with most other sorts of retail stores, but he has a special problem in the variety of lengths and widths common to the foot of man. The United States army's schedule of GI service shoes lists 239 combinations of size and width. This is, of course, a singular wealth of selection. Most feet fall in a relatively narrow range of sizes. A survey of several hundred thousand pairs of shoes sold by a group of large shoe factories indicated that about 85 per cent of the sales were in 45 combinations of size and width (about 33 per cent of a manufacturer's full line); moreover, 66 per cent of the sales were in 16 (or about 12 per cent). For the most part, retailers will stock a reasonably full line in 60 or more sizes.

To the four dimensions—price, style, color, and size—in terms of which a retailer must plan his stocks, we may add a fifth—time. Both the volume of sales and the sorts of shoes featured change from one season of the year to the next, and retailers must build their stocks in anticipation of these seasonal requirements. Especially for women's shoes, the short life of a style number—often no more than six weeks—creates serious merchandising problems. Stocks are typically built to a maximum in April and May and again in the fall; they are reduced to a minimum in January and about six months later, in midsummer. At their minimum, they may average three quarters of their maximum size.

The multidimensional character of a shoe retailer's stocks suggests that they must be large. But it is equally true that they must be small. "It is essential," the prospective shoe retailer is warned, "that you maintain the proper relationship between inventory and sales. If your stock is too low, you lose sales; if too high, you lose profits." They must be small because a retailer makes money by buying and selling merchandise. At any given time, he has a limited amount of capital invested in the business. One important criterion by which bankers, investors, and colleagues evaluate his success is the amount of profit on invested capital. If a shoe retailer makes a 2 per cent profit on sales, and stocks turn twice a year, as they do in many shoe stores, he will make a 6 per cent profit on capital invested in merchandise, assuming a gross margin percentage of $33\frac{1}{3}$ per cent (on retail). If they turn five times a year, a figure probably attained by some chain systems, he will make 15 per cent profit on capital invested in merchandise, assuming the same gross margin percentage of $33\frac{1}{3}$. Since capital invested in stock in trade constitutes a very substantial portion of the total investment in most retail businesses, the effect on overall return on capital of changes in the rate of turnover is great.

Another reason for the rigid limitation of stocks, particularly of women's shoes, is style obsolescence. The selling life of a high-style shoe is short. The need to prepare ahead for peak-season sales, the uncertainty that a model will be accepted, and the short span of its life even if it proves popular mean that a retailer's stocks can be cluttered with unsalable goods in a twinkling. The pressure to hold stocks of high-style goods at a minimum is apparent in the difference between usual stock-turnover ratios of women's and men's shoes. Because of the greater variety in women's shoe styles, one would suppose that a greater assortment and therefore a larger stock, would be required per unit of sales in women's shoe departments than in men's. Actually, the figures indicate the reverse: stocks of women's shoes turn more rapidly than those of men's. The reason, in part, may be a tendency for manufacturers of style merchandise to attract customers by supplying rapid factory-to-store deliveries; stores therefore need smaller stocks. For the more staple men's shoes, a low price may be relatively somewhat more attractive than fast deliveries. In part, the faster turnover of women's shoe stocks seems to be a function of a larger scale of operations, which permit adequate selections without necessarily causing stocks to be high relative to sales. In any event, the challenge with which proper stock control confronts management is visible in the surprising difference in average turnover achieved in independent and chain shoe stores or in profitable and unprofitable shoe stores.

The burden of all this is simply that the size of stocks must be a matter of central importance to a shoe retailer. Consequently enforcement of stock objectives, whatever they are, must rank high among the many necessarily conflicting objectives that management pursues.

Mack summarizes the stock-size policies which are designed to meet the pressures described in the preceding paragraphs as follows:

. . . It is difficult to get a clear picture of just how the proper size of stocks is determined by shoe retailers or, more particularly, how the size of stocks is intended to change from time to time. Retailers with whom I have spoken claim that they aim to keep the ratio of sales to stocks about constant from season to season—constant, that is, between successive fall-winter seasons or spring-summer seasons.

. . . The amount of staple, nonseasonal shoes to be carried in stock is, for seasonal shoes, a function of expected sales. The merchandising manuals say that adequate stocks will, on the average, represent a specified multiple of usual weekly sales. Because shoes are not bought by retailers every hour or day, the actual size of stock must vary, and a proper minimum and maximum figure will be set. The minimum figure depends on the cushion thought necessary to meet variations in the sizes and models that customers require and unexpected spurts in sales or delays in delivery, as well as on the usual time required for an order to be delivered. Thus, if for a certain line of shoes a two-week cushion is thought advisable, and it takes three weeks to get delivery, a five-week supply represents the minimum stock; replenishment is called for when stock drops to this figure. The amount ordered depends on the maximum figure, which, in turn, depends on the factors already mentioned plus the frequency with which it is practical to place new orders (or the minimum acceptable size of an order). For a fast-moving staple line, these sizing-up orders may be placed every week or two weeks, thus (continuing with our example) causing maximum stocks to be a six-to-seven-week supply.

This procedure yields an implicit stock objective that is somewhere between a fixed absolute amount and a fixed ratio to sales (and is a function also of delivery periods). Which it approaches will depend on how a week's sales are estimated. If a planned and unchanged sales figure is used, planned stocks will tend to be held at a fixed level; if actual sales are the basis of the calculation, planned stock will maintain a more or less fixed ratio to expected sales. In actual practice, the sales figure probably has some stability, but may be altered whenever sales seem to establish themselves at a new level.

The vital importance of proper stock policy is vividly underscored in the following remarks of Mack:

In a large store, forecasting sales and setting up the budget is likely to be a full-dress affair undertaken at least twice a year. I have mentioned these forecasts in connection with the designing of model stocks, but they form the basis of a wide variety of other plans, including the amount of money to be spent on merchandise each month.

In the fall, executives start to compute figures for the period of, perhaps, February to August or January to July; those for the second six-month period are typically undertaken in early spring. The basic starting figure is likely to be the sales for the corresponding period of the previous year or few years. The figures may then be adjusted for the amount by which the store or department has been going ahead or behind. Finally, further corrections may be made on the basis of evaluations of a wide variety of special or general business conditions. In a large store, executives of many subdivisions are asked to submit estimates of what their sales are likely to be. These guesses, often oversanguine, are likely to be pared by the next higher groups to which they are submitted. The sum of the estimates will be scrutinized by top executives studying its component parts, the sales history of the entire company and business conditions expected to influence sales and prices. The guess concerning the future will be based on a variety of sources: Salesmen's reports, trade gossip, and personal contacts with manufacturers or competitors; market services and conferences with trusted advisers. Pet statistical indicators may also be scrutinized. For example one national organization reported that sales of stores in certain industrial towns show early trends; another company, selling popular-priced men's shoes, found the trend in industrial payrolls (as revealed by a twelve-month moving average) a good prognostication of its own sales. In small stores in which management techniques are less formalized, the guess about sales for a given month in the future may be little more than the sales of the corresponding month of the previous year, adjusted for any known peculiarities of that month and sometimes also by the percentage amount by which sales for the past half year or so have seemed to exceed or fall short of those of the corresponding months of the previous year.

The detailed workings of the order-and-shipment mechanism for finished shoes are described as follows by Mack:

When the new lines are first assembled and shown by shoe manufacturers, usually in November and December or early January for Easter styles, and in May or June for the fall models, retailers place "preseason" advance orders which may cover between 35 and 65 per cent of estimated sales for the next six months. (When and why they move through this range is the subject of the following chapter.) As the season progresses, "secondary" orders are placed for delivery in perhaps two months, more or less. In addition, retailers typically order some goods for "at-once" delivery; and in this case the receipt of the order may be expected within a few weeks or even less, sometimes in a few days if the shoe is carried by the "in-stock" department of a manufacturer or wholesaler, or it may not be expected for six weeks or so if it must be made to order and factories are active. These orders for immediate delivery may take care of unexpected developments, or they may simply be quite routine fill-in orders, or they may represent the slack in the "open-to-buy" position intentionally left to "sweeten stocks" at the latest possible moment.

Before leaving this most valuable work of Mack, we may profitably digress to quote some of her remarks on the procurement of the basic raw material for the whole shoe industry: leather. The following passage gives a description of the specific origin of those nonconstant returns to scale, characteristic for raw materials in general, whose existence we came to suspect in Chapter III, where we noted the wide price fluctuations of raw materials prices over the business cycle.

Hides and skins come from three major kinds of sources: from meat-packing plants; from a wide variety of domestic sources associated with the meat industry broadly defined; and from abroad.

The meat-packing industry, according to the Census of Manufactures, 1939, consisted of 1,478 establishments averaging eighty-one employees. But most of the work done in these buildings had little to do with hides, which are, of course, only a by-product. Many of the establishments were members of single corporate entities. Four of these—Swift, Armour, Cudahy, and Wilson, known as the "Big Four"—produced about 67 per cent of domestic packer hides in 1935. These companies, together with the Argentine subsidiaries of some of them, occupy a position of strategic importance in the raw hides market. Hides from large slaughterhouses and packing plants, known as "packer hides," have been estimated as constituting about two thirds of the total hide supply in this country. It was possible to tabulate systematically only the portion coming from slaughterhouses that deal in interstate commerce—"hides from federally inspected slaughter." They averaged 52 per cent of the total hide supply on American markets during the interwar period. Hides are typically the most valuable of the many by-products of the packing industry, averaging somewhere between 10 and 12 per cent of the value of different classes of carcasses, though they constitute only around 7 per cent of the body weight. Nevertheless, it seems clear that demand for hides could not materially influence the supply of cattle moving toward the slaughterhouses of the country. The supply of domestic packer hides is governed by conditions in the meat industry and constitutes a relatively steady stream within the fluctuating total hide supply.

Such hides also constitute the elite, for their "take off" and cure are commonly superior to that of the rest. The work is done at the large slaughterhouses by a team of men, each of whom sets to work on his assigned section of the carcass immediately after slaughter. When the hide has been cut off, it is removed to a cellar, cooled, spread out with others, and covered with rock salt; another layer of hides is placed on top and likewise sprinkled, until the pack reaches a height of about 40 inches. The edges are turned up to prevent the pickle from escaping. 'It is then "closed" with an extra cover of salt and allowed to remain at a temperature of 40 to 60 degrees for about thirty days. Since, in a small establishment, it may take time to assemble a complete pack, the process may take as long as six weeks. The adequacy of both take-off and cure has high commercial importance. As a possible cause of blemishes and poor trim, take-off determines the intensity with which the hide surface may be utilized for the manufacture of leather goods. Cure influences the quality of the leather and the length of time for which a hide may be safely kept before tanning—an interval that may range between one and perhaps ten months.

The second major source of hides with a statistical record are "hides from uninspected slaughter." They constituted 34 per cent of the interwar supply. Some of these are packer hides, but the large slaughterhouses from which they come deal within state lines and therefore are not federally inspected. But most are "country hides" and come from smaller packers or slaughterhouses, butchers, ranchers, or farmers. Though strictly speaking, these hides are also by-products of the meat industry, their supply on the commercial markets of the country is not rigidly geared to the supply of beef. If conditions are not favorable, they do not move through the complicated marketing channels to the central markets. Also hides of fallen cattle, typically about 2 per cent of the cattle population, may or may not be removed and marketed since the carcasses can be sold as glue stock, hides and all. Consequently this segment of the total hide supply fluctuates considerably from year to year. Many country hides are of poor quality, since their take-off, trim, and cure are usually inferior to the systematic work of the slaughterhouses.

Even more sensitive to domestic demand is the supply of imported hides which, in American markets, is entirely free of the by-product character. On the average, 14 per cent of the interwar supply of cattle hides came from other countries, though the figure varied widely: it was only slightly over 3 per cent in 1954 or 1958 and between 25 and 30 per cent in 1928, 1929, and 1941. Some of the imported hides, mostly from the Argentine, are high-quality packer hides. But when supplies are scarce, dried hides from remote corners of the earth may move to American markets. These hides are typically of inferior quality because of both the unskilled take-off and the character of the cure. It is interesting that some of them may be primary products rather than by-products even at their original source; this is true in Hindu countries, where beef is not eaten and hides are the chief salable product from the carcass.

4. A Dynamic Model of an Economy

In this section a simple dynamic model of the business cycle, incorporating some of the empirical facts noted in the previous section, will be introduced. The analysis of the model and the implications of the simplifying assumptions built into it will be discussed in the later lectures.

We consider an economy in which the commodities produced are $C_1, \cdots, C_n$, together with labor commodities $C_0, C_{-1}, \cdots, C_{-L}$. The model economy is taken to operate on a day-to-day basis as follows: Each morning the manufacturer of each commodity (for simplicity, we will assume that there is only one manufacturer per commodity, and that each manufacturer produces only a single commodity) takes inventory of his present stock. Having taken this inventory, he then schedules an amount of production which will bring his inventory to a certain level (which for other reasons he regards as optimum); we shall take this optimum inventory to be given by a formula

optimum inventory = constant $\times$ expected sales + basic inventory.

In order to calculate the amount of production to schedule, the manufacturer uses his estimate of optimum inventory, estimates the expected day's sales as being equal to the previous day's sales, and aims to produce an amount which, in addition to covering estimated sales, will just bring inventories to their optimum level. Having thus determined the desired production schedule for the day, the proper amounts of the various commodities $C_1, \cdots, C_n$ required to meet that schedule are ordered. Since our model refers with the greatest cogency to material commodities and the stocks thereof, we will absorb wage-payments into the formulation of our model, thereby eliminating the explicit occurrence of labor commodities. This elimination may be understood to take place as follows.

Let the total production of all commodities, including the labor commodities $C_0, \cdots, C_{-L}$, in a given period be $a_N, \cdots, a_{-L}$. Let the complete input-output matrix, including the inputs to the labor commodities determined by the various wage-rates, be π_{ij}, so that i and j vary from N to $-L$. Then the amount of commodity j produced net of consumption is

$$(5.1) \qquad a_j - \sum_{i=-L}^{N} a_i \pi_{ij}, \quad j = -L, \cdots, N.$$

Since labor commodities cannot be stored in inventory, but are consumed at the moment of production, we have

$$a_j - \sum_{i=-L}^{0} a_i \pi_{ij} = \sum_{i=1}^{N} a_i \pi_{ij}, \quad j = 0, \cdots, -L.$$

We may solve these equations for the amounts a_j of the commodities $C_0, \cdots, C_{-L}$ produced by letting $(I - \overset{\circ\circ}{\Pi})_{ij}^{-1}$ denote the entries of the inverse of the $(L + 1) \times (L + 1)$ matrix whose elements are $\delta_{ij} - \pi_{ij}$, $i,j = 0, \cdots, -L$. Our solution is then

$$(5.2) \qquad\qquad a_j = \sum_{i=1}^{N} \sum_{k=-L}^{0} a_i \pi_{ik} (I - \overset{\circ\circ}{\Pi})_{kj}^{-1}.$$

If we replace the quantities $a_0, \cdots, a_{-L}$ in the equations (5.1) by their expressions as given by (5.2), we may write the amount of commodity j produced net of consumption as

$$a_j - \sum_{i=1}^{N} a_i \tilde{\pi}_{ij}, \quad j = 1, \cdots, N,$$

where the matrix $\tilde{\pi}_{ij}$ is defined by

$$(5.3) \qquad \tilde{\pi}_{ij} = \pi_{ij} + \sum_{k,l=-L}^{0} \pi_{ik} (I - \overset{\circ\circ}{\Pi})_{kl}^{-1} \pi_{lj}, \quad i,j = 1, \cdots, N.$$

The reader will not fail to notice that the labor-eliminated input-output matrix $\tilde{\pi}_{ij}$ which is defined by (5.3) is a direct generalization of the same matrix defined in the case in which we had only a single labor sector by (1.8). We may now ignore the labor sectors entirely, and consider production to take place in a closed economy of material commodities with input-output matrix $\tilde{\pi}_{ij}$. (Compare the corresponding remarks in the paragraph following formula (1.8).) While the elimination of labor-commodities from our model involves a considerable distortion of the sociological form of the economy, it is important to realize that it involves only a mild distortion of the effect of wage-payments on sales and on inventory accumulation; and it is the relation between sales and inventory accumulation which will be decisive in the model which we are in the process of formulating. A large part of what would ordinarily be tabulated as "personal consumption" is hidden away in our model by the mathematical reduction which has just been described. In a subsequent improvement of the model we will introduce what does not at all feature in the present simpler model, additional luxury or nonproductive consumption in the form of explicit terms in our equations. The reader should not confuse this explicit contribution to personal consumption with the additional contributions to personal consumption which, as we have explained, are implicit. Our treatment, of course, involves the assumption that wages are spent, in some fixed fraction, on personal consumption; the statistical reliability of this assumption will be discussed in a later lecture. The assumption that labor is never in significantly short supply is also involved.

At any rate, a set of orders for factor input are transmitted, as explained. Each manufacturer is thereby called upon to supply out of inventory certain amounts of the commodity which he produces; in general he will only be able to supply a certain fraction of the total demand. It is assumed that if demand cannot be fully satisfied, the same fraction of each order received is to be confirmed.

Finally, each manufacturer upon notification of what fractions of his various orders can be filled, selects the smallest of such fractions and cancels orders for commodities in amounts larger than that fraction of his original order. Shipment then takes place instantaneously and the new day of production begins.

The scheme which has been described verbally in the preceding paragraphs may be given a precise mathematical formulation as follows. Let c_j be the number of day's sales regarded as the optimum inventory level for the commodity C_j. We shall assume for the time being that desired inventory is simply c_j times estimated sales; use of a slightly more general formula of the sort described four paragraphs above will be deferred for a short while. Let $a_j(t)$ be the amount of C_j produced on the tth day, and let $\bar{\pi}_{ij}$ be, as previously and in the sense indicated above, the amount of C_j consumed in the production of a unit of C_i. Fixed capital will be ignored in the present model. The sales of C_j on the $t - 1$ day are then given by the expression $\sum_{i=1}^{n} \bar{\pi}_{ij} a_i(t - 1)$. Let $b_j(t)$ be the actual inventory of C_j on the morning of the tth day. Then a_j and b_j are in the relation

$$(5.4) \qquad b_j(t) = b_j(t - 1) + a_j(t - 1) - \sum_{i=1}^{n} \bar{\pi}_{ij} a_i(t - 1).$$

The desired production $d_j(t)$ for the tth day is then given by

$$(5.5) \quad d_j(t) = \left\{ c_j \sum_{i=1}^{n} \tilde{\pi}_{ij} a_i(t-1) + \sum_{i=1}^{n} \tilde{\pi}_{ij} a_i(t-1) - b_j(t-1) \right.$$

$$\left. - a_j(t-1) + \sum_{i=1}^{n} \tilde{\pi}_{ij} a_i(t-1) \right\} +$$

(remember that an allowance for expected sales is made, and use (5.4)). Here, the notation x^+ is defined by $x^+ = 0$ if $x < 0$, $x^+ = x$ if $x \geq 0$. It is necessary to define desired production as the positive part, in this sense, of the expression in curly brackets on the right of (5.5), since desired production cannot be less than zero, the machinery of production being unidirectional. Equation (5.5) simplifies immediately to

$$(5.6) \quad d_j(t) = \left\{ (c_j + 2) \sum_{i=1}^{n} \tilde{\pi}_{ij} a_i(t-1) - a_j(t-1) - b_j(t-1) \right\} +.$$

Desired production levels having been computed by formula (5.6), the next step, according to the heuristic account of the model given above, is for the manufacturer of commodity i to send out orders for each commodity C_k in the amounts $\tilde{\pi}_{ik} d_i(t)$. In this way, the manufacturer of commodity C_k receives from all sources a total order for $\sum_{i=1}^{n} \tilde{\pi}_{ik} d_i(t)$ units of C_k. We may then calculate the fraction $\mu_k(t)$ of total orders received which can be filled by the manufacturer of C_k; this quantity may be called the "kth *market strain coefficient*" and is given by the ratio of inventory of C_k to total orders, i.e. by

$$(5.7) \qquad \mu_k(t) = b_k(t) / \sum_{i=1}^{n} \tilde{\pi}_{ik} d_i(t).$$

Let K_j be the set of indices k for which $\tilde{\pi}_{jk} > 0$. Then the severest restriction upon the production of C_j coming from difficulties in factor procurement is measured by that index k in the set K_j for which $\mu_j(t)$ is smallest. Thus, in accordance with the heuristic account of the model given above, we assume that the manufacturer cancels all orders in excess of this smallest fraction of his initial orders. This procedure may be described mathematically as follows. Let

$$(5.8) \qquad \sigma_j(t) = \min_{k \, \epsilon \, K_j} (1, \mu_k(t)).$$

This number may be called the "supply strain factor for the jth producer." The jth producer's actual production is then finally given by the formula

$$(5.9) \qquad\qquad a_j(t) = d_j(t)\sigma_j(t).$$

We have now a closed dynamic model. Application of equations (5.4) through (5.9) determine $a_j(t)$ and $b_j(t)$ in terms of $a_j(t-1)$ and $b_j(t-1)$, which is to say, determine the present day's production and inventory levels recursively as a function of the previous day's production and inventory and inventory levels.

Thus our model describes a dynamic economy in which specification of an initial state determines the whole subsequent motion of the economy. What are the motions of the model economy like? The next few lectures will be devoted to an analysis of this question. We shall see that our attempts to describe these motions lead us to the discovery of important over-all inventory-production cycles which resemble the empirical business cycle in many features.

Mathematical Analysis
of a Cycle-Theory Model.
Expansive and Depressive Cases

1. Aggregation of the Model of the Preceding Lecture

Equations (5.4)–(5.9) define a dynamic model economy in which specification of the initial state of all inventory and production levels determines the subsequent motion of the economy. If there are N commodities, the state of the economy at any time t is determined by $2N$ parameters, N for production level and N for inventory level. Thus the economic motion is, mathematically, a motion in $2N$ dimensional space. The general motion of the model can be quite complicated. For this reason, we shall begin our analysis by showing that the general model defined by equations (5.4)–(5.9) always admits a special motion which can be described by 2 rather than $2N$ parameters. Analysis of this special motion will allow us to make a fundamental distinction, separating our model economies into *depressive* and *expansive* cases. In a subsequent lecture, we shall return to the study of general motions of the model, indicating the significance for these general motions of the distinction to be introduced.

Let $\tilde{\Pi}$ be the input-output matrix of (5.4)–(5.9), with elements $\tilde{\pi}_{ij}$. In all that follows, we shall assume that $\tilde{\Pi}$ is connected, and, of course, that dom $(\tilde{\Pi}) < 1$. Let $\gamma = \text{dom}(\tilde{\Pi})$. Then by the results of Lecture 2, there exists an eigenvector $\mathbf{v}'$ satisfying

$$(6.1) \qquad \mathbf{v}'\tilde{\Pi} = \gamma\mathbf{v}', \quad \mathbf{v} > 0.$$

We may now obtain a radical simplification of the recursions (5.4)–(5.9) by making the strong assumption of "initially balanced production and inventory," i.e., by assuming the initial production levels and initial inventory levels are both proportional to the components of the vector $\mathbf{v}'$. (The vector $\mathbf{v}'$ represents a "balanced" list of commodities, in the heuristic sense that if $\mathbf{v}'$ is used as input to the economy, the outputs produced will again be, by (6.1), in the same proportion.) We assume that initially both production and inventory are separately in balanced proportions, i.e., that

(6.2a) $$a_j(t-1) = a(t-1)v_j$$
(6.2b) $$b_j(t-1) = b(t-1)v_j,$$

where a and b now denote a general "production level" and "inventory level" respectively.

We assume further that the coefficients expressing the optimal inventory levels in terms of a day's sales (compare Section 4 of the preceding lecture) are equal in all lines of industry, i.e., that

$$c_1 = c_2 = \cdots = c_n = c.$$

With these assumptions, the expression $c_j \sum_{i=1}^{n} a_i(t-1)\tilde{\pi}_{ij}$ for target inventory on the tth day reduces to $c\gamma a(t-1)v_j$, the expression (5.4) for inventory on the morning of the tth day reduces to

(6.3) $$b_j(t) = \{b(t-1) + [(1-\gamma)a(t-1)]\}v_j,$$

and the expression (5.5) for desired production on the tth day reduces to

(6.4) $$d_j(t) = \{[(c+2)\gamma - 1]a(t-1) - b(t-1)\}^+v_j.$$

From (6.3), and putting $\epsilon = 1 - \gamma$, we have

(6.5) $$b_j(t) = (b(t-1) + \epsilon a(t-1))v_j.$$

This shows that if we define $b(t)$ by the expression

(6.6) $$b(t) = b(t-1) + \epsilon a(t-1),$$

we have

(6.7) $$b_j(t) = b(t)v_j.$$

The market strain coefficients $\mu_k(t)$ given by (5.7) are plainly independent of the commodity C_k (by (6.7) and (6.4)), and are given by

(6.8) $$\mu(t) = [b(t)/\gamma]/[\tilde{\gamma}a(t-1) - b(t-1)]^+,$$

where $\bar{\gamma} = ((C - 2)\gamma - 1)$. The supply strain factor (5.8) is then plainly independent of the commodity C_j and is given by $\sigma(t)$ $= \min (1, \mu(t))$. The production levels on the tth day are now given by (5.9) as

$$a_j(t) = d_j(t)\sigma(t)$$

or

$$a_j(t) = d_j(t) \min \{1, (b(t)/\gamma)/[(\bar{\gamma}a(t - 1) - b(t - 1))^+]\}$$

which we may write more simply as

(6.9) $a_j(t) = \min (\{\bar{\gamma}a(t - 1) - b(t - 1)\}^+, b(t)/\gamma)v_j.$

If we define $a(t)$ by the value of the coefficients of v_j in (6.9), we have

(6.10) $a_j(t) = a(t)v_j.$

From equations (6.7) and (6.10) we can now conclude by induction that the assumption (6.2a,b) that initial inventory and production are separately in balanced proportion implies that the inventory and production will (separately) remain in balanced proportion, i.e., that both $\mathbf{a}'(t)$ and $\mathbf{b}'(t)$ will remain scalar multiples of $\mathbf{v}'$ for all t. The problem of computing the $2N$ numbers $a_j(t)$, $b_j(t)$ for each t is thus reduced to the problem of computing the 2 numbers $a(t)$ and $b(t)$ for each t.

Equations (6.6) and (6.10) show the recursion relations which must be satisfied by the inventory and production levels $a(t)$ and $b(t)$ are

(6.11a) $b(t) = b(t - 1) + \epsilon a(t - 1)$
(6.11b) $a(t) = \min (\{\bar{\gamma}a(t - 1) - b(t - 1)\}^+, b(t)/\gamma).$

Thus we have demonstrated that the general model defined by (5.4)–(5.9) has a particular motion described by the much simpler recursions (6.11a)–(6.11b). Our next task is to study these recursions.

We make, however, the general remark: it is interesting to note that we will find aspects of the business cycle phenomenon in a model in which both production and inventory are always in natural proportions. This constitutes preliminary evidence against the views of many classical economists who held that the necessary factor, indeed the essential factor, in business cycles is the imbalance of various lines of production, and that a business recession is simply a correction of proportions in the economy. The view that the business cycle simply reveals "anarchy of production" is one on which our model throws doubt.

2. The Aggregative Equations

Equations (6.1) may be called *aggregative* equations, since they refer to aggregate levels of production and inventory. In the previous section we showed that these aggregate recursions could be derived from the disaggregated cycle model of Lecture 5, Section 4, on the basis of a simplifying assumption of "initially balanced proportion"; thus the aggregate recursions describe a particular motion of the disaggregated model. Since aggregate equations have been much emphasized in the literature since Keynes, and the "aggregate approach" has even been taken to be characteristic of Keynesian economics, it is interesting to note that these aggregate recursions may be obtained directly if we think of the economy as turning out a single (aggregative) "commodity." Then γ represents the amount of the (single) "commodity" required to produce a unit of the "commodity," and the statement $0 < \gamma < 1$ is the same as our restriction dom $(\tilde{\Pi}) < 1$. For a single commodity, the inventory of the commodity on the morning of the tth day must be equal to the inventory of the commodity on the morning of the $(t-1)$st day plus the amount $a(t-1)$ produced on the $(t-1)$st day minus the amount $\gamma a(t-1)$ consumed on the $(t-1)$st day. This gives equation (6.11a). The amount of sales on the $(t-1)$st day (the amount consumed), is again used to determine the target inventory, yielding $c\gamma a(t-1)$ as the target inventory level on the tth day. The desired production on the tth day is the desired inventory of the commodity plus the expected sales minus the inventory on the $(t-1)$st day, if this difference is positive. If the difference is negative, the amount of production desired is zero. Moreover, the actual production is as close as it can be to the desired production, but not more than $b(t)/\gamma$, since production of a unit of the commodity requires an initial inventory of γ units of the commodity for its production. These considerations yield the aggregative equations (6.1) directly. We remind the reader once more that in our model we have neglected any consumption except that automatically generated (in the framework of the present model) by wage payments.

The relationship between the aggregative equations and the equations for individual commodities is worth pondering. It has been common since Keynes to write aggregative equations directly, using considerations like those immediately above to justify the equations. We see that this procedure is basically sound, yielding directly equations that could also have been derived from individual-commodity equations by use of a suitable simplifying assumption.

3. Properties of the Aggregative Equations

Equations (6.11) may be regarded as describing a motion in the $[a,b]$ plane, each successive point being determined by the preceding point: $[a(t), b(t)] = \tilde{\Lambda}[a(t-1), b(t-1)]$, the transformation $\tilde{\Lambda}$ being defined by the equations (6.11). It is plain from examination of these formulae that equations (6.11) limit the motion to the sector in the nonnegative quadrant bounded by $a = 0$ and $b = \gamma a$. These lines may be called the "*production cutoff line*" and the "*scarcity line*" respectively, and the region between these may be called the *accessible*

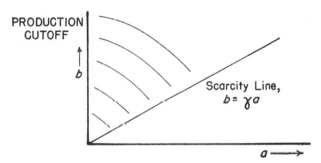

Fig. 2.   The accessible region for the motion $\tilde{\Lambda}$.

region.   (See Fig. 2.)   If the point $[a(t), b(t)]$ is not on a boundary, the recursions (6.1) reduce to the linear recursion relations

(6.12a) $b(t) = b(t-1) + \epsilon a(t-1)$
(6.12b) $a(t) = \bar{\gamma} a(t-1) - b(t-1)$

(where, as before, we have put $\epsilon = 1 - \gamma$, $\bar{\gamma} = ((c+2)\gamma - 1)$.   This pair of equations defines a linear transformation Λ which sends $[a(t-1), b(t-1)]$ into $[a(t), b(t)]$:

(6.13) $[a(t), b(t)] = \Lambda[(a(t-1), b(t-1))].$

The transformation Λ can be represented by the matrix

(6.14) $L = \begin{bmatrix} \bar{\gamma} & -1 \\ \epsilon & 1 \end{bmatrix}.$

The relationship between the transformation $\tilde{\Lambda}$ and the linear transformation Λ is described by stating that if the point $[\tilde{a}(t), \tilde{b}(t)]$ $= \Lambda[a(t-1), b(t-1)]$ lies to the left of the production cutoff line, $\tilde{\Lambda}[a(t-1), b(t-1)] = [0, b(t)]$, while if $[\tilde{a}(t), \tilde{b}(t)]$ is to the right of the scarcity line, $\tilde{\Lambda}[a(t-1), b(t-1)] = [\gamma b(t), b(t)]$. If $\Lambda[a(t-1), b(t-1)]$ lies in the accessible region, $\tilde{\Lambda}[a(t-1), b(t-1)] = \Lambda[a(t-1), b(t-1)]$ (cf. Fig. 3).

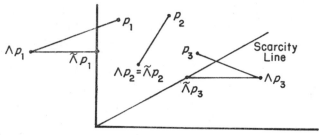

Fig. 3.   Relation between $\tilde{\Lambda}$ and the linear transform Λ.

Starting from an interior point p_0, of our admissible region, we wish to study the successive points $p_j = \tilde{\Lambda}^i p_0$. It is not hard to see that, for all j up to a certain value k, we will have

(6.15) $p_j = \tilde{\Lambda}^i(p_0) = \Lambda^i(p_0).$

Thus we must begin by studying the iterates of the linear transformation Λ; to this end, we have only to apply the standard techniques of linear analysis.

We treat the $[a, b]$ plane as a two-dimensional vector space W of column vectors, the points of the plane being vectors in W and the coordinates of any point being the components of the corresponding vector referred to the natural basis $[1, 0]$, $[0, 1]$ of W. Then Λ is a transformation of W onto itself, which has the matrix given by (6.14).

To study the result of repeated application of a linear transformation to a vector of W, we first find a new basis $\mathbf{W}_1$, $\mathbf{W}_2$ for W in terms of which the matrix representing the transformation is diagonal. In order that the matrix representing the transformation Λ in terms of the basis $\mathbf{W}_1$, $\mathbf{W}_2$ be diagonal, there must exist two constants λ_1, λ_2 such that

(6.16)
$$\Lambda\mathbf{W}_1 = \lambda_1\mathbf{W}_1; \quad \Lambda\mathbf{W}_2 = \lambda_2\mathbf{W}_2,$$

that is, the vectors $\mathbf{W}_1$ and $\mathbf{W}_2$ must be the *eigenvectors* of Λ; the corresponding numbers λ_1 and λ_2 being the *eigenvalues*.

The standard principles of linear algebra tell us that the condition that an equation of the form $\Lambda\mathbf{W} = \mathbf{W}$ have a nontrivial solution $\mathbf{W}$ is that

$$\det (L - \lambda I) = 0,$$

i.e.,

$$\lambda^2 - (\bar{\gamma} + 1)\lambda + (\bar{\gamma} + \epsilon) = 0$$

from which we deduce that

(6.15a)　$\lambda_1 = [(\bar{\gamma} + 1)/2] + [(\bar{\gamma} - 1)/2]\{1 - [4\epsilon/(\bar{\gamma} - 1)^2]\}^{\frac{1}{2}}$

(6.15b)　$\lambda_2 = [(\bar{\gamma} + 1)/2] - [(\bar{\gamma} - 1)/2]\{1 - [4\epsilon/(\bar{\gamma} - 1)^2]\}^{\frac{1}{2}}$

so that for ϵ small enough, λ_1 and λ_2 are real and distinct.

Since it would hardly be good practice for a manufacturer to carry less than one day's sales as inventory, we shall assume $c \geq 1$. We will take ϵ to be small, so that γ is only slightly less than 1, and $\bar{\gamma} = (c + 2)\gamma - 1$ has a lower bound which is only slightly less than 2. Since ϵ is small, the approximation

$$\{1 - [4\epsilon/(\bar{\gamma} - 1)^2]\}^{\frac{1}{2}} \sim 1 - [2\epsilon/(\bar{\gamma} - 1)^2]$$

can be used, yielding for the eigenvalues the approximate values

(6.16a)　　　　　$\lambda_1 \sim \bar{\gamma} - [\epsilon/(\bar{\gamma} - 1)]$

(6.16b)　　　　　$\lambda_2 \sim 1 + [\epsilon/(\bar{\gamma} - 1)].$

Thus the large eigenvalue λ_1 is a little less than $\bar{\gamma}$ and hence not much less than 2 while the small eigenvalue λ_2 is a little more than 1.

The eigenvectors $\mathbf{W}_1$ and $\mathbf{W}_2$ corresponding to these eigenvalues satisfy

$$\lambda_i a_i = \bar{\gamma} a_i - b_i$$
$$\lambda_i b_i = b_i + \epsilon a_i, \quad i = 1,2$$

(we have written a_i and b_i for the components of W_i). We may then solve, obtaining an expression for the component b_i in terms of a_i:

$$b_i = (\bar{\gamma} - \lambda_i)a_i, \quad i = 1,2$$

and also

$$b_i = [\epsilon/(\lambda_i - 1)]a_i, \quad i = 1,2.$$

Thus the eigenvector W_1 corresponding to the large eigenvalue λ_1 is the vector whose components are a and $a/(\lambda_1 - 1)$, and the other eigenvector W_2 is the vector whose components are a and $(\bar{\gamma} - \lambda_2)a$.

This completes our description of the eigenvalues λ_1 and λ_2 and the corresponding eigenvalues W_1 and W_2. To apply all the information to the study of the iterates of the linear transformation Λ, it is convenient to let T denote the transformation which takes the vector $[1,0]$ into W_1 and the vector $[0,1]$ into W_2. Then it is plain that $T^{-1}\Lambda T$ takes $[1,0]$ into $[\lambda_1,0]$ and $[0,1]$ into $[0,\lambda_2]$. Thus $T^{-1}\Lambda T$ has the matrix

(6.17)
$$\begin{bmatrix} \lambda_1 & 0 \\ 0 & \lambda_2 \end{bmatrix}.$$

This transformation is readily iterated; its jth power plainly has the matrix

(6.18)
$$\begin{bmatrix} \lambda_i{}^j & 0 \\ 0 & \lambda_2{}^j \end{bmatrix}.$$

Since $(T^{-1}\Lambda T)^2 = T^{-1}\Lambda^j T$, this shows us how the iterates of Λ behave. Application of the transformation Λ expands every vector lying along the W_1-axis by the large factor λ_1 and expands every vector lying along the W_2-axis by the smaller factor λ_2. The linear transformation T interchanges the oblique W_1, W_2 axes with the more familiar orthogonal a,b axes; the transformation $T^{-1}\Lambda T$ expands every point lying along the a-axis by the large factor λ_1 and expands every vector lying along the b-axis by the smaller factor λ_2. The geometric effect of $T^{-1}\Lambda T$ is then readily comprehended; this effect is perhaps represented most plainly if we recognize the fact that since

$$b_0\lambda_2{}^j = b_0 \exp{(j \log \lambda_2)} = b_0 (\exp{(j \log \lambda_1)})^{(\log \lambda_2/\log \lambda_1)}$$
$$= (b_0 a_0{}^{-(\log \lambda_2/\log \lambda_1)})(a_0 \exp{(j \log \lambda_1)})^{(\log \lambda_2/\log \lambda_1)}$$

the points $[a_0\lambda_1{}^j, b_0\lambda_2{}^j]$ lie along the curves whose equation is $b = k_0 a^\chi$, where $\chi = \log \lambda_2/\log \lambda_1$. Since λ_2 and λ_1 both exceed 1 while $\lambda_1 \geq \lambda_2$, we have $0 < \chi < 1$. Thus the curves of the family $b = k_0 a^\chi$, $0 < k_0 < \infty$, have the following configuration in the $[a,b]$ plane (cf. Fig. 4).

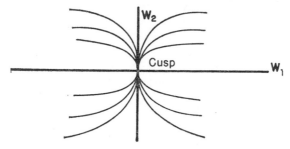

Fig. 4. The family of curves $|b| = b_0 |a| \chi$.

The configuration is that which is commonly called a node (the appropriate curves in the 2nd, 3rd, and 4th quadrants have been constructed from those in the first quadrant by reflection). The effect of the linear transformation $T\Lambda T^{-1}$ is then to push points outward along the curves of Fig. 4, always expanding the a-coordinate of a point by the factor λ_2. Since Λ has the same effect relative to the W_1, W_2 axes as $T^{-1}\Lambda T$ has relative to the a,b axes, Λ

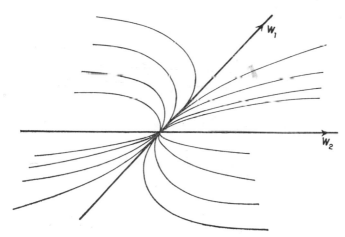

Fig. 5. The oblique node.

must push points outward along the family of curves obtained from the family of Fig. 4 by the transformation T, as in Fig. 5.

This pattern of curves is ordinarily known as an *oblique node*. To complete our analysis, we must know how to superimpose the oblique node of Fig. 5 upon the accessible region of Fig. 2; that is, we must know how the eigenvectors $\mathbf{W}_1$ and $\mathbf{W}_2$ are oriented relative to the boundaries of that region.

Since $\mathbf{W}_1$ is the vector $[1, \epsilon/(\lambda_1 - 1)]$, ϵ is small, and λ_1 is not much less than 2, $\mathbf{W}_1$ points below the scarcity line (i.e., the lower boundary of the accessible region). Since $\mathbf{W}_2$ is the vector $[1, \{(c+2)\gamma - 1 - \lambda_2\}]$, $\mathbf{W}_2$ may point either into the accessible region or below its lower boundary, depending on whether

$$(6.19a) \qquad\qquad (c+2)\gamma - 1 - \lambda_2 > \gamma$$

or

$$(6.19b) \qquad\qquad (c+2)\gamma - 1 - \lambda_2 < \gamma.$$

These inequalities may be written as

$$(6.20a) \qquad\qquad (c+1)\gamma > 1 + \lambda_2$$
$$(6.20b) \qquad\qquad (c+1)\gamma < 1 + \lambda_2.$$

We may make this distinction in an equivalent and more transparent if less geometrical manner as follows. Our model will be expansive or depressive according as, at levels of inventory and production lying along the scarcity line, manufacturers desire to increase or to decrease production. That is, our model is expansive or de-

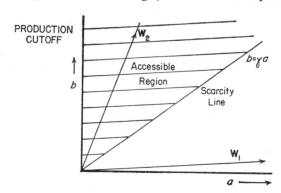

Fig. 6. The eigenvectors and accessible region in the expansive case.

pressive according as to whether $(\bar{\gamma}a - b) - a$ is positive or negative when $b = \gamma a$, i.e., according as $[(c + 2)\gamma - 1] - \gamma - 1 = (c + 1)\gamma - 2$ is positive or negative. Since γ is slightly less than 1 while c is more than 1, either inequality may hold, depending on the size of c. We shall call the first case (6.20a), in which the eigenvector $\mathbf{W}_2$ points into the accessible region, the *expansive case*, and the second case (6.20b), in which the eigenvector $\mathbf{W}_2$ points below the scarcity line, the *depressive case*. Let us first study the expansive case. Here the configuration of the eigenvectors and the accessible region is as in Fig. 6.

The accessible region thus includes the portion of the curves of Fig. 5 indicated in the following Fig. 7.

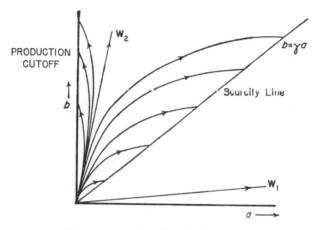

Fig. 7.   The curves of motion in the expansive case.

It is now easy to discuss the effect of the transformation $\tilde{\Lambda}$. Starting with a point p_0 interior to the accessible region and applying $\tilde{\Lambda}$, we see from Fig. 3 and the paragraph of text which this figure illustrates that the points $\tilde{\Lambda}^i p_0$ will coincide with the points $\Lambda^i p_0$ until a boundary of the accessible region is reached. Thus, $\tilde{\Lambda}$, like Λ, will, to begin with, push points upward from position to position along the curves indicated in Fig. 7. The effect of $\tilde{\Lambda}$ once the boundary has been reached follows in the same way from Fig. 3 and the attendant text. Points along the scarcity line $b = \gamma a$ of Fig. 2 are mapped to higher positions along the scarcity line (cf. Fig. 3). Points on the production cutoff line correspond to production levels $a = 0$; according to (6.11) any such point is mapped by $\tilde{\Lambda}$ into itself.

The result of successive application of $\tilde{\Lambda}$ to a point p is shown in Fig. 8.

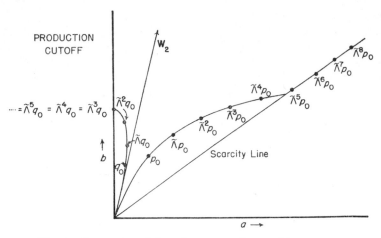

Fig. 8. Successive states of an expansive model economy.

If the initial point p_0 is to the right of $\mathbf{W}_2$ the successive applications of Λ will carry the point fairly rapidly to the right until it reaches the scarcity line, after which, according to our previous statements, the succeeding points must fall on the scarcity line going upward to the right. This corresponds to the happy situation of stable prosperity in which production is limited only by the supplies which can be obtained from other manufacturers and in which everyone has more orders for commodities than he can possibly fill. If, on the other hand, the initial point q_0 is to the left of $\mathbf{W}_2$, successive applications of Λ will soon bring the point to the production cutoff line, where it will stay. This corresponds to an "absolute depression" in which production is completely shut down, nobody gets any orders for commodities, and thus nobody schedules any production.

Motion to the right of $\mathbf{W}_2$ corresponds to the situation in which each manufacturer initially finds that his sales are high compared to his inventory, and so schedules more production. Since all manufacturers are doing this, of course sales go up, and each manufacturer falls further behind on inventory, and so must schedule even more production. The motion to the left of $\mathbf{W}_2$ describes the situation in which each manufacturer initially finds his inventory level too high relative to sales, and so cuts back production. Since every other manufacturer follows suit, sales drop and get even more out of line with inventory. Thus production is cut even more and so repeatedly until it halts completely.

A paradoxical fact about the above described motion of the model is worth noting. If we are initially on the left of $\mathbf{W}_2$ so that a halt of production, i.e., a depression, has begun to develop, then if some "external" disaster occurs and destroys a sufficiently large part of the current inventory (but has no other effect), this disaster will have the happy effect of transferring us to the region to the right of $\mathbf{W}_2$, and hence ensuring that we will go on to prosperity. This striking, if somewhat surprising, consequence of our analysis has been discussed at length by Keynes and others; discovery of this phenomenon, so much at variance with the prejudices of classical economics, is the basic step toward Keynesianism. When inventories are threatening, a horde of locusts can bring economic salvation!

It will often be convenient in what follows to discuss the motion of a point under successive applications of a transformation like $\tilde{\Lambda}$ by making use of terminology borrowed from mechanics. In general, if the state of a certain system is described by certain quantities x_i, $i = 1, \cdots, n$, each of which is a function of time, the equations $x_i = x_i(t)$ specifying the variation of those quantities x_i with time are known as the *equations of motion*. (The range of t may include negative as well as zero and positive values.) The equations of motion specify a relationship among the x_i with t as parameter. If t is eliminated this relationship determines a set of points in the n-dimensional space of the coordinates x_i. This set of points is variously known as the *orbit*, the *trajectory line*, or simply the *trajectory* of the motion. That is, the orbit or trajectory is the set of points representing states which are sooner or later taken on by the system. If the orbit depends upon initial conditions, we have a family of orbits, filling out the whole of x_i-space. In the example which we have just studied the orbit is a discrete set of points of the kind represented in Fig. 8; the continuous curves of Figs. 7 and 8 are merely convenient curves of interpolation. We will sometimes find it convenient in what follows to refer somewhat imprecisely to such continuous curves as the orbits of the model. Since we will always be interested in the over-all nature of the motion of our model, and never in the exact details of this motion, such slight imprecision will not involve us in any significant errors.

Figures 7 and 8 describe the motion of our model in the expansive case. As equation (6.20) shows, the model will be expansive for c sufficiently large. For c sufficiently close to 1, however, the fact that λ_2 is slightly larger than 1 and that $\gamma < 1$ implies that (6.20b) will be satisfied, and we will find ourselves in the *depressive case*. We now turn to the examination of this case. The eigenvector $\mathbf{W}_2$ now points below the scarcity line, so that configuration of eigenvectors, accessible region, and nodal curves now appears as in the following Fig. 9.

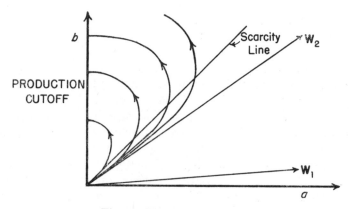

Fig. 9. The depressive case.

The entire accessible region is now to the left of the eigenvector $\mathbf{W}_2$, and all orbits, even those beginning on the scarcity line, proceed to, and remain at, the production cutoff line. Thus our model in these cases shows an economy in which permanent depression is inevitable.

Our model economy will be expansive or depressive depending on the size of the constant c: the number of day's sales held as inventory. The "day" in our model is best viewed as that period defined by the property, assumed in our model, that at peak prosperity inventories can turn over in a "day," but not in a smaller length of time. That is, our "day" is the minimum turnover period for the economy; in empirical fact, this "day" would be about two months. Our model is then expansive or depressive depending on how much more than a necessary minimum inventory (in ratio to sales) manufacturers will, on the average, desire to carry. The larger the value of c the less likely a depression becomes; which is to say that the higher in terms of sales the individual manufacturers set their target inventories the better off is the entire economy. Of course, this over-all desideration is not necessarily in harmony with the policy that would be followed by the manufacturer individually, since individual maximum profits are generally obtained by maintaining as low an inventory as possible; this minimum inventory policy is that recommended by the efficiency economist. It is then clear that a manufacturer who tries to keep his inventories turning over as rapidly as possible, that is, a maximally efficient manufacturer, would be described in terms of our model by a value of c approximating to 1.

We have here a situation, like that prevailing in the game of "majority," where what is *best individually* can actually be far from a collective optimum. We are led by the present model to the depressing conclusion that the recommendations of efficiency experts, if generally followed in the whole economy, will lead inevitably to a permanent depression. Of course, the depression is only permanent because excess inventories once accumulated remain forever; in a situation of no production, they are forever excessive relative to sales. This eternal stagnation is thus a consequence of the absence of any consumption not generated by production in our model. We shall next introduce such consumption, and note also that desired inventories are likely to contain, besides a term proportional to sales, a constant term (basic inventory) independent of sales. It is not hard to come to terms with the modifications this introduces into our model; we will find, however, a qualitatively different outcome.

Consumption in the Cycle-Theory Model.
Say's Law

1. Mathematical Analysis of Consumption as an Additional Feature. The Model Cycle.

We saw at the conclusion of the preceding lecture that the inexorable rise and permanent oversupply of inventories in our model was due to the fact that no inventory-reducing consumption was introduced in the model. We now wish to modify the earlier model by supposing that in each production day, a certain fixed amount e_j of commodity c_j is consumed by the manufacturers who collectively constitute our model. We shall also make our description of inventory policy somewhat more realistic by adding an amount h_j of commodity c_j as basic inventory to the inventory which the manufacturer of commodity c_j wishes to carry; thus, we will now have

desired inventory = basic inventory + $c_j \times$ day's sales.

Instead of introducing these assumptions into the disaggregated equations of Lecture 5, we shall, in order to obtain the simplest aggregative model, assume at once that e_j and h_j are proportional to the "balanced" eigenvector V of equation (5.7). Making use of the technique for direct elaboration of aggregative equations explained at the beginning of the previous lecture, we then obtain the following modification of the recursions (6.1a) and (6.1b):

(7.1a) $$b(t) = b(t-1) + (1-\gamma)a(t-1) - e$$

(7.1b) $$a(t) = \min\left[\{((c+2)\gamma - 1)a(t-1) - b(t-1) \\ + (c+2)e + h\}^+, \quad (b(t)/\gamma)\right].$$

It should be explained that in writing the final term in (7.1b), we assume that the whole of the inventory available at the beginning of a "day" is available for production; one may for instance take the subtraction from stocks for the purposes of consumption to occur "in the evening" after the day's production has taken place. In writing equation (7.1a) as simply as we do, we are assuming in similar fashion that $(1 - \gamma)a(t) + b(t)$ always exceeds e, so that the whole economy is not eventually devoured by the consumers. It will be necessary for us to check the correctness of this assumption when we examine the detailed orbit of our model.

Our analysis may now follow the paths marked out in the preceding lecture. As long as this transformation keeps us between the "production cutoff line" $a = 0$ and the "scarcity line" $a = b/\gamma$ of the preceding lecture (cf. Fig. 2), the equations (7.1a–b) bid us iterate the *inhomogeneous linear* map defined by

(7.2a) $$b(t) = b(t - 1) + \epsilon a(t - 1) - e$$

(7.2b) $$a(t) = \bar{\gamma}a(t - 1) - b(t - 1) + \tilde{h}.$$

Here we have put $\epsilon = 1 - \gamma$, $\bar{\gamma} = (c + 2)\gamma - 1$, and $\tilde{h} = (c + 2)e + h$. If this transformation takes us out of the admissible region of Fig. 2, we are to return to this region in the same way as in Lecture 6 (cf. Fig. 3).

We may now make use of the simple mathematical principle that *an inhomogeneous linear transformation is simply a homogeneous linear transformation referred to a displaced center*, namely, to the fixed point of the inhomogeneous transformation. The fixed point of the transformation defined by (7.2a–b) is the solution $[a_K, b_K]$ of the equations

(7.3a) $$b_K = b_K + a_K - e$$

(7.3b) $$a_K = \bar{\gamma}a_K - b_K + \tilde{h}.$$

Thus

(7.4a) $$a_K = e/\epsilon$$

(7.4b) $$b_K = (\bar{\gamma} - 1)(e/\epsilon) + \tilde{h}.$$

We note that this *Keynes point* $[a_K, b_K]$ lies above the scarcity line $\gamma a = b$, since $c > 1$ and thus

(7.5) $\gamma(e/\epsilon) \leq (c\gamma e/\epsilon) - 2e + (c+2)e$
$\leq (c\gamma e/\epsilon) + (2\gamma - 2)(e/\epsilon) + (c+2)e + h$
$= ((c+2)\gamma - 1 - 1)(e/\epsilon) + \tilde{h}$
$= (\bar{\gamma} - 1)(e/\epsilon) + \tilde{h}.$

The Keynes point $[a_K, b_K]$ is by definition the level of inventory and production at which production exactly balances consumption, and actual inventory is exactly equal to desired inventory. If we now let $\tilde{a}(t) = a(t) - a_K$ and $\tilde{b}(t) = b(t) - b_K$ denote the deviations of actual production and inventory at time t from the Keynes point, we find from (7.3a–b) that (7.2a–b) are equivalent to

(7.6a) $\tilde{b}(t) = \tilde{b}(t-1) + \epsilon\tilde{a}(t-1)$

(7.6b) $\tilde{a}(t) = \bar{\gamma}\tilde{a}(t-1) - \tilde{b}(t-1).$

These, however, are *exactly the recursions which were governing in the preceding lecture.* We find in consequence that the pattern of orbits in our new model is exactly like the pattern of orbits in the preceding model, except that the center of the oblique node of Fig. 5 is shifted from the origin to the Keynes point. We are consequently examining the very same node sections of which are portrayed in Figs. 5, 6, and 9, but looking at a different section of the picture! This remark enables us to construct the corresponding figures for our new model with a minimum of effort. We have again a dichotomy between an "expansive case" and a "depressive case" as in the preceding lecture. The case corresponding to the expansive case portrayed in Fig. 7, defined by the property that the small-eigenvalue eigenvector of the transformation defined by (7.6a–b) points into the angle between the production cutoff and the scarcity lines, appears as in the following Figure 10. (Compare Fig. 7.)

The "recovery point" marked in Fig. 10 is at the level of inventory where sales for the purpose of consumption bring about a rise in production from the zero level; according to equation (7.1b), this is at the level $b = (c+2)e + h$ of inventory. Geometrically, this point is the unique point at which an orbit curve proceeding down from the Keynes point is tangent to the b-axis. The "danger point" marked on the diagram is the point at which full employment of existing inventory in production just barely yields a surplus of e; it is consequently at the level $b = e/\epsilon$. If inventories ever fall below this danger level, they will inevitably be reduced without limit by per-

sistent consumption, and eventually the whole economy will be
devoured by the consumers (in our oversimplified model; in a more

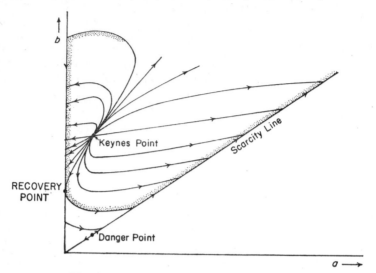

Fig. 10.   Consumption in an expansive case.

realistic model this would lead to "inflation" and the restriction of
consumption).   Points above the danger point on the scarcity line
proceed upward in successive periods of time; points below the
danger point proceed downwards.   In order that our model, with
fixed (nonproductive) consumption in the sense we have assumed,
be reasonable, it is then necessary that $(c + 2)e + h$ should distinctly
exceed e/ϵ.

We have marked a typical orbit in Fig. 10; it shows a recession
beginning, production falling to zero to permit the decline of inventories to recovery levels, recovery, and, in accordance with the
basically "expansive" nature of the case under examination, a
permanent prosperity thereafter, with inventories engaged in a per-
petual race to keep up with each other, and consumption, having once
led to recovery, playing an ever smaller role.   This illustrates the
mechanism of recovery, but evidently not that of recession.   To
study this latter mechanism, we must examine the case corresponding
to the depressive case portrayed in Fig. 9, in which the small-
eigenvalue eigenvector of the transformation defined by (7.6a–b)

points out of the angle between the production cutoff and the scarcity lines. Here we have Fig. 11 (cf. Fig. 9).

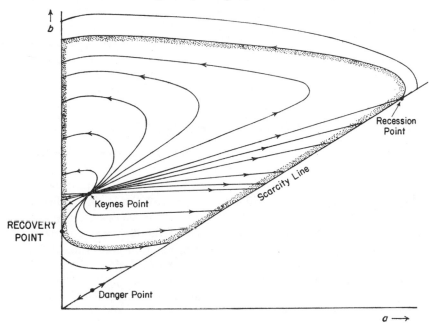

Fig. 11. Consumption in a depressive case.

The indicated "recovery point" and "danger point" have here the same significance as previously. The new feature is the occurrence of a "recession point," which may be defined as that point where, even at prosperity levels of production, existing inventory is just barely desired. Geometrically, it is the unique point at which an orbit curve proceeding up from the Keynes point is tangent to the scarcity line. Noting that desired production is $\{\bar{\gamma}a(t-1) - b(t-1) + \tilde{h}\}^{+}$, and that along the scarcity line we have $a = b/\gamma$, it follows that the recession-point inventory level is determined by

$$(7.7) \quad [\{(\bar{\gamma} - 1)/\gamma\} - 1]b = -\tilde{h}, \quad \text{i.e.,} \quad b = [\gamma/(\gamma - \bar{\gamma} + 1)]\tilde{h}$$
$$= \gamma\tilde{h}/[2 - (c + 1)\gamma].$$

We have marked a significant orbit in Fig. 11: it shows recession, inventory reduction, recovery, inventory buildup, and new recession. Examination of the configuration of orbits in Fig. 11 shows that (except for orbits beginning at dangerously low inventory levels), any initial motion will, after a first recession, trace out the cyclic motion which has been marked. In the terminology of orbit-theory, the orbit marked is a *stable limit cycle*. This conclusion is true to the extent that the small inaccuracies in the motions at the production-cutoff line and the scarcity line occasioned by our use of continuous curves rather than discrete sequences of points in Fig. 11 may be ignored.

2. A Qualitative Account of the Preceding Results

Our cycle-theory model is, of course, a monstrous oversimplification of the complex of factors which play a rule in the cycles of the actual economy. Perhaps our greatest error is to assume instantaneous and sharp reaction in all sections of the economy to a change in conditions, which, coupled with the assumption of instantaneous transmission of orders and shipments from one point of the economy to another and with the assumption of a standard production-period in all lines of industry and of a perfect "lockstep" coordination of industries gives our model recession an all-encompassing violence foreign to the actual recession. Nevertheless, our model uncovers a central mechanism whose significance is generally acknowledged. Let us review the main features of this mechanism, as they follow from our model and as they would follow from any similar model.

1. Once a recession has begun, the *desired inventory levels* fall below *actual inventory levels;* a rapid falling-off of production leads to a correspondingly rapid fall of desired inventory. The lowered production levels and the continuation of a reasonable level of consumption imply the slower but progressive decrease of inventories. The recession will continue until a certain surplus of inventory is "burnt off." When this point is reached, recovery will begin.

2. Widespread attempts to sustain inventory then begin, leading to a pick-up in sales, and to a consequent upward revision of notions as to what constitutes desirable levels of inventory. In an effort to build up inventories, production is rapidly advanced, desirable inventories rise still more, and shortages (symptomatized, say, by difficulty in getting quick delivery) develop. Production then continues at a high level, inventories gradually being built up. Production is sustained beyond the requirements of consumption by a general desire to increase inventories. Prosperity will continue until inventories reach their falling-off point.

3. As inventories increase, the part of inventory size justified by consumption grows relatively smaller, a larger fraction of their size being justified by the collective efforts to increase inventory. Eventually this unstable sustaining force collapses, and a new recession begins. (Note that the "expansive" and the "depressive" cases which we have been led to distinguish are defined precisely by the stability vs. instability of this sustaining force.)

The following quotations from the December, 1960, *Survey of Current Business* will indicate the extent to which the inventory cycle mechanism of our model is observed empirically:

Production is currently being held back to pare inventories. While stocks in trade channels have undergone little net change in the aggregate since midyear, manufacturers' holdings have been reduced moderately. The cutback—amounting to about $800 million from June through October—has been concentrated so far in working stocks; this reduction was not significantly different on a relative basis from the 4 per cent decline in sales over this period. Accumulation of finished goods at the factory level has continued through 1960, and in view of the current volume of sales, business seems to regard them as being on the high side at the present time.

Factory Orders and Output Drop

Incoming orders to manufacturers declined in October following a two-month spurt due largely to accelerated defense order placement. For both durable and nondurable goods producers, new orders were once more close to earlier lows. With incoming new business flowing at a seasonably adjusted pace about equal to sales in the last several months, backlogs were unchanged at a volume $5 billion, or 10 per cent below a year ago. . . .

The reduction of inventories of finished steel in the hands of consumers and producers has been under way for the past 6 months or so. For producers, the inventory liquidation has been moderate with the book value of current stocks of finished goods inventories—intermediate and finished steel products as well as other finished materials—just moderately under the high point. Though actual figures are not available, it appears that the reduction has been on a much larger scale for the metal fabricating industries.

3. The Keynes Theorem

The cycle, regarded as an entity, is then a mechanism preventing the unrestricted rise of inventories; thus, on the average, adjusting production to consumption. We can obtain a more satisfactory view of the over-all significance of this principle by using the tautologous relation between inventory and production levels, incorporated in our model, but relatively independent of its special features:

$$(7.8) \qquad b_j(n) - b_j(n-1) = a_j(n-1) - \sum_{i=1}^{n} a_i(n-1)\tilde{\pi}_{ij} - e_j.$$

If we sum this equation from $n = 1$ to $n = K$ and divide by K, we find that

$$(7.9) \qquad \bar{a}_j^{(K)} - \sum_{i=1}^{n} \bar{a}_i^{(K)}\tilde{\pi}_{ij} = e_j + K^{-1}(b_j(K) - b_j(1));$$

here, $\bar{a}^{(K)}$ denotes the average of the quantity $a(n)$ over the period $n = 1$ to $n = k$. In situations like the one we have been examining, in which *there exists an obstacle to the unbounded increase of inventories, so that inventories will remain bounded* (or increase relatively slowly) over long periods of time, we get the essential force of this last relationship by letting $K \to \infty$, and writing $\bar{a}_j$ for the long-time average of $a_j(n)$; doing this, we obtain the *Keynes Theorem:*

$$(7.10) \qquad \bar{a}_j - \sum_{i=1}^{n} \tilde{\pi}_{ij}\bar{a}_i = e_j;$$

matricially expressed

$$(7.11) \qquad (I - \tilde{\Pi})\bar{\mathbf{a}} = \mathbf{e}.$$

This shows the way in which, abstracting from the dynamic details of the business cycle, consumption determines production. In a model in which consumption e was not fixed but variable, and in which we also had investment f, this relationship, under the same assumption of bounded inventories, would be modified to

$$(7.12) \qquad (I - \tilde{\Pi})\bar{\mathbf{a}} = \bar{\mathbf{e}} + \bar{\mathbf{f}}.$$

If we solve this equation for ($\bar{\mathbf{a}}$) we get

$$(7.13) \qquad \bar{\mathbf{a}} = (I - \tilde{\Pi})^{-1}(\bar{\mathbf{e}} + \bar{\mathbf{f}}),$$

the first of a number of *multiplier relations* which we shall discuss. Let us remark that the prototype of these relationships is the equation $a_K = e/\epsilon$ which in our preceding discussion located one coordinate of the Keynes point.

4. General Reflections on Theories of the Business Cycle. Say's Law

The success of a model like the one that has been presented has, if we are willing to take it seriously, implications for the theory of the business cycle. In the first place, in our model cycle all industries are at all times in perfect proportionate balance: *thus the cycle is not a cycle of disproportions, but a cycle of general overproduction.* This may justly make us skeptical of the host of theories which insist that a recession is only a correction of disproportions that have developed in a previous boom period. Of course, in empirical fact, the various lines of production will behave differently and disproportions will continually develop and be corrected; nevertheless, the basic movement is that of a general aggregate of production. Our model indicates no reason why the correction of disproportions should characterize recessions more than periods of boom.

It will be noted that our discussion of cycle theory has been carried out entirely in "real" terms, no question of prices entering. That, with this exclusion of all monetary considerations, any theory is possible, leads us to infer that *the business cycle is not primarily a monetary phenomenon* (though it surely has important monetary aspects). Since this conclusion is disputed by various "monetary theorists" of the business cycle, we may regard it as nontrivial. In order to strengthen our inference, it is well to have at least a glance at the neglected monetary side of the phenomenon visible in our model. We may ask: do the exchanges which we have assumed in our model lead to a progressive deficit at one or another point, until one or another manufacturer runs out of means of payment?

We find it easiest to answer this question for the simplest orbit of our model: the orbit along which production and inventory remain fixed. Note first that, in models like the one which we have been studying, the Keynes relation (7.10) implies that only one level of production may be assigned to such an orbit: the commodity-by-commodity level of production which exactly supports the assigned level of autonomous consumption. We must now see whether the even turnover of material commodities which characterizes the Keynes point also meets the fiscal conditions of our model. Let the vector of total consumption have the components e_j. Let the vector describing the consumption of the ith manufacturer in a single period have the components $e_j{}^{(i)}$. We have, of course, $\sum_i e_j{}^{(i)} = e_j$. Let $\bar{a}_j$ be the levels of production, so that (7.10) is satisfied. The difference between sales and expenditures for the ith manufacturer is

$$(7.14) \qquad \sum_{j=1}^{n} \bar{a}_j \tilde{\pi}_{ji} p_i + p_i e_i - \sum_{j=1}^{n} \bar{a}_i \tilde{\pi}_{ij} p_j.$$

By the Keynes relation (7.10), this may be written as

$$(7.15) \qquad \bar{a}_i p_i - \sum_{j=1}^{n} \bar{a}_i \tilde{\pi}_{ij} p_j,$$

which, by (1.9), is equal to

$$(7.16) \qquad \rho \sum_{j=1}^{n} \bar{a}_i \tilde{\phi}_{ij} p_j.$$

Plainly, then, if the ith manufacturer's autonomous consumption expenditures are restricted by the ordinary budgetary condition

$$(7.17) \qquad \sum_{j=1}^{n} e_j{}^{(i)} p_j = \rho \sum_{j=1}^{n} \bar{a}_i \tilde{\phi}_{ij} p_j,$$

all the conditions of exchange are met: income balances outgo and the rate of profit is uniform. If we interpret the quantities $\bar{a}_i$ not as the invariable Keynes levels of production, but as average levels of production over the course of the business cycle, we see by this computation that even for the dynamic motion each manufacturer's income and outgo will be in balance over the business cycle.[1] Thus no financial obstacle need arise in our model.

The identity of all the expressions (7.14)–(7.16), that is, the equation

(7.18)   cash value of industrial sales = cash value of industrial
purchases

may be called *Say's law*. The principle properly extrapolated from this somewhat trivial identity is the principle tentatively put forward above; that the business cycle is basically a real and *not a monetary*

---

[1] A closer examination will show that if there are significant disparities in the capitalisation of different lines of industry, as measured by differences in the ratio (profit/unit sales), there will be a tendency for the highly capitalised industries to accumulate bank-balances from the less capitalised industries during boom periods, and vice-versa during recessions.

phenomenon. This correct inference has often been overextended in the economic literature to the inference that there can be no cycle of general overproduction at all. But the most fundamental fact of which our model informs us is the fact that *recessions can exist,* indeed, that in economies approximately describable by our model, which are in addition depressive rather than expansive, recessions *must* take place from time to time. This conclusion, while evident empirically, has in the past been the subject of theoretical dispute. Let us therefore dwell on this matter at greater length.

The definition which we have just given to "Say's law," and the phenomenon which we observe in the cycle-theory model which we have just studied, reveals the persuasive fallacy involved in Say's law as traditionally interpreted. This traditional if mistaken statement of the false "law," which we have repeated just above, amounts to a denial of the possibility of general overproduction; hence it denies the existence of the phenomena which we have just examined. We can, in consequence, use these phenomena to discover the defects in the "law." We shall quote statements of the false Say's law from a number of classical sources. It is worth noting in this connection that the most trenchant statements of the erroneous law come in the early 1800's, that is, early in the history of political economy. The "law," once stated, seemed so self-evident as to pass entirely out of the sphere of discussion, and to become a general, generally unspoken underlying preconception of economics. We may remark that fundamental scientific errors often perpetuate themselves in this form—the analogy with Newton's notion of absolute space and time and its overthrow by Einstein is striking. Discussion of Say's law began again, though, in somewhat unsatisfactory form, early in the twentieth century; the decisive overthrow comes with Keynes's *General Theory* (1936). Even today, a residual opinion clings to the error, as witness Mr. Henry Hazlitt:

Such a hulabaloo has been raised about Keynes's alleged "refutation" of Say's law that it seems desirable to pursue the subject further. One writer has distinguished "the four essential meanings of Say's law, as developed by Say and, more fully, by Mill and Ricardo." It may be profitable to take her formulation as a basis of discussion. The four meanings as she phrases them are:

(1) Supply creates its own demand; hence, aggregate overproduction or a "general" glut is impossible. . . . I shall contend that . . . 1 is correct,

properly understood and interpreted. . . . There is still need and place to assert Say's law when anybody is foolish enough to deny it. It is itself, to repeat, essentially a negative rather than a positive proposition. It states that a *general* overproduction of *all* commodities is not possible. And that is all, basically, that it is intended to assert.

We quote a number of classical statements of the false Say's law.
(A) *J. B. Say, Treatise on Political Economy*, (1801).

It is production that creates a demand for products. To say that sales are dull, owing to the scarcity of money, is to mistake the means for the cause. Sales cannot be said to be dull because money is scarce, but because other products are so. . . . A product is no sooner created than it, from that instant, affords a market for all other products to the full extent of its own value. Thus the mere circumstance of the creation of one product immediately opens a vent for other products.

(B) *James Mill, Commerce Defended*, (1808).

The production of commodities creates, and is the universal cause which creates a market for the commodities produced. . . . A nation's power of purchasing is exactly measured by its annual produce. The more you increase the annual produce, the more by that very act you extend the national market. The demand of a nation is always equal to the produce of a nation.

(C) *John Stuart Mill, Principles of Political Economy*, (1848).

What constitutes the means of payment for commodities is simply commodities. Each person's means of paying for the production of other people consist of those which he himself possesses. All sellers are inevitably, and by the meaning of the word, buyers. Could we suddenly double the productive powers of the country, we should double the supply of commodities in every market, but we should by the same stroke, double the purchasing power. . . .

The central confusion here is between *ability to purchase* and *desire to purchase:* each author proves, quite correctly, that an increase in the scale or production must be matched by a general increase in the ability of manufacturers to purchase other commodities. This is then fallaciously identified with a corresponding desire to purchase; so that the whole mechanism of a (possibly deficient) desire to purchase (on the part of manufacturers) which is basic to our cycle-model is carelessly ruled out. We find this error in Say's first sentence (Does "demand" mean "ability to purchase" or "desire to purchase"? In the first sense Say is substantially correct, in the second sense substantially incorrect); in Say's third sentence (sales in our model are dull because others lack the desire to purchase, not the ability); in Say's fourth and fifth sentences (ability to purchase vs. desire to purchase again). We note the same error in James Mill's too facile transition from "power of purchasing" to "extend the national market"; and in J. S. Mill's evident inference from "purchasing power" to desire to purchase, an inference whose fallacy is evident in our model.

This confusion is of remarkable persistence. Perhaps its final form is to be found in the work of Keynes himself, in the sections of the *General Theory* where he tries to attach a financial mechanism (based upon the rate of interest and "liquidity preference") to the basic real-term phenomenon, so as to complete his analysis. What is basically involved, however, is not the inability of manufacturers to produce without borrowing, but the lack of desire on the part of a manufacturer in possession of all the elements of production, to go ahead with this production. Later Keynesians have largely discounted these specifically fiscal ideas of Keynes, either explicitly or in practice, and either on empirical or on theoretical grounds.

Is not all this clear evidence of the theoretical utility of proper mathematical method?

General Reflections on Keynesian Economics. The Numerical Value of the Multiplier

1. Over-all Significance of the Keynes Theorem

The Keynesian notions which we have approached through the simplified cycle-theory model of the last three lectures are so central to all current economic thinking that it is appropriate to dwell upon them, even if this requires us to interrupt our strictly mathematical development.

To write

(*) total production − total industrial consumption of elements of production

     = personal consumption + collective consumption + desired and executed investment + growth of inventories,

is to write a tautology that follows from the definitions of the terms involved. But to supplement this tautology with the fact, taken from our cycle-theory model, that definite obstacles can exist to the growth of inventories (as also to the size of other categories of investment), is to make the basic step to the Keynesian theories.

A succinct formulation of classical economics might be *Consumption adjusts to the limits imposed by production;* Keynesian economics on the contrary insists that *Production adjusts to the limits imposed by consumption* (and, of course, investment).

The classical economics is then the *economics of scarcity* (no general overproduction of commodities possible), the Keynesian economics is *the economics of affluence* (general overproduction of commodities a recurrent phenomenon). There is, of course, something paradoxical in describing a recession or depression, which is a period of exceptional hardship and of production in amounts insufficient for general satisfaction, and hence is superficially a period of apparent underproduction, by the word "overproduction." That we do so, and that recessions appear in this way in our cycle-theory model, comes from the circumstance that we have formulated our model in a labor-eliminated form; i.e., as a model involving material commodities only. To reconstruct the effect of wage-payments, we must unravel this mathematical simplification. Suppose, for the sake of simplicity, that we have only one single labor sector. Let π_{ij} be the extended input-output matrix, including the labor-input row and the input-to-labor column. Let $\overset{\circ}{\pi}_{ij}$ denote the matrix with this row and column deleted. Then $\tilde{\pi}_{ij}$ is the matrix $\overset{\circ}{\pi}_{ij} + (1 - \pi_{oo})^{-1}\pi_{io}\pi_{oj}$; thus, in using the matrix $\tilde{\pi}_{ij}$, the commodities consumed by laborers out of wage payments accruing to the labor required to produce one unit of commodity i are being counted directly as a commodity input required to produce a unit of commodity i. The "consumption" (assumed constant) in our model is consequently nonwage-generated private consumption plus government consumption. Personal consumption, as it ordinarily figures in gross product tables, would then be the fixed autonomous consumption e_j *plus* the wage-generated consumption

$$a(n) \sum_{i=1}^{n} v_i(1 - \pi_{oo})^{-1}\pi_{io}\pi_{oj}.$$

Calling this latter sum u_j, we find personal consumption as ordinarily reckoned to be represented in our model by the expression $e_j + a(n)u_j$. The fluctuations of consumption during the cycle thus come from the fluctuations of $a(n)$. The "affluence" aspect of a recession is visible to those whose consumption is relatively independent of production and forms a part of the terms e; a rather opposite aspect appears however to those whose consumption is directly dependent upon production and in our grossly simplified model forms part of the terms $a(n)u$. Demand, if expressed by persons in this later category, may constitute ineffective demand.

With this understanding then of the meaning of the terms involved, we may state the Keynes relation (7.11) as

$$(8.1) \qquad \bar{a}_j - \sum_{i=1}^{n} \tilde{\pi}_{ij}\bar{a}_j = e_j$$

or with the inclusion of average investment

$$(8.2) \qquad a_j - \sum_{i=1}^{n} \tilde{\pi}_{ij}\bar{a}_i = \bar{e}_j + \overline{(\text{investment})}_j$$

the bars denoting time-averages.

This equation, taken not as an average but as an indicator of the effect of one or another policy (ignoring dynamic complications), is the basis of many Keynesian policy recommendations. Thus, in order to avoid the stresses of recession, one can

1. Increase e, through "spend now" or "spend more" exhortations and programs, civil and military, and through unemployment relief, etc.

2. Increase investment by fast tax write-offs, guarantees against loss, public works programs, etc.

3. Increase the elements of $\tilde{\pi}_{ij}$ through wage increases of one or another sort.

The difference between the Keynesian and the classical view is dramatically evidenced by the familiar dispute over point *3* above. The classicist argues that wage cuts in depressions are prime means of bringing the depression to an end; the Keynesian considers that by reducing the elements $\tilde{\pi}_{ij}$ in (8.1) (and perhaps, through reflex, reducing investment) such an act will tend to make a depression worse. According to the Keynesian theory, the production levels are determined by solving the equations (8.2):

$$(8.3\text{a}) \qquad \mathbf{a} = (1 - \tilde{\Pi})^{-1}(\mathbf{e} + \mathbf{investment});$$

since

$$(8.3\text{b}) \qquad (1 - \tilde{\Pi})^{-1} = 1 + \tilde{\Pi} + \tilde{\Pi}^2 + \tilde{\Pi}^3 + \cdots,$$

it is then plain that $\mathbf{a}$ increases with $\tilde{\Pi}$, and hence with the wage level. This result is in *direct contradiction* to the non-Keynesian economic theory which makes the claim that the proper thing to do in time of depression is to *cut wages*. To illustrate the definiteness of the difference between Keynes and the classicists on this score, we quote such an opinion from the book of Mr. Henry Hazlitt:

> If I were put to it to name the most confused and fantastic chapter in the whole of the *General Theory*, the choice would be difficult. But I doubt that anyone could successfully challenge me if I named Chapter 19, on "Changes in Money-Wages."
>
> Its badness is after all not surprising. For it is here that Keynes sets out to challenge and deny what has become in the last two centuries the most strongly established principle in economics—to wit, that if the price of any commodity or service is kept too high (i.e., above the point of equilibrium) some of that commodity or service will remain unsold. This is true of eggs, cheese, cotton, Cadillacs, or labor. When wage rates are too high there will be unemployment. Reducing the myriad wage rates to their respective equilibrium points may not in itself be a sufficient step to the restoration of full employment (for there are other possible disequilibriums to be considered), but it is an absolutely necessary step.
>
> This is the elementary and inescapable truth that Keynes, with an incredible display of sophistry, irrelevance, and complicated obfuscation, tries to refute.

The difference is evidently marked. We shall return in later lectures to this passage from Hazlitt. Let us only remark here that "classical" conclusions of this type are obtained by arguing that by driving down labor costs a larger total of labor will be used, essentially because manufacturers will use labor more freely. In our theory we have assumed fixed production coefficients, including the coefficients π_{io}: which is to say that the amount of labor is in proportion to production. Thus, we have assumed away Mr. Hazlitt's grounds of argument; the differing conclusions of the present Keynesian theory and the classical non-Keynesian theory can be traced to differing fundamental assumptions about the operation of an economy. We shall later put the two theories on common ground and be able to make a fairer comparison. We will see that by determining from actual statistics the extent to which production tends to use definite amounts of labor irrespective of wages paid, it is in principle possible to settle this dispute.

2. An Heuristic Model of the Keynesian Conclusions

Certain significant features of classical economics appear vividly when presented in terms of a "Robinson Crusoe" model; in which

Crusoe, faced with scarcities of almost everything, allocates his efforts to maximize his satisfaction. It is instructive to set up a similar "Crusoe" picture of the central Keynesian phenomena. This may be done as follows. Crusoe has now occupied his desert island for many years, and, developing his own considerable initial endowments as an engineer, installed a complete variety of automatic machinery to supply all his needs. (Note the transition from scarcity to affluence.) It is then quite plain that the statistics for any typical activity of the automatic machinery, as e.g., electric power consumed, foot-pounds hoisted, etc., will be determined proportionately by Crusoe's desire to consume. If he lives frugally in a given month, the machinery will hardly turn; if he is possessed of a desire to construct a road, a palace, or what have you, the machinery will turn more vigorously. If included among the components of this machinery are found the humanoid robots beloved of science fiction, then the number of hours of labor performed by robots, their employment or unemployment, would be similarly proportional to Crusoe's desire to consume. Now if Crusoe's man Friday found himself classified among the robots, and paid at a fixed wage rate, he would of course prefer that Crusoe consume more rather than less, and might even try to insist, if he could, that Crusoe regularly engage in activities, wasteful for Crusoe, but sustaining for himself. Crusoe's affluence, if manifested in the too-ready satisfaction of Crusoe's desire to consume, would of course correspond to Friday's difficulties, to Friday's being left out in the economic cold. In an actual economy, of course, people partake of the "Crusoe" and "Friday" character in degrees spread over a wide spectrum and in many qualitatively different ways. Thus the simple phenomenon becomes more complex, and is only to be reconstructed through a certain quantitative effort of analysis. A depression certainly does not appear superficially as a period characterized by exceptional affluence: nevertheless, our analysis shows that part of its basic cause is the too-ready satisfaction of the consumption demands of too large a segment of those controlling the disposition of resources (together with, of course, the fact that this control is very unevenly distributed in the real population, that is, together with the lack of all title to resources among the depressed segment of the population). An additional complication comes from the fact that "Crusoe" is in actuality replaced by a highly fragmented committee who fall very readily into panicky paralysis of a kind which we have observed in our study of the game of "majority." Thus, a depression, which we have regarded theoretically as revealing economic affluence, will appear to the bulk of the population as a period of exceptional deprivation, and to many others as a period of relative, even of mild deprivation, and unnerving confusion. The situation is highly paradoxical; but our theoretical analysis, as well as the success of the Keynesian economic policies, points clearly to social wealth and not social poverty as the root cause of depressions.

The paradoxical features of the situation which we have been examining are emphasized by Keynes in a brilliant and famous passage:

If this is accepted, the above reasoning shows how "wasteful" loan expenditure may nevertheless enrich the community on balance. Pyramid-building, earthquakes, even wars may serve to increase wealth, if the education of our statesmen on the principles of the classical economics stands in the way of anything better.

It is curious how common sense, wriggling for an escape from absurd conclusions, has been apt to reach a preference for wholly "wasteful" forms of loan expenditure rather than for partly wasteful forms, which, because they are not wholly wasteful, tend to be judged on strict "business" principles. For example, unemployment relief financed by loans is more readily accepted than the financing of improvements at a charge below the current rate of interest; whilst the form of digging holes in the ground known as gold-mining, which not only adds nothing whatever to the real wealth of the world but involves the disutility of labour, is the most acceptable of all solutions.

If the Treasury were to fill old bottles with banknotes, bury them at suitable depths in disused coal-mines which are then filled up to the surface with town rubbish, and leave it to private enterprise on well-trained principles of laissez-faire to dig the notes up again (the right to do so being obtained, of course, by tendering for leases of the note-bearing territory), there need be no more unemployment and, with the help of the repercussions, the real income of the community, and its capital wealth also, would probably become a good deal greater than it actually is. It would, indeed, be more sensible to build houses and the like; but if there are political and practical difficulties in the way of this, the above would be better than nothing.

The analogy between this expedient and the gold-mines of the real world is complete. At periods when gold is available at suitable depth experience shows that the real wealth of the world increases rapidly; and when but little of it is so available, our wealth suffers stagnation or decline. Thus gold-mines are of the greatest value and importance to civilisation. Just as wars have been the only form of large-scale loan expenditure which statesmen have thought justifiable, so gold-mining is the only pretext for digging holes in the ground which has recommended itself to bankers as sound finance; and each of these activities has played its part in progress—failing something better.

Ancient Egypt was doubly fortunate, and doubtless owed to this its fabled wealth, in that it possessed two activities, namely, pyramid-building as well as the search for the precious metals, the fruits of which, since they could not serve the needs of men by being consumed, did not stale with abundance. The Middle Ages built cathedrals and sang dirges. Two pyramids, two masses for the dead, are twice as good as one; but not so two railways from London to York. Thus we are so sensible, have schooled ourselves to so close a semblance of prudent financiers, taking careful thought before we add to the "financial" burdens of posterity by building them houses to live in, that we have no such easy escape from the sufferings of unemployment. We have to accept them as an inevitable result of applying to the conduct of the State the maxims which are best calculated to "enrich" an individual by enabling him to pile up claims to enjoyment which he does not intend to exercise at any definite time.

3. The Matrix Multiplier, the Vector Multiplier, and the Average Multiplier

The linear relationship (8.3a) has evidently the form of a (matricial) multiplier, and is one of a number of related equations of this type which are known as "multiplier" or "accelerator" relationships. Noting, for instance, that real national income is by definition total production *minus* industrial consumption, hence $(a_j - \sum_{i=1}^{n} \mathring{\pi}_{ij} a_i)$, we may deduce from (8.3) that

$$(8.4) \qquad \mathbf{NI'} = (\mathbf{e'} + \mathbf{investment'})(I - \mathring{\Pi})^{-1}(I - \mathring{\Pi}),$$

an equation in real terms valid in the case of a single labor sector which provides a Keynesian relation for determining the components of national income in terms of final output. It should be noted that each of the matrices in this equation is an "institutional" characteristic of the economy; this makes it plain "why the multiplier is constant."

Equation (8.4), simplified to a simple numerical (aggregative) equation relating total money value of final output to total money value of national income by conversion to money terms and averaging, is often called the Keynes multiplier equation. Of course, this drastic simplification neglects the variation in per dollar contributions to national income of the various different commodities which can constitute final output, as also the variations in relative production levels upon variation of the material composition of final output. Nevertheless, it will have considerable utility in rough policy discussions neglecting these finer effects.

In applying an equation like (8.4) or an aggregated form of that equation to data taken from an actual economy, we need a generalization of (8.4) taking account of the circumstance that there will be more than a single labor commodity, and that certain labor commodities (as personal efforts of military defense) are included in final output. In writing such a generalization, it is well to use the input-output matrix in its original form, rather than in the labor-eliminated form which was convenient in the last three lectures, and in terms of which we have written equation (8.4). Thus, let π_{ij} be the input-output matrix including labor sectors, so that i and j vary from N to $-L$. Let $\ddot{\pi}_{ij}$ denote the matrix of inputs to material sectors (industrial consumption) so that $\ddot{\pi}_{ij} = \pi_{ij}$ if $i = 1, \cdots, N$, while $\ddot{\pi}_{ij} = 0$ if $i = 0, \cdots, -L$. Then if $\omega' = [\omega_N, \cdots, \omega_{-L}]$ is the vector of final output (real components of national dividend), and $\mathbf{a}' = [a_N, \cdots, a_{-L}]$ is the vector of total production of the commodities $C_N, \cdots, C_{-L}$, we have plainly

$$(8.5) \qquad \omega_j = a_j - \sum_{i=-L}^{N} a_i \pi_{ij}, \quad j = -L, \cdots, N$$

so that

$$(8.6) \qquad \omega'(I - \Pi)^{-1} = \mathbf{a}'.$$

This is evidently a direct generalization of equation (8.3). Knowing the components of total output $\mathbf{a}'$, as they appear in (8.6), we must now make a subtraction for industrial consumption in order to obtain national income. Since total production minus industrial consumption is $\mathbf{a}'(1 - \ddot{\Pi})$, we have plainly

$$(8.7) \qquad \mathbf{NI}' = \omega'(I - \Pi)^{-1}(I - \ddot{\Pi})$$

for the total components of national income. This is the appropriate generalization of equation (8.4).

Let us now discuss the aggregation of equation (8.7). Let $\mathbf{p}$ be the vector of prices, including labor-commodity prices (after correction for the effects of excises). Then, from (8.7), the value of national income is given by

$$(8.8) \qquad NI = \mathbf{NI}' \cdot \mathbf{p} = \omega'(I - \Pi)^{-1}(I - \ddot{\Pi})\mathbf{p}.$$

Let $\mathbf{R}$ be the vector $(I - \Pi)^{-1}(I - \ddot{\Pi})\mathbf{p}$, with components $[R_N, \cdots, R_{-L}]$. Then (8.8) may be written

$$(8.9) \qquad NI = \sum_{k=-L}^{N} \omega_k R_k,$$

showing the way in which final output determines national income at the Keynesian equilibrium. The vector $\mathbf{R}$ may be called the *Keynes Vector Multiplier* for converting final output (in real terms) into national income.

If we write $K_j = R_j/p_j$, so that

$$(8.10) \qquad NI = \sum_{j=-L}^{N} K_j(\omega_j p_j),$$

we have a corresponding Keynes vector multiplier for converting the components of final output (expressed in money terms) into national income. If we neglect the variation from one commodity to another of the coefficients K_j, more precisely, if we replace the coefficients K_j by their average K weighted according to the proportional value of each commodity in final output, we may write (8.10) as

$$(8.11) \qquad NI = K\omega' \cdot \mathbf{p},$$

or

(8.12) national income = Keynes multiplier · national output.

Our derivation shows that the components K_j are defined by the technological conditions of production and the wage-rates; the average multiplier K however might vary somewhat with variations in the composition of final output.

4. Estimation of the Multiplier

The multiplier then is the factor relating final output of the economy to national income. To make a quick if crude estimation of the multiplier, we segregate the entries in the gross national product tables (given in a previous lecture) into three general sub-headings *national dividend* (as previously reckoned); *maintenance and fixed charges* (i.e., items making a long-term economic contribution, and insensitive to the business cycle; these items would be cut back significantly only in severe and protracted recession and ought for the present purposes be reckoned as an addendum to the national output) and *direct current expenses of production*. Note in particular that since replacement of old equipment is an important form of investment, it is convenient to include gross rather than net investment in final output. Thus, we shall estimate the multiplier as the ratio of Gross National Product, less excises, rather than of National Income, to total output. Approximate totals, taken from our earlier tables, would be as shown in Table XI (taken in billion dollars, year 1957).

TABLE XI
National Dividend and National Maintenance

A1. National Dividend; Estimate of Sources

Noncorporate profits	8
Corporate dividends	9
Corporate retained profits	9
Net private interest	10
Government interest payments	6
State and local government net investment	4
Federal military expenses	44
Total national dividend	90

A2. National Dividend; Rough Estimate of Disposition

Federal military expense	44
State and local government net investment	4
Corporate investment, net	15
Farm and noncorporate investment, net	6
Net housing investment (rental construction and mortgage financed)	10
Personal consumption (financed out of dividends and interest)	10
Total	89

B. Maintenance and Fixed Charges

Depreciation charges	38
Additional state and local expenditures	32
Additional federal nonmilitary expenditures	6
Total	76

The total of A and B is 166; the gross national product (less in_direct business taxes) is 402. *Thus the multiplier is* $\frac{402}{166}$, *or approxi*-mately 2.4. We may check this estimate in a simple way by taking the yearly series of *gross national product*, estimating output by sub-tracting the yearly series, *personal consumption expenditures*, making a subtractive correction for the item *indirect business tax liability*, and estimating the multiplier as a ratio. Table XII contains the relevant data. (Source: U. S. Department of Commerce.)

TABLE XII

Alternate Estimates of the Keynesian Multiplier

	(A)	(B) Personal	(C)	(D)	(E)	(F)	(G)
Year	GNP	Consumption	(A) − (B)	(A)/(C)	Excises	(A) − (E)	(F)/(C)
1951	329	210	119	2.74	26	303	2.55
1952	347	220	127	2.68	28	319	2.50
1953	365	233	132	2.76	30	335	2.54
1954	363	238	130	2.78	30	333	2.57
1955	397	257	140	2.83	33	364	2.60
1956	419	269	150	2.79	36	383	2.56
1957	440	284	156	2.82	38	402	2.60

This leads us to estimate the multiplier computed on this "con-sumption" basis with corrections for excise taxes as 2.55; the excess of this estimate over our earlier estimate of 2.4 comes from the heading "personal luxury consumption" formerly reckoned as output, and reckoned above as excluded from output. Without correction for excise taxes, we would have the larger estimate 2.8. The figures for years before 1951 are not strictly comparable, owing to the significant changes in tax law that took place in 1950.

With the value 2.4 of the multiplier, we may make computations of hypothetical recessions; computations of this sort stand behind many of the economic policy recommendations currently being made. Suppose, e.g., that in consequence of difficulties in housing credit or for some other reason the housing investment item under (A2) above fell to zero. Then

(a) If net corporate investment, item under (A2) in Table X1 were unaffected, GNP (after correction for excises) would fall 24 bil-lion or 6%, and employment a like amount, approximately 3.6 of

60 million workers additional unemployment, which, added to the normal 3 million minimal unemployment would lead to unemployment figures of 6.6 million.

(b) If the housing fall contemplated in (a) led to cutbacks of fixed and inventory investment of 50%, GNP less excises would fall 42 billion or 10%, leading to unemployment of 9 million.

Such a reflex is quite possible (as, on the side of *inventory* investment, our model insists). For example, in the recession year 1954 net corporate investment fell to 7 from a previous figure of 14 and with a subsequent rise to 15; in 1949 net corporate investment fell to 5 from a previous figure of 17 and with a subsequent rise to 14.

Conversely, we may reckon how much of a fall in our two output categories, (A) and (B) above, is necessary to produce a given level of unemployment. Thus, for instance, to have 20 million unemployed (on the 1957 economic basis) a fall of $\frac{17}{60}$ or 28% in the categories (A) and (B) is required; this is approximately 50 billion. Elimination of the item "Federal military expense" and corollary reduction of the item "Corporate investment" would do it. This consideration throws light on the widespread belief that the economy is currently dependent on military production.

5. A Remark

In the present lecture we have, in order to present the Keynesian conclusions in their starkest form, taken a rigidly "bimodal" attitude toward consumption, dividing consumption into two parts, one of which we took to be automatically and proportionately determined by wages, the other part of which we took to be autonomous and constant. In subsequent lectures, we will improve our treatment by interpolating a more realistic spectrum of consumption practices between these two extremes. This will introduce us to considerations centering about the "propensity to consume" which, since Keynes, have been repeatedly stressed in the literature. We shall at that time indicate a set of assumptions which are sufficient in order that the more general cases to be treated reduce to the simple case studied in the present lecture. In this way, our analysis will return us to the conclusions of the present chapter, modified however in the direction of a greater realism, and seen from a different point of view and against a more general background.

LECTURE *9*

A Modified Cycle-Theory Model

1. Some Semi-empirical Considerations

The preliminary cycle-theory model presented and analyzed in Lectures 6 and 7 greatly exaggerates the violence of the business cycle, which, typically, involves fluctuations of 15–20% in the levels of industrial output, rather than the periodic total cutoff of production which we find for the model cycle of Lecture 7 (cf. especially Fig. 11, Section 7.1). In the present lecture we shall aim at indicating the direction in which a qualitatively improved model might lie, without, however, pretending to construct anything like an economic model sufficiently complete to be of predictive value.

Let us first note that the sales-production linkage on which the operation of the model of Lectures 6 and 7 was based is far more rigid in the sphere of industrial than in the sphere of trade activities. There is a very basic reason for this. Industrial activity is the production of commodities at a point not in immediate contact with their ultimate destination; trade is the disposition of commodities. Industrial production proceeds in any given hour with a given intensity; trade adjusts from moment to moment to the participation of the consumer. If industrial production runs a few per cent above the rate at which its products are consumed, the consistently positive difference, output minus consumption, *cumulates*, and significant masses of unsold inventory must inevitably appear. Not so in the sphere of trade. If, for instance, the sales force of a trade enterprise is a few per cent larger than what sales figures might indicate as optimum, the average salesman will simply sell a few per cent less: there will surely develop no "excess inventory of completed salesmanship"! Nor will it be possible for the entrepreneur in trade to envisage drastic reductions in the size of his operations, justifying these, in the manner of the industrial manufacturer, by reference to an already produced excessive stock of "finished sales." Thus, in trade enterprise, neither will the pressure to bring operations into line with consumption take on the acute form which it may in industrial enterprise, nor will sudden drastic changes in the scale of activity be feasible. Instead of adjusting so forcefully as industrial activity to a changing general business atmosphere, trade activity will adjust by moderate degrees to the requirements of the economy at large, trade enterprise gradually growing or shrivelling as average economic conditions indicate. We may deduce from this that the presence of nonindustrial activities in the economy will dampen the oscillations of production generated in the industrial sphere. Let us examine some statistical information which indicates the relevance of the effects described above and gives a rough indication of their magnitude. In the first place, it is appropriate to examine the proportion within total activity of industrial activity: such information is given in Table XIII, taken, like the other tables to be presented in the present chapter, from the *Business Statistics* of the Office of Business Economics.

TABLE XIII

Employment by Principal Economic Categories—U. S. 1955

	(millions)
Durable goods manufacturing	9.5
Nondurable goods manufacturing	7.0
Mining	0.8
Contract construction	2.8
Agriculture	6.7
Transportation and utilities	4.0
Wholesale and retail trade	10.8
Finance, insurance, and real estate	2.2
Service and miscellaneous	5.9
Government	6.9
Total employment	63.2
Unemployed	2.7
Total labor force	65.9

The cycle-sensitive manufacturing, mining, and construction sectors give employment to 20 million of 63 million total employed, or 31% of the total.

We take the figures in Table XIV from the 1957–8 recession. They show that approximate oscillation of employment in various economic categories, measured from the pre-recession levels to the lowest recession levels.

TABLE XIV

Seasonally Adjusted Employment in Principal Economic Categories
Per cent of variation in the recession of 1957–8 (millions)

Category	Pre-recession	Recession minimum	Approx. variation
Durable goods manufacturing	9.9	8.5	15%
Nondurable goods manufacturing	7.0	6.7	4%
Mining	0.8	0.7	12%
Contract construction	2.9	2.5	15%
Agriculture	7.5	6.9	10%
Transportation and utilities	4.2	3.9	8%
Wholesale and retail trade	11.3	11.1	2%
Finance, insurance, and real estate	2.4	2.4	0%
Service and miscellaneous	6.3	6.3	0%
Government	7.6	7.8	−3%

We note the extent to which nonagricultural employment fluctuations are concentrated within the manufacturing, mining, and construction spheres, and within manufacturing within the durable manufacturing sphere. The employment-stability of the trade, finance, service, and government sectors, accounting for 27 of 66 million persons employed, roughly 40% of the total economic effort, is especially noteworthy. For comparison, we give similar figures for a number of other principal statistical series in Table XV.

Again, the concentration of fluctuations in the industrial sphere is evident, as also the fact that a large part (something like half) the burden of recession is borne by corporate pre-tax profits and ultimately by corporate retained profits and corporate investment (particularly inventory investment), dividend distribution being maintained at a reasonably constant rate.

TABLE XV

Various Seasonally Adjusted Economic Indices
Per cent of variation in the recession of 1957–8

	Pre-recession	Recession minimum	Approx. variation
Industrial production	145	126	15%
Manufactures	147	128	15%
Durable manufactures	160	131	20%
Nondurable manufactures	131	124	6%
Food manufactures	113	112	1%
Textile mill products	100	91	9%
National income	371	358	4%
Gross national product	447	431	4%
Corporate profits before tax	44	32	20%
Private wages and salaries	200	193	4%
Gross investment	68	51	30%
Dividend income	128	126	2%

Trade activities (which we take as typical of the cycle-insensitive class of economic activities) then adjust not to an immediately preceding sales situation but to an average sales situation, as computed over several preceding economic "days" or "planning periods." We may incorporate an aspect of this judgment into a mathematical model in a conveniently simple if Procrustean fashion by replacing the expression "previous day's sales" in the basic formula (5.5) for desired production in the jth commodity sphere by the expression "average sales over previous Δ_i days," i.e., replacing the expression

$$(9.1) \qquad c_j \sum_{i=1}^{n} a_i(t-1)\tilde{\pi}_{ij}$$

by the expression

$$(9.2) \qquad c_j \Delta_j^{-1} \sum_{\delta=1}^{\Delta_j} \sum_{i=1}^{n} a_i(t-\delta)\tilde{\pi}_{ij}.$$

The integer Δ_j is a characteristic of the jth industry, heuristically, a "rate of response" index, which, for the reasons which we have indicated above, may be taken as larger for trade sectors and smaller for industrial sectors. The complete set of recursions of the final section of Lecture 5 may then be carried over to yield the modified dynamic model defined by the following recursive formulae (we shall include consumption and base inventory from the outset).

$$(9.3) \qquad b_j(t) = b_j(t-1) + a_j(t-1) - \sum_{i=1}^{n} \tilde{\pi}_{ij} a_i(t-1) - e_j$$

$$(9.4) \quad d_j(t) = \left\{ (c_j + 2)\Delta_j^{-1} \sum_{\delta=1}^{\Delta_j} \sum_{i=1}^{n} \tilde{\pi}_{ij} a_i(t-\delta) - a_j(t-1) - b_j(t-1) \right.$$
$$\left. + (c_j + 2)e_j + h_j \right\}^+$$

(This is the equation for desired production; e_j is autonomous consumption and h_j is base inventory.)

$$(9.5) \qquad\qquad \mu_k(t) = \frac{b_k(t)}{\displaystyle\sum_{i=1}^{n} \tilde{\pi}_{ik} d_i(t)}$$

(market strain factor in kth commodity market).

$$(9.6) \qquad\qquad \sigma_j(t) = \min\,(\min_{\pi_{jk}>0} \mu_k(t),\, 1)$$

(supply strain factor in jth commodity production).

$$(9.7) \qquad\qquad a_j(t) = d_j(t)\sigma_j(t)$$

(actual production of jth commodity).

These recursions give us a closed model; we now turn to the analysis of a special case of the model.

2. Stability of the Keynes Point for Large Λ

It is apparent heuristically that as the constants Δ_j increase, our model economy becomes less prone to sudden or wide shifts in the levels of production; for Δ_j large *on the average* we consequently expect production and inventory levels which are initially in the vicinity of the Keynes point to hover about these invariant levels for extended periods of time. In the present section we will justify this tentative conclusion by giving a complete analysis of the particularly tractable case $\Delta_1 = \cdots = \Delta_n = \Delta$, $c_1 = \cdots = c_n = c$. Thus, we wish to find the fixed point of the transformation defined by (9.3)–(9.7) and to study the transformation in the vicinity of its fixed point.

This may be done as follows. In the first place, we conclude from (9.3) that fixed-point production levels must be given by

$$(9.8) \qquad a_j{}^K - \sum_{i=1}^{n} a_i{}^K \tilde{\pi}_{ij} = e_j;$$

(9.8), of course, is merely our old friend the Keynes relation. It follows in the same way from (9.4) that the fixed-point inventory levels are given by

$$(9.9) \qquad (c_j + 2) \sum_{i=1}^{n} a_i{}^K \tilde{\pi}_{ij} - 2a_j{}^K + (c_j + 2)e_j + h_j = b_j{}^K,$$

so that using (9.8) we have the unsurprising formula

$$(9.10) \qquad c_j a_j{}^K + h_j = b_j{}^K,$$

for the equilibrium inventory levels. Note that at these production and inventory levels we have $d_j = a_j{}^K$ by (10.4); $\sum \tilde{\pi}_{ik} a_i{}^K = a_j{}^K - e_j$; so that

$$(9.11) \qquad \mu_k = (c_k a_k{}^K + h_k)/(a_k{}^K - e_k) > 1,$$

since we always assume $c_k \geq 1$; hence $\sigma_j = 1$ for all j. Thus (9.7) gives $d_j = a_j{}^K$ again and confirms the fact that (9.8) and (9.10) define a fixed point $a_j{}^K$, $b_j{}^K$ of our dynamic model, *and that for all a_j, b_j in the vicinity of this fixed point the transformation defined by (9.3)–(9.7) reduces to the linear transformation defined by the two following equations:*

$$(9.12) \qquad b_j(t) = b_j(t-1) + a_j(t-1) - \sum_{i=1}^{n} \tilde{\pi}_{ij} a_i(t-1) - e_j$$

$$(9.13) \qquad a_j(t) = (c+2)\Delta^{-1} \sum_{\delta=1}^{\Delta} \sum_{i=1}^{n} \tilde{\pi}_{ij} a_i(t-\delta) - a_j(t-1) - b_j(t-1)$$
$$+ (c+2)e_j + h_j.$$

We may at once adapt the techniques employed in Lecture 7 to the study of these inhomogeneous recursions. In the first place, if we write $\tilde{b}_j(t) = b_j(t) - b_j{}^K$ and $\tilde{a}_j(t) = a_j(t) - a_j{}^K$ for the deviations of inventory and production levels from their equilibrium value, then $\tilde{a}_j$ and $\tilde{b}_j$ satisfy the homogeneous linear recursions

$$(9.14) \qquad \tilde{b}_j(t) = \tilde{b}_j(t-1) + \tilde{a}_j(t-1) - \sum_{i=1}^{n} \tilde{\pi}_{ij} \tilde{a}_i(t-1)$$

$$(9.15) \quad \tilde{a}_j(t) = (c+2)\Delta^{-1} \sum_{\delta=1}^{\Delta} \sum_{i=1}^{n} \tilde{\pi}_{ij} a_i(t-\delta) - \tilde{a}_j(t-1) - \tilde{b}(t-1).$$

These recursions are *of order* Δ in the sense of the theory of difference equations, i.e., they relate the values of certain variables at a given time to the values of the variable in Δ preceding periods. Such a system of recursions may trivially be reduced to a system of recursions which is of first order (i.e., defines the values of its variables at a given time in terms of their values in the immediately preceding period) by using a device entirely analogous to a device familiar in the theory of differential equations. Namely, we introduce $\tilde{b}_{j,\nu}(t) = \tilde{b}_j(t - \nu + 1)$, $\nu = 1, \cdots, \Delta$, and $\tilde{a}_{j,\nu}(t) = \tilde{a}_j(t - \nu + 1)$, $\nu = 1, \cdots, \Delta$ as a new set of variables; it is immediately seen that the recursions (9.14)–(9.15) are equivalent to the following recursions in our newly introduced variables:

$$(9.16) \quad \tilde{b}_{j,\nu}(t) - \tilde{b}_{j,\nu-1}(t-1), \quad \nu = 2, \cdots, \Delta;$$

$$\tilde{b}_{j,1}(t) = \tilde{b}_{j,1}(t-1) + \tilde{a}_{j,1}(t-1) - \sum_{i=1}^{n} \tilde{\pi}_{ij} \tilde{a}_{i,1}(t-1);$$

$$(9.17) \quad \tilde{a}_{j,\nu}(t) = \tilde{a}_{j,\nu-1}(t-1), \quad \nu = 2, \cdots, \Delta;$$

$$\tilde{a}_{j,1}(t) = (c+2)\Delta^{-1} \sum_{\delta=1}^{\Delta} \sum_{i=1}^{n} \tilde{\pi}_{ij} \tilde{a}_{i,\delta}(t-1) - \tilde{a}_{j,1}(t-1)$$
$$- \tilde{b}_{j,1}(t-1).$$

We have now to study the result of repeated application of the linear transformation defined by (9.16)–(9.17) to the variables $\tilde{a}_{j,\nu}$, $\tilde{b}_{j,\nu}$. The principles of linear analysis tell us that this aim may most effectively be carried out by finding the eigenvalues and eigenvectors of this linear transformation. Our linear transformation operating in $2n\Delta$ dimensions, we must find $2n\Delta$ eigenvalues and eigenvectors; i.e., $2n\Delta$ sets of variables $\tilde{a}_j$, $\tilde{b}_j$, and λ for which the recursions (9.16)–(9.17) or the equivalent recursions (9.14)–(9.15) lead to a period-to-period multiplication of the variables $\tilde{a}_j$ and $\tilde{b}_j$ by the constant factor λ.

Once having this aim clearly in mind, we may readily carry it out, as follows. We make the ansatz $\tilde{a}_j(t) = \tilde{a} v_j \lambda^t$, $\tilde{b}_j(t) = \tilde{b} v_j \lambda^t$ in (9.14)–(9.15), where $\mathbf{v}'$ is an arbitrary eigenvector of the matrix $\tilde{\Pi}$, the corresponding eigenvalue being γ, so that

$$(9.18) \qquad \sum_{i=1}^{n} \tilde{\pi}_{ij} v_i = \gamma v_j, \quad j = 1 \cdots n.$$

With the ansatz, the equations (9.14)–(9.15) reduce to

$$(9.19) \qquad \tilde{b} = \lambda^{-1}\tilde{b} + \lambda^{-1}(1 - \gamma)\tilde{a},$$
$$\tilde{a} = ((c + 2)\Delta^{-1}(\lambda^{-1} + \cdots + \lambda^{-\Delta})\gamma - 1)\tilde{a} - \tilde{b}\lambda^{-1},$$

and the equations (9.16)–(9.17) to

$$(9.20) \qquad \lambda\tilde{b}_\nu = \tilde{b}_{\nu-1}, \quad \nu = 2, \cdots, \Delta;$$
$$\lambda\tilde{b}_1 = \tilde{b}_1 + (1 - \gamma)\tilde{a}_1;$$

$$(9.21) \qquad \lambda\tilde{a}_\nu = \tilde{a}_{\nu-1}, \quad \nu = 2, \cdots, \Delta;$$

$$\lambda\tilde{a}_1 = (c + 2)\Delta^{-1}\gamma \sum_{\delta=1}^{\Delta} \tilde{a}_\delta - \tilde{a}_1 - \tilde{b}_1.$$

The $n \times n$ matrix $\tilde{\Pi}$ will have n eigenvalues γ. For each such γ, the eigenvalue problem (9.20)–(9.21), which has 2Δ variables, will have 2Δ solutions. Thus our procedure yields $2n\Delta$ solutions in all; we know, however, that $2n\Delta$ is the correct total number of eigenvalues of our original linear transformation (9.16)–(9.17). We may conclude at once that all the eigenvalues λ of the transformation (9.16)–(9.17) satisfy a pair of equations of the form (9.19).

Now, the pair (9.19) of homogeneous linear equations will have a solution if and only if its determinant vanishes, i.e., if and only if

$$(9.22) \qquad \lambda^2 + [(c + 2)\gamma/\Delta] (1 - \lambda^{-\Delta+1}) - \gamma = 0.$$

If we solve this equation for each eigenvalue γ of the matrix $\tilde{\Pi}$, we will therefore obtain the full set of eigenvalues of the linear transformation (9.16)–(9.17).

By Lemma 3.1 of Lecture 3, each such eigenvalue γ is bounded by $\gamma_0 = \text{dom}(\tilde{\Pi})$. Moreover, $\gamma_0 < 1$. Can (9.22) have a root λ such that $|\lambda| \geq 1$? If this were the case then $|1 - \lambda^{-\Delta+1}| \leq 2$, so that it would follow from (9.22) that

$$(9.23) \qquad 1 \leq |\lambda|^2 \leq \left(\frac{2(c + 2)}{\Delta} + 1\right) \gamma_0,$$

which, for Δ sufficiently large, is a contradiction. Thus, we conclude that if Δ *is sufficiently large, all the eigenvalues, real or complex, of the transformation* (9.16)–(9.17) *are smaller than 1.*

Hence, repeated applications of the transformation (9.16)–(9.17) to its eigenvectors reduces each of these eigenvectors by a power of a factor which is always less than one; so that the eigenvectors are successively mapped into a sequence of vectors approaching zero with geometric rapidity. Since, according to the principles of linear analysis, an arbitrary vector can be written as a linear combination of these eigenvectors, it follows that the transformation (9.16)–(9.17), repeatedly applied to any vector, maps it into a sequence of vectors approaching the zero vector with geometric rapidity. But then, arguing from the relationships between the homogeneous recursions (9.16)–(9.17), the inhomogeneous linear recursions (9.12)–(9.13), and the full set of recursions (9.3)–(9.7) defining the present dynamic model which have already been established, we find that every orbit beginning in the vicinity of the Keynes point (9.8)–(9.10) of our model converges toward the Keynes point with geometric rapidity. Thus, in the present model, the business cycle oscillations are damped out with time. More realistically, one might expect a sporadic recurrence of damped oscillations, "excited" by external influences. The "pure components" of the general oscillation correspond to the eigenvalues λ found above; a component corresponding to an eigenvalue λ with $|\lambda|$ much smaller than 1 will damp out rapidly; a component corresponding to an eigenvalue λ with $|\lambda|$ nearly 1 will damp out only slowly, and appear as an easily excited, often observed cyclical mode. In the present case there is of course no "problem of economic stability"—the economy, however, can still be "sluggish"—the validity of the Keynes formula is self-evident.

3. Additional Remarks

The cyclical oscillations of the model presented immediately above are damped and thus the Keynes point is *stable;* the oscillations of the model presented in Lectures 6 and 7 are undamped and the Keynes point is *unstable.* To what extent is each of these two polar possibilities relevant to the actual economy? This question may be formulated as follows. It may be expected, in accordance with the statements of the first section of the present chapter, that the relatively slow response of, let us say, employment in the nonindustrial sectors of the economy will tend to moderate and confine the fluctuations which take place in the industrial sector. In order that the industrial fluctuations not be damped out entirely by the stable non-industrial sector it is necessary that the industrial sector be sufficiently sensitive to fluctuations in sales generated by its own varying levels of activity that the cyclical mechanism described in Section 2 of Lecture 7 can operate. If, in this sense, there is sufficient "feedback" from the industrial economy into itself, one could expect recurring "unstable" fluctuations of the type of Lecture 7 centering in the industrial sector, while the stabilizing mechanism of the present lecture will limit the reach of these fluctuations. For such "feedback" to occur, it is of course necessary that the 4% fluctuations in national income typical of a recession lead to concentrated

TABLE XVI

Fluctuations in Various Seasonally Adjusted Manufacturing Production Indices

Per cent of variation in the recession of 1957–8

	Pre-recession peaks	Recession low	Approx. variation
Motor vehicles and parts	132	86	42%
Primary metal manufacturing	143	86	55%
Total transport equipment manufacturing	220	178	21%
Electrical machinery	215	166	25%
Rubber	141	112	24%
Nonelectrical machinery	155	122	18%
Fabricated metal, total manufacturing	141	118	18%
Stone, clay, and glass	159	134	16%
Industrial chemicals	207	182	13%
Petroleum and coal	143	127	12%
Fixtures and furniture	123	110	12%
Lumber	118	107	10%
Textiles	101	91	10%
Paper	163	149	9%
Tobacco	114	115	−1%
Food and beverage manufacturing	114	116	−2%

shifts of consumer purchases away from the industrial sector, so that a fall in industrial production may be associated in a sufficiently forceful way with a fall in *industrial* sales. We shall not attempt to construct a model reflecting all these suggested features, but shall merely present some statistics taken from the 1957–58 recession which tend to support the diagnosis just made.

Table XVI gives a more detailed breakdown of production fluctuations than are available in Table XV. The theory of Lectures 6

TABLE XVII

Fluctuations in Various Seasonally Adjusted Manufacturing Inventory Indices

Per cent of variation in the recession of 1957–8

	Pre-recession peaks	Recession low	Approx. variation
Motor vehicles and parts	340	250	30%
Nonelectrical machinery	674	556	19%
Total transport equipment manufacturing	804	653	20%
Electrical machinery	395	335	17%
Fabricated metal	322	278	15%
Petroleum and coal	364	327	11%
Rubber	110	98	11%
Lumber and furniture	191	172	11%
Tobacco	206	183	11%
Textiles	269	245	9%
Primary metals	436	401	5%
Stone, clay, and glass	127	120	6%
Chemicals, total	382	373	4%
Paper	147	141	4%
Food and beverage	488	459	5%
Durable manufactures, total	317	279	13%
Nondurable manufactures, total	224	214	5%
Durable wholesale inventories	65	63	3%
Nondurable wholesale inventories	63	58	8%
Durable retail inventories	110	103	7%
Nondurable retail inventories	133	131	2%

and 7 suggests that high production fluctuations ought to be corre-
lated with high inventory and sales fluctuations. Table XVII
gives some statistics on inventory fluctuations by industry. Note
that six of the highest ranking seven sectors are common to Tables
XVI and XVII.

Next, it is appropriate to inquire whether the industries in which
production and inventory fluctuations are high are also forced to
bear the burden of conspicuously high shifts in consumer buying.
For this purpose, we present the data in Table XVIII on retail sales

TABLE XVIII

Fluctuations in Various Seasonally Adjusted Retail Sales Indices
Per cent of variation in the recessions of 1957–8 and 1953–4

	1957–8			1953–4
	Pre-recession peaks	Recession low	Approx. variation	Approx. variation
Automobiles and parts	305	250	19%	12%
Appliances	350	295	17%	20%
Hardware	245	212	10%	14%
Lumber	690	610	12%	16%
General merchandise	186	170	9%	8%
Furniture	570	540	6%	6%
Clothing	105	100	5%	12%
Eating establishments	125	120	4%	3%
Drugs and sundries	550	535	3%	0%
Liquor	360	350	3%	6%
Groceries	365	368	−1%	−3%
Automobile repair	127	128	−1%	−5%
Shoes	175	180	−2%	6%

in the 1957–8 recession, with some comparable figures for the 1953–4
recession as a check.

It is plain from Table XVIII that a reduction in consumer expenditures tends to be concentrated in the automobile and appliance
sectors.

We may now summarize the view of business cycles to which the
above empirical evidence and the theoretical models which have

been presented point, as follows. The industrial sector is subject to cyclical fluctuations qualitatively like those described in Lecture 7. The slow response of employment in trade and other nonindustrial sectors to changing business conditions greatly moderates the over-all impact of the industrial fluctuations, adding a "stable sector" in which a large fraction of economic activity is maintained at equilibrium levels. Industrial instability results from the fact that consumer economies made necessary by a falling-off of over-all activity tend to be concentrated in automobile and large durable goods purchases, so that the industrial economy is to a certain extent an "unstable closed system."

4. Graphical Representations

An extremely wide variety of charts, constructed so as to emphasize one or another feature of economic activity, are used as aids in eco-

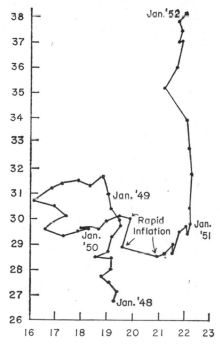

Fig. 12. Recession of 1949–50 and Korean boom. Plane of production and inventory.

nomic diagnosis. The foregoing analysis suggests that charts in which the orbit of the economy in a production-inventory plane is plotted should be useful. The most useful plot might be based on over-all seasonally adjusted indices of production and inventory in those sectors which appear as cyclically sensitive in the foregoing tables. Sales-inventories plots might also be useful. In the following pages, we shall reproduce a number of such charts, picturing the cycles of 1948–9, 1953–4, 1957–8, and also the cycle of 1960–1, which at the present writing is still in process. The production-inventory diagrams are plots of the seasonally adjusted FRB index of industrial production against seasonally adjusted manufacturers' inventories deflated by the BLS wholesale price index; the sales-inventory diagrams use the same inventory series but plot it against seasonally adjusted manufacturers' sales, deflated in the same way.

Figure 12 shows the characteristic counterclockwise motion of the economy in the inventory-production plane which our theory leads us to expect (cf. Fig. 3). The apparent decrease of physical inventories in the part of the graph marked "rapid inflation" is an illusion produced by our crude method of deflating book value of stocks by wholesale price index.

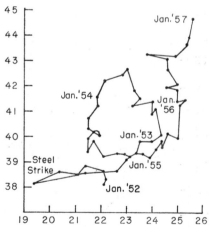

Fig. 13. Recession of 1954. Plane of production and inventory.

The motion described by Fig. 13 shows a marked similarity with that of Fig. 12. Fig. 13 also suggests that the course of economic motion tends to be quite stable against external influences: the steel strike of 1952 appears as a passing episode leaving hardly any discernible trace.

The over-all pattern of motion seen in Figs. 12 and 13 repeats itself in the following Fig. 14; we see the same pattern beginning to

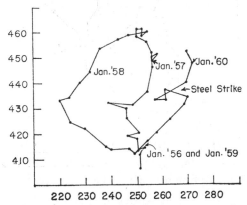

Fig. 14.   Recession of 1958.   Plane of inventory and production.

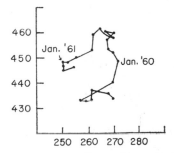

Fig. 15.   Recession of 1960–1.   Plane of inventory and production.

develop in Fig. 15, which depicts the start of the 1960–1 recession, still in process at the time of writing.

Figure 16 superimposes the graphs given in the three preceding figures. The pattern of motion suggests a rather slow upward secular progress of the Keynes point, which seems from Fig. 16 to have moved from an FRB Industrial Production Level of about 90 to a level of about 107 between 1953 and 1960.

Figure 17 gives the economy's orbit between June 1952 and Janu-

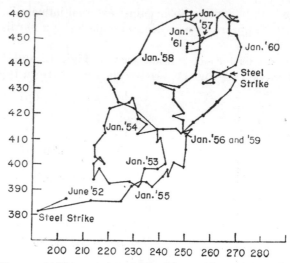

Fig. 16. Three post-Korean recessions. Plane of inventory and production.

ary 1961 in the plane of inventory and sales. The over-all resemblance of Figs. 16 and 17 is plain, though the inventory-sales orbit is evidently somewhat more erratic than the inventory-production orbit.

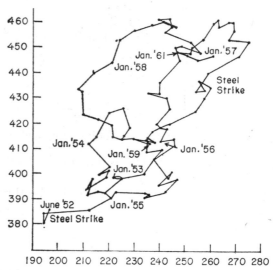

Fig. 17. Three post-Korean recessions. Plane of inventory and sales.

Additional Discussion of Cycle Theory

In the present lecture, we shall present three theoretical fragments, two of which are intended to round out our study of the unstable cycle-theory model of Lectures 6 and 7, and the third of which applies this model to illuminate a much-discussed point of economic policy.

1. Contracyclical Policy

Various systems of "automatic stabilization" have been proposed for moderating the amplitude of those cyclic fluctuations of production to which the economy has been repeatedly subject and of which we may take the model of Lecture 7, qualified as in the preceding lecture, to be roughly descriptive. A typical scheme of this sort is the unemployment insurance system, whereby a certain tax on income of employed persons is imposed and certain benefits are paid to the unemployed, thereby maintaining personal consumption in times of high unemployment. We shall use the simple aggregate model of Lecture 7 (depressive case) to give an approximate description of the workings of such a scheme over the phases of the business cycle.

In such a scheme, then, wages are taxed at a certain rate, and benefits paid at a certain rate to the unemployed. If A is that "peak" level of general production at which unemployment is zero, then the benefits paid in any period would have the form $\beta(A - a)$, β being a coefficient describing the benefit rate and a the actual level of production. We may assume that these benefits enter immediately into our model (particularly equations (7.1a)–(7.1b)) as an addendum to autonomous consumption (the term e in equation 7.1b). The effect of the taxes or premiums collected is also easy to describe. These taxes may be taken as a deduction from disposable wages, i.e., as a lowering by a few per cent of the wage rate. We saw in the first section of Lecture 8 that a reduction of the wage rate reduces the elements of the matrix $\tilde{\Pi}$ and hence of the quantity $\gamma = \mathrm{dom}\,(\tilde{\Pi})$ which enters as a coefficient in the recursion (7.1a)–(7.1b). Hence, the collection of unemployment insurance payments will reduce the coefficient γ to a slightly smaller coefficient γ'. Thus the over-all effect of the unemployment insurance scheme is to modify the equations (7.1a)–(7.1b) of aggregate motion to the following equations.

(10.1a) $b(t) = b(t-1) + (1 - \gamma')a(t-1) - e - \beta(A - a(t-1))$

(10.1b) $a(t) = \min\left[\{((c+2)\gamma' - 1)a(t-1) - b(t-1) + (c+2)e \right.$
$\left. + (c+2)\beta(A - a(t-1)) + h\}^{+},\ (b(t)/\gamma')\right]$

These equations may be written after introduction of the coefficients $\gamma'' = \gamma' - \beta$, $e'' = e + \beta A$ as

(10.2a) $b(t) = b(t-1) + (1 - \gamma'')a(t-1) + e''$

(10.2b) $a(t) = \min\left[\{((c+2)\gamma'' - 1)a(t-1) - b(t-1) + (c+2)e'' \right.$
$\left. + h\}^{+},\ (b(t)/\gamma')\right]$

Comparison of the equations (10.2a)–(10.2b) with the equations (7.1a)–(7.1b) reveals such a close similarity of form as to make it evident without further ado that the motions of the two models are qualitatively the same. To emphasize this point, we shall merely remark that since $\gamma > \gamma' > \gamma''$ the calculations given in Lecture 6, especially formula (6.16) and the following formulae, show that the two eigenvectors of the linear transformation whose matrix is

(10.3) $$\begin{bmatrix} (c+2)\gamma'' - 1 & -1 \\ 1 - \gamma'' & 1 \end{bmatrix}$$

point *between* the eigenvalues of the corresponding unmodified linear transformation, whose matrix is

(10.4) $$\begin{bmatrix} (c+2)\gamma - 1 & -1 \\ 1 - \gamma & 1 \end{bmatrix}.$$

Indeed, the eigenvalues λ_2 and λ_2 of the matrix (10.4) are given approximately by equations (6.16) as

(10.5a) $\lambda_1 \sim (c+2)\gamma - 1 - [1 - \gamma]/[(c+2)\gamma - 2]$

and

(10.5b) $\lambda_2 \sim 1 + [1 - \gamma]/[(c + 2)\gamma - 2],$

which makes it plain that lowering γ lowers λ_1 and raises λ_2. More-over, the eigenvectors of (10.4) are given by the immediately follow-ing equations of Lecture 6 as

(10.6a) $b_2 = ((c + 2)\gamma - 1 - \lambda_2)a_2 \sim (c + 2)\gamma - 2$
$$- [1 - \gamma]/[(c + 2)\gamma - 2]$$

and

(10.6b) $b_1 = \dfrac{1 - \gamma}{\lambda_1 - 1} a_1 \sim (1 - \gamma)/\{(c + 2)\gamma - 2$
$$- [1 - \gamma]/[(c + 2)\gamma - 2]\}$$

so that it is also plain that lowering γ lowers the slope of $[a_2,b_2]$ and raises the slope of $[a_1,b_1]$. Hence, if the unmodified model (7.1a)–(7.1b) belongs to the depressive case, the modified model belongs even more definitely to the depressive case.

Thus our cycle-theory model, modified by the introduction of the unemployment scheme, undergoes repeated cycles of the same quali-tative form as the unmodified model (cf. especially Fig. 11). How do the modified and the unmodified cycles compare quantitatively? This question has two aspects: where is the new Keynes point, and how do the modified and unmodified cyclical amplitudes compare with each other? To locate the new Keynes point, we must discuss the relation between the rate of benefit payment coefficient β and the reduction in the coefficient γ which follows from the insurance de-ductions.

For the insurance scheme to be actuarially balanced, the benefits and deductions must stand in a relation which implies a zero net outflow or inflow of funds over the cycle, so that personal consump-tion averaged over the various phases of the cycle remains unchanged. Now, if the input-output matrix for the nonlabor sectors of an economy is π_{ij}, $i = 1, \cdots, n$, then it is tautologous that if $a_j(t)$, $b_j(t)$, and $e_j(t)$ denote the varying components of production, inven-tory, and total personal consumption, we have

(10.7) $b_j(t + 1) = b_j(t) + a_j(t) - \sum\limits_{i=1}^{n} a_i(t)\pi_{ij} - e_j(t);$

we may deduce exactly as in Section 3 of Lecture 7 that in a model in which inventories remain bounded, average production is technologically determined from average consumption. This means, however, that in order for our unemployment-insurance model to be actuarially balanced, it must have the same Keynes-point production level as was found before the introduction of the unemployment-insurance scheme. But then, since the Keynes-point production level is unchanged, it follows that such an actuarially balanced scheme must support the same level of personal consumption at the Keynes point as would be attained in the absence of the insurance system. That is, at the Keynes point, an actuarially balanced insurance system must reduce to a pure transfer operation: taxing the employed at a certain rate and distributing the collections *per capita* to the unemployed. Conversely, this condition of balance at the Keynes point may be used to establish the ratio between premium rate and benefit rate which would lead to a cyclically balanced scheme.

Since at the Keynes point the insurance scheme reduces to a transfer operation, it follows that the Keynes point inventory must also be the same for the cycle-theory model, whether modified by an actuarially balanced unemployment system or no. Thus actuarial balance and invariance of the Keynes point are equivalent.

We have seen above however that the operation of the insurance system diminishes the angle between the two eigenvectors of the linear transformation (10.4). Thus, the geometric construction given in the first section of Lecture 7 shows that the cycle for the modified model will be shallower, bearing the relation to the unmodified cycle indicated in Fig. 18.

We may give a qualitative account of the result represented graphically in Figure 18 as follows: on the upswing of the cycle, the collection of insurance premiums reduces disposable income and hence sales, so that excess inventories build up more rapidly than in the absence of the insurance scheme, and so that the unstable inventory-accumulation boom phase collapses earlier than it would otherwise have. On the downswing, the payment of benefits sustains purchasing power, leading to a more rapid consumption of excess inventories and thus a more rapid recovery than would otherwise take place. The over-all effect should then be milder, more frequent recessions, the long-term trend of economic growth being affected relatively little.

It is evident heuristically that the analysis of any other automatic

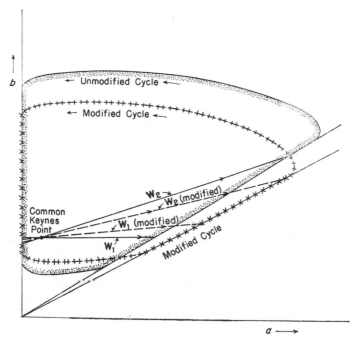

Fig. 18. Modification of model cycle by contracyclical stabilization. (Compare Fig. 11.)

stabilizer of the same general nature as the unemployment insurance system, as, e.g., a cyclically balanced budget with extra-heavy expenditures or with temporary tax cuts in recession periods, would be much the same as the analysis given above, and would lead to similar conclusions. We may note in this connection that many of the proponents of automatic stabilization schemes have noted with concern the apparent fact that while recessions seem to be getting milder, they seem to be occurring more frequently, and that the long-term trend of economic growth seems deficient.

We may remark on leaving the present topic that the above conclusions are based upon the assumption that the contracyclical scheme is cyclically balanced. A fiscally unbalanced unemployment insurance scheme, say, may function as a backdoor method for either raising or lowering the average wage rate. In either case, however, it will be equivalent in the sense of the above analysis to a balanced contracyclical scheme corresponding to a modified wage rate, rate of deficit accumulation, etc.

2. Variable Consumption

It is entirely plausible that cyclical fluctuations of production lead to changes in personal consumption independent of these fluctuations automatically and implicitly generated in the model of Lectures 6 and 7 by fluctuations in wage payments. In the present section, we shall study a modified aggregate model into which this possibility is introduced. It will appear that none of the principal conclusions which we have drawn from the simpler model require substantial modification.

We generalize our model by introducing variable nonproductive consumption into the model, tying nonproductive consumption to previous income and hence to previous production. We shall write an aggregative scheme directly. In our previous aggregative model (cf. Lecture 6) the increase in total inventory from day $t - 1$ to day t is $(1 - \gamma)a(t - 1)$. Let us now suppose that the nonproductive consumption $\beta(t)$ is equal to a constant e_0 plus some constant fraction α (the propensity to consume) of the quantity $(1 - \gamma)a(t - 1)$. The function $e(t)$ may then be introduced as an unknown function of time on the same basis as production and inventory level, and by appropriate easy generalizations of the arguments outlined in Section 2 we obtain the recursion relations

$$(10.8a) \qquad e(t) = \alpha(1 - \gamma)a(t - 1) + e_0$$

$$(10.8b) \qquad b(t) = b(t - 1) + \epsilon a(t - 1) - e(t - 1) - e_0$$

$$(10.8c) \quad a(t) = \min\left[\{\bar{\gamma}a(t - 1) - b(t - 1) + (c + 2)e(t - 1) \\ + (c + 2)e_0\}^+, (b(t)/\gamma)\right];$$

(here $\bar{\gamma} = (c + 2)\gamma - 1$, $\epsilon = 1 - \gamma$). We have assumed that production takes priority over consumption, i.e., have assumed, just as in Section 1 of Lecture 7, that subtractions from stocks for the purpose of consumption occur in "in the evening" after the day's production. For simplicity we assume to begin with that $e_0 = 0$; this assumption will be removed later.

We shall not undertake to study the detailed orbits of the three dimensional system (10.8). Rather, we intend to show that a depressive case like the depressive case of the model of Lectures 6 and 7 exists for this generalized model also.   The depressive case is characterized by the fact that inventories remain bounded along every orbit; hence, by the argument of the third section of Lecture 7, a Keynes relation connecting average production and average consumption must hold, and hence the motion must involve a repeated slowing down of production during which accumulated inventories are consumed.

From (10.8) we have

$$\gamma a(t-1) \le b(t-1)$$
$$a(t) \le \bar{\gamma} a(t-1) + (c+2)e(t-1) - b(t-1)$$

so that we obtain, using (10.12a),

(10.9) $a(t) \le (\bar{\gamma} - \gamma)a(t-1) + (c+2)\alpha(1-\gamma)a(t-2)$

as a recursive inequality satisfied by the number $a(t)$.   (10.9) is a recursion in which $a(t)$ is bounded by an expression involving $a(t-2)$ as well as on $a(t-1)$.   Here we may make convenient use of a device analogous to the device of introducing a new unknown to allow replacement of a single second-order differential equation by two first-order differential equations.   (Compare the procedure employed in Section 2 of Lecture 9.)   We introduce the two-dimensional vector $\mathbf{v}(t)$ whose components are $a(t)$ and $a(t-1)$.   Let M be the 2×2 matrix

(10.10) $M = \begin{bmatrix} \bar{\gamma} - \gamma & (c+2)\alpha\epsilon \\ 1 & 0 \end{bmatrix}.$

Then (10.9) is equivalent to the statement that $\mathbf{v}(t)$ satisfies

$$\mathbf{v}(t) \le M\mathbf{v}(t-1).$$

Since M is connected, it has a positive eigenvector $\mathbf{m}'$ corresponding to the eigenvalue $\mu = \text{dom}\,(M) > 0$, i.e.,

$$\mathbf{m}'M = \mu\mathbf{m}'.$$

Therefore

(10.11) $\mathbf{m}' \cdot \mathbf{v}(t) \le \mu\mathbf{m}' \cdot \mathbf{v}(t-1)$

from which it is clear that $\mathbf{m}' \cdot \mathbf{v}(t) \to 0$ (and therefore that $\mathbf{v}(t) \to 0$) if $\mu < 1$; however $\mathbf{m}'\mathbf{v}(t)$ can approach infinity if $\mu > 1$.

The case $\mu < 1$ then corresponds to our former depressive case;

we shall confine our attention to this case. Since $v(t)$ is bounded and from the definition of $v(t)$, it follows that $a(t)$ is bounded. Therefore, by (10.8a), $e(t)$ is also bounded.

We may now establish the boundedness of $b(t)$. Since $e(t)$ and $a(t)$ are already known to be bounded, it follows at once from (10.8b) and (10.8c) that there exists a constant β sufficiently large so that

   (i) $a(t) \leq \beta$, all t;
   (ii) $b(t) \geq \beta$ implies $a(t) = 0$, all t;
  (iii) $b(0) \leq 2\beta$.

We will show by induction that $b(t) \leq 2\beta$ for all t. From (10.8b) we have $b(t) \leq b(t-1) + a(t-1)$ (since inventory increase cannot exceed production). Hence, if $b(t-1) \leq \beta$, then $b(t) \leq 2\beta$ follows from (i); if $\beta \leq b(t-1) \leq 2\beta$, then $b(t) \leq 2\beta$ follows similarly from (ii). Thus $b(t) \leq 2\beta$ follows by induction, and $b(t)$ is therefore bounded. Therefore $\mu = \text{dom}\,(M) < 1$ implies the boundedness of production, consumption and inventory levels, and implies that the Keynes relation holds.

From the form (10.10) of the matrix M we see that its dominant μ is the larger of the roots of

$$\phi(x) \equiv x^2 - ((c+1)\gamma - 1)x - (c+2)\alpha(1 - \gamma) = 0.$$

Since $\phi(0) = -(c+1)\alpha(1 - \gamma) < 0$, $\phi(x)$ has one negative root and one positive root. The positive root μ will be less than 1 if and only if $\phi(1) \geq 0$, i.e.,

$\mu < 1$ is equivalent to $1 - ((c+1)\gamma - 1) - (c+2)\alpha(1 - \gamma) > 0$

or

(10.12) $\mu < 1$ is equivalent to $(c+1)(\gamma + \alpha(1 - \gamma)) + \alpha(1 - \gamma) < 2$.

If $c = 1$, this condition is equivalent to the condition $\alpha < \frac{2}{3}$. Hence, if c is sufficiently close to 1, and α is sufficiently far below the critical level $\alpha = \frac{2}{3}$, we will have dom $(M) < 1$ and it will follow that inventories and production in the economy will remain bounded and hence that a Keynes relation between production and average consumption is valid.

It is readily seen that the introduction of an inhomogeneous term e_0 representing constant autonomous consumption would not affect our conclusion, and would affect our argument only slightly. The same assertion may be made about the introduction of a constant representing basic inventory as in the first section of Lecture 7.

We may assert in summary that the present model possesses a depressive case showing the same qualitative features as the simpler model of Lecture 7.

3. The Depressive Case in the Disaggregated Model

The preceding lectures, and especially the Keynesian statics developed in Lecture 8, have served to emphasize the central significance of the Keynes relation (7.11), and hence, if we recall the derivation of (7.11), the importance for dynamic theory of the qualitative question: do inventories remain bounded along the dynamic orbits, or do they not? In the present section, we will attempt to study this question in the context of the general disaggregated dynamic model introduced in the final section of Lecture 5, but with autonomous consumption introduced. In this way, we shall hope to gain a certain additional insight into the inventory-recession mechanism, without making the strong simplifying assumptions on which the analysis of Lectures 6 and 7 was based.

If we re-examine the description of the model without autonomous consumption introduced in the final section of Lecture 5, we see that the corresponding model with autonomous consumption introduced would be as follows.

We must assume first that the optimum inventory policy followed by the manufacturer of commodity C_j is described by the formula

$$(10.13) \qquad \text{target inventory} = c_j s_j(t-1) + h_j$$

for the target inventory established for the evening of the tth day. Here, h_j is a basic inventory required just to stay in business and c_j is the incremental amount by which inventories should be increased due to a unit increase in sales on the previous day; $s_j(t-1)$ is the volume of actual sales on the previous day. Note that equation (10.13) is the most general linear relationship possible between target inventory levels and previous day's sales.

Desired production on the tth day is then the amount of production required to bring inventories up to the desired level, allowing for anticipated present-day sales (which is estimated by the manufacturer to be equal to the previous day's sales). If $a_j(t)$ is the actual amount of production on the tth day, then, since we are dealing with a closed economy, $a_j(t)$ is related to $s_j(t)$ by

$$(10.14) \qquad s_j(t) = \sum_{j=1}^{n} \tilde{\pi}_{ij} a_i(t) + e_j,$$

e_j denoting the amount of commodity j sold for purposes of (autonomous) consumption. We shall suppose that inventories never run so low as to make this consumption impossible. We can therefore write the following formula for desired production $d_j(t)$ on the tth day:

$$(10.15) \quad d_j(t) = \left\{ c_j \left[\sum_{i=1}^{n} \tilde{\pi}_{ij} a_i(t-1) + e_j \right] + h_j \right.$$
$$\left. + \left[\sum_{i=1}^{n} \tilde{\pi}_{ij} a_i(t-1) + e_j \right] - b_j(t) \right\}^{+},$$

where the sum of the first two terms in square brackets is desired inventory, the third term is volume of estimated sales, and the last term is inventory on the morning of the tth day. Let

$$(10.16) \qquad \check{\pi}_{ij} = c_j \tilde{\pi}_{ij} \quad i, j = 1, \cdots, n$$

and note that

$$b_j(t) = b_j(t-1) + a_j(t-1) - s_j(t-1) - e_j$$

i.e.,

$$b_j(t) = b_j(t-1) + a_j(t-1) - \sum_{i=1}^{n} \tilde{\pi}_{ij} a_i(t-1) - e_j.$$

We can also introduce market and supply strain factors $\mu_k(t)$ and $\sigma_j(t)$, cf. formulae (5.7) and (5.8).

Then, in terms of vectors, equations (10.15) become

$$(10.17) \quad \mathbf{d}'(t) = \{ \mathbf{a}'(t-1)(\check{\Pi} + 2\tilde{\Pi} - I) - \mathbf{b}'(t-1) + \mathbf{g}' \}^{+},$$

where $\mathbf{g}'$ is the vector with components $(c_j + 2)e_j + h_j$. Since the factors $\sigma_j(t)$ are bounded above by 1, we will also have

$$(10.18\mathrm{a}) \qquad\qquad \mathbf{a}'(t)\check{\Pi} \leqq \mathbf{b}'(t)$$
$$(10.18\mathrm{b}) \qquad\qquad \mathbf{a}'(t) \leqq \mathbf{d}'(t)$$

in our completed model. We shall not repeat the precise definition
of the factors $\sigma_j(t)$ since we intend to carry out only a qualitative
investigation of the orbits, for which purpose the inequalities already
written are sufficient.

Let us now make the assumption that there is no component of
the production vector $\mathbf{a}(t)$ which vanishes. Then

$$\mathbf{d}'(t) = \mathbf{a}'(t-1)(\check{\Pi} + 2\tilde{\Pi} - I) - \mathbf{b}'(t-1) + \mathbf{g}'$$

and hence

$$\mathbf{a}'(t) \leqq \mathbf{a}'(t-1)(\check{\Pi} + 2\tilde{\Pi} - I) - \mathbf{b}'(t-1) + \mathbf{g}'.$$

Using (10.18a) with argument $t-1$ we get

(10.19) $$\mathbf{a}(t) \leqq \mathbf{a}(t-1)(\check{\Pi} + \tilde{\Pi} - I) + \mathbf{g}.$$

Our task is now to analyze this recursive inequality on $\mathbf{a}(t)$, making
it our goal to discover the conditions under which $\mathbf{a}$ remains bounded
in all of its components.

We take $\check{\Pi} + \tilde{\Pi}$ to be a connected matrix, and let $\mathbf{v}$ be the eigenvector corresponding to the dominant K of $\check{\Pi} + \tilde{\Pi}$, i.e.,

(10.20) $$(\check{\Pi} + \tilde{\Pi})\mathbf{v} = K\mathbf{v}.$$

Then, since $\mathbf{v} > 0$,

(10.21) $$\mathbf{v} \cdot \mathbf{a}'(t) \leqq (K-1)\mathbf{v} \cdot \mathbf{a}'(t-1) + \mathbf{v}\mathbf{g}'.$$

We may now make use of the following simple lemma.

LEMMA. *Let*
$$a_n \leq \tau a_{n-1} + f$$

be a recursive inequality satisfied by a sequence $\{a_1, a_2, \cdots\}$, *where* τ
and f are constants. Then if $\tau < 1$ the a_n are bounded.

Proof: Let ϕ be a number such that

(i) $\phi > a_1$
(ii) $\phi > f/(1 - \tau)$.

Then it follows that

$$a_{n-1} < \phi \quad \text{implies} \quad a_n < \tau\phi + f$$

and hence implies $a_n < \phi$.

Therefore, by induction, ϕ is a bound on the a_n. Q.E.D.

It follows that if, in equation (10.21), the coefficient $K - 1$ is less than 1 (corresponding to what has been called the depressive case in our former discussions) the sequence of scalar products $\mathbf{v} \cdot \mathbf{a}'(t)$ is bounded, and this means that the sequence $\mathbf{a}(t)$ itself is bounded, since $\mathbf{v}$ does not depend on t and all the components of $\mathbf{v}$ are positive. Thus it follows from our assumptions that all production levels remain bounded. We wish to show next that the boundedness of production implies the boundedness of each inventory level.

To show that inventories remain bounded we can adopt an argument used in the preceding section. From equations (10.17) and (10.18) and from the boundedness of the $\mathbf{a}(t)$ it follows readily that there exists a number β sufficiently large so that

(i) $a_j(t) \leq \beta$, $j = 1, \cdots, n$; all t

(ii) $b_j(t) \geq \beta$ implies that $a_j(t) = 0$; $j = 1, \cdots, n$; all t

(iii) $b_j(0) \leq 2\beta$ $j = 1, \cdots, n$.

We will show by induction that $b_j(t) \leq 2\beta$. From equations (10.17) we certainly have

$$(10.22) \qquad\qquad b_j(t+1) \leq b_j(t) + a_j(t);$$

this simply says that the increase in inventory cannot be more than production. (Equality could occur only when there are no sales of the jth commodity in period t.) We take as the induction hypothesis the statement $b_j(t) \leq 2\beta$. Then, if $b_j(t) \geq \beta$, it follows from (ii) and (10.22) that we have

$$(10.23) \qquad\qquad b_j(t+1) \leq 2\beta;$$

if $b_j(t) < \beta$, relation (10.23) follows from (i) and (10.22). Therefore 2β is a bound for the inventory levels $b_j(t)$.

Thus, in a depressive model economy, i.e., in a model economy in which increments to sales generate sufficiently small increments to desired inventory, any orbit along which every component of production remains nonzero is forever confined to a bounded region of the inventory-production space. This conclusion is valid quite without any assumption as to the initial proportions of inventory and production along the orbit, i.e., independent of any initial or continuing and continually adjusted disproportion of production along the orbit. It follows that along such an orbit, the conditions which in Lecture 7 were seen to be sufficient for the validity of the Keynes relation (7.11) are seen to hold.

We can summarize as follows:

THEOREM. *Let* dom $(\breve{\Pi} + \tilde{\Pi}) < 2$. *Then on each orbit either* $\mathbf{a}'(t)$ *has some component which vanishes infinitely often, or production and inventories are forever bounded so that the Keynes relation* (7.11) *holds* (*or inventories eventually fall so low that autonomous consumption must be reduced from its stated level*).

The analyses of Lecture 7, of the preceding section, and of the present section all point in the same direction; toward a tendency for inventories to remain bounded. The boundedness of production and inventory in a model with a stable Keynes point, like that of Lecture 9, is even more obvious.

Thus a general inference to the effect that

(a) depending on the size of a certain key eigenvalue a model economy may be distinguished as being expansive or depressive;

(b) in a depressive economy inventories remain bounded and consequently a suitably generalized version of the Keynes relation (7.11) is valid;

seems warranted.

4. Delays in Production and Shipment

Our previous models have always assumed shipment to be instantaneous, so that it is important to ask whether any fundamental changes in results can occur if the equations are reformulated to include shipment delays and varying production delays.

How would the models of Lectures 6 and 7 be changed if these additional effects were considered? Let us suppose, for instance, that delays in shipping or in production are approximately included into the model by requiring that each manufacturer is allowed to sell (i.e. ship out) only a certain fraction q of his inventory. In this case it is readily seen that the aggregative equations without consumption become

$$b(t) = b(t-1) + \epsilon a(t)$$
$$a(t) = \min\left[\{\bar{\gamma}a(t-1) - b(t-1)\}^+, qb(t)/\gamma\right]$$

which reduce, of course, for the case $q = 1$ to our former equations (6.11). Referring to our previous theory, we find that the nature of the orbits is governed by the position of the two eigenvectors $\mathbf{W}_1$ and $\mathbf{W}_2$ of the matrix

$$\begin{bmatrix} 1 & \epsilon \\ -1 & \bar{\gamma} \end{bmatrix},$$

corresponding to the large and small eigenvalues of this matrix. Compared to our previous case, the only change will be in the slope of the scarcity line. As q gets smaller the scarcity line rises higher and higher until above some value of q the entire admissible region lies to the left of the $\mathbf{W}_2$-line. This configuration describes a completely depressive economy. Compensating for this rise of q, of course, would be a rise in c, the number of days sales held as inventory; production and shipment delays would make each manufacturer set c higher, which in turn raises the slope of the eigenvector $\mathbf{W}_2$. On balance, the model can be either expansive or depressive.

Empirically, it appears that manufacturers' inventories tend to be adjusted to slightly more than 1.6 months sales, after an allowance for basic inventory; and that this is close to their rate of turnover under boom conditions. Thus, if in our earlier model of the economy we take our "day" to be 1.6 months, we can take $c \cong 1$ without grave error.

To reemphasize our point, however: the *decisive relation* in unstable cycle-theory models like those of Lectures 6 and 7 is that between *the inventory which must be carried in order to avoid delays in shipment* and the *inventories which will be carried as extra protection*.

A Model of Liquidity Preference

1. Establishing the Model

A key element in the cycle-theory presented in Lectures 5–10 was the "decision to reduce inventories" which we built into our models, basing ourselves on reasonable empirical grounds, but which we left largely unanalyzed. When manufacturers reduce inventories they free resources for other uses: how does this affect the conclusions developed in the preceding lectures? In the present lecture and in the one which follows, we shall attempt to illuminate this question. Our method will be to construct a model of production and exchange within which a decision to expand or to reduce inventories can be studied as a problem of the "optimization" type familiar from efficiency economics. We will find that optimum adjustment to the conditions of the model to be constructed may lead to decisions to reduce inventory in the manner assumed in the preceding lectures. In this way, we will confirm our earlier conclusions and establish them upon a more ample basis.

Our model is as follows: we take, as usual, an economy involving n material commodities $C_1, \cdots, C_n$, and $L+1$ labor commodities $C_0, \cdots, C_{-L}$. Again, as usual, we take the input-output matrix to be $\pi_{i,j}$, where $1 \leq i \leq n$ and $-L \leq j \leq n$. In addition, we introduce a money commodity C_{n+1} which cannot be produced; this money commodity is taken to consist of a collection of identical, infinitely divisible, legal-tender bonds issued by a central authority and bearing interest, at a rate $100s$ per cent per "day" or "planning period," payable in additional bonds. Thus, the possessor of x bonds will at the end of one day's uninterrupted possession be awarded sx additional bonds. We shall assume that $s \geq 0$.

Let the (instantaneous) price of one unit of commodity C_k be p_k; we assume that all prices are positive. Revising our otherwise arbitrary physical units of each commodity, we may suppose that $p_j = 1$ for all j; these "price units" will be used throughout the present lecture unless the contrary is explicitly indicated.

With this normalization, the essential features of the present model may be described as follows. Each individual entrepreneur is assumed to be in possession, at the start of a typical day, of holdings of the commodities $C_1, \cdots, C_{n+1}$ in certain amounts $b_1, \cdots, b_{n+1}$. This being his situation, the entrepreneur is assumed to have the option of dividing his holding of bonds into $n + 1$ parts, using the jth part, $1 \leq j \leq n$, for the purchase of the inputs to the production of C_j in appropriate proportions and then immediately using these inputs completely, thereby producing a certain well determined number of units of C_j. The $n + 1$st part into which the entrepreneur's holding of bonds is divided is assumed to be retained in order to earn interest at the given rate s. Moreover, the entrepreneur is assumed to have the additional option of dividing his holding of each sort of commodity into two parts, one of which is retained in storage, the other of which is offered for sale. We assume that conditions in the C_j-market are such that of each unit of C_j offered for sale, σ_j units of C_j will be sold, and $1 - \sigma_j$ units will remain unsold; thus σ_j is a parameter between 0 and 1 which measures the instantaneous "state of the market" for the commodity C_j, as reflected in the rate of stock turnover which an optional sales policy is capable of achieving. In order to take account within our model of style obsolescence and technical obsolescence, spoilage, and fixed overhead costs, we assume that each unit of C_j which is either retained or unsold decays after one day to a certain number τ_j of units; here $0 \leq \tau_j < 1$. The coefficient τ_j then is a general spoilage and carrying charge loss parameter.

Let the number of units of commodity C_j which can be produced by expending one bond on the necessary inputs in correct proportion and using them to produce C_j be η_j; η_j is of course determined not merely by the input-output matrix but also by the prices; we have $0 < \eta_j$. Then, starting with holdings of $C_1, \cdots, C_{n+1}$ equal to the components of the vector $\mathbf{b} = [b_1, \cdots, b_{n+1}]$, and dividing it in accordance with the above-described options into a sum of nonnegative terms

$$(11.1) \quad \mathbf{b} = [b_{11} + b_{12}, \, b_{21} + b_{22}, \, \cdots, \, b_{n1} + b_{n2}, \, b_{n+1,1} + \cdots + b_{n+1,n+1}],$$

the entrepreneur will upon exercise of these options find himself at the end of the day in possession of inventories of $C_1, \cdots, C_{n+1}$ equal to the components of the following vector $\mathbf{c}$:

$$(11.2) \quad \mathbf{c} = [\tau_1 b_{11} + \tau_1(1 - \sigma_1)b_{12} + \eta_1 b_{n+1,1}, \, \tau_2 b_{21} + \tau_2(1 - \sigma_2)b_{22}$$
$$+ \, \eta_2 b_{n+1,2}, \, \cdots, \, \tau_n b_{n1} + \tau_n(1 - \sigma_n)b_{n2} + \eta_n b_{n+1,n}, \, \sigma_1 b_{12}$$
$$+ \, \sigma_2 b_{22} + \cdots + \sigma_n b_{n2} + (1 + s)b_{n+1,n+1}].$$

Let $\phi(\mathbf{b})$ denote the set of all vectors $\mathbf{c}$ which can be derived from a given vector $\mathbf{b}$ after the fashion of (11.1)–(11.2); then ϕ is a (one-to-many, i.e., many-valued) transformation defined in the positive orthant.

Of course, ϕ depends upon the constants σ_j reflecting the instantaneous state of the market for C_j and upon the instantaneous prices p_j; were we at the present moment aiming at the direct integration of the transformation ϕ into a dynamic model of prices and production, we would have to deal at once with this dependence. Our idea, however, is somewhat different. We wish to analyze an entrepreneur's projection of his future operations, assuming, as in the cycle-theory of Lectures 5, 6, and 7, that these projections are based upon the simplest of all hypotheses, the hypothesis that market conditions will remain unchanged. In a more complete model the specific action taken by an entrepreneur on any particular day would still be determined by this projection, but the projection would be revised each day as the actual motion of the economy changes the data upon which the entrepreneur bases his projections.

We may consider, however, that the phenomena of cyclic expansion and contraction of production which would occur in such a dynamic model have been portrayed with at least qualitative fidelity in Lectures 7 and 10. Thus, in the present lecture, we forego the dynamic problem in order to develop a detailed "still photograph" of instantaneous market conditions and of the instantaneous optimal adjustment to the conditions which may correspond either to a decision to increase or to reduce inventories. The parameters σ, τ, s of (11.2) should then be taken as descriptive of a given "state of business" which entrepreneurs expect to persist for a period of time sufficiently long so as to compel them to make at least a temporary adjustment. What we wish to find is this adjustment. For the present, then, it is appropriate for us to take the constants σ_j and η_j as fixed, and hence to study the iterates of the fixed multivalued transformation ϕ.

We will show in what follows that this study leads in a natural manner to a systematic ranking of inventory positions as more or less favorable. It is then heuristically plausible to suppose that a manufacturer always strives to attain the most favorable position in the sense of this ranking; this assumption enables us to discover his optimal action in the given situation. The analysis leads by a technically complicated path to very simple conclusions; the reader may prefer to read the main statements and preliminary definitions which are to follow immediately, and to ignore the technical mathematics of their proof.

2. Basic Lemmas and Definitions, Statement of Main Results

Let $\mathbf{b} = [b_1, \cdots, b_{n+1}]$ be a vector (necessarily of dimension $n + 1$) describing the inventory holdings of an entrepreneur. It is plain that if $\mathbf{b}_1 \geq \mathbf{b}$, the holdings $\mathbf{b}_1$ are definitely preferable to the holdings $\mathbf{b}$. This ordering of vectors is, however, only a *partial ordering*, in the sense that there exist noncomparable pairs of vectors, i.e., pairs of vectors $\mathbf{b}_1$, $\mathbf{b}_2$ for which both assertions $\mathbf{b}_1 \geq \mathbf{b}_2$ and $\mathbf{b}_2 \geq \mathbf{b}_1$ are false. We will show in what follows how a linear ordering may be derived from the ordering $\geq$ and the mapping ϕ, i.e., we will show how to derive a transitive relationship $\mathbf{b}_1 \succ \mathbf{b}_2$ such that one of the two alternatives $\mathbf{b}_1 \succ \mathbf{b}_2$ or $\mathbf{b}_2 \succ \mathbf{b}_1$ necessarily holds for each pair of vectors $\mathbf{b}_1$, $\mathbf{b}_2$. In order to be able to describe this construction, we must first give some preliminary definitions and lemmas. We begin by extending the ordering $\geq$ of vectors to sets of vectors.

DEFINITION 11.1. *Let E and F be two sets of vectors. Then we will write $E \geqq F$ if for each $\mathbf{b}_1 \in F$, there exists a $\mathbf{b}_2 \in E$ such that $\mathbf{b}_2 \geqq \mathbf{b}_1$.*

The statement $E \geqq F$ has then the following heuristic significance: the set of options E is preferable to the set of options F.

Next we give a more convenient form to the definition (11.1)–(11.2) of the mapping ϕ. It is evident, in the first place, that the set of vectors $\mathbf{c}$ in (11.2) is identical with the set of vectors $\mathbf{d}$ such that

(11.3) $\quad \mathbf{d} = [\tau_1(1 - \sigma_1)b_{11} + \tau_1(b_{12} + b_{13} + \cdots + b_{1,n+1}) + \eta_1 b_{n+1,1},$
$\quad\quad \tau_2(1 - \sigma_2)b_{22} + \tau_2(b_{21} + b_{23} + \cdots + b_{2,n+1}) + \eta_2 b_{n+1,2}, \cdots,$
$\quad\quad \tau_n(1 - \sigma_n)b_{nn} + \tau_n(b_{n1} + \cdots + b_{n,n-1} + b_{n,n+1}) + \eta_n b_{n+1,n},$
$\quad\quad \sigma_1 b_{11} + \sigma_2 b_{22} + \cdots + \sigma_n b_{nn} + (1 + s)b_{n+1,n+1}]$

where

(11.4) $\quad \mathbf{b} = [b_{11} + b_{12} + \cdots + b_{1,n+1}, b_{21} + b_{22} + \cdots + b_{2,n+1}, \cdots,$
$\quad\quad\quad\quad\quad\quad b_{1,n+1} + b_{n+1,2} + \cdots + b_{n+1,n+1}],$

each of the terms b_{ij} being nonnegative. Thus, if we define $(n + 1)$ $\times (n + 1)$ matrices $M_1, \cdots, M_n$ and M_{n+1} by the equations

(11.5) $\quad (M_k)_{i,j} = \tau_j \delta_{ij}$ if $1 \leq i,j \leq n$ and $i,j \neq k;$
$\quad\quad (M_k)_{i,j} = 0$ in every other case $1 \leq i,j \leq n + 1$ unless (i,j)
$\quad\quad\quad\quad\quad\quad = (k, n + 1), (n + 1, k),$ or $(k, k);$
$\quad (M_k)_{k,n+1} = \eta_k; \quad (M_k)_{k,k} = \tau_k(1 - \sigma_k); \quad (M_k)_{n+1,k} = \sigma_k;$

and

(11.6) $\quad\quad (M_{n+1})_{i,j} = \tau_j \delta_{ij}, j = 1, \cdots, n, i - 1, \cdots, n + 1$
$\quad\quad\quad\quad\quad\quad (M_{n+1})_{i,n+1} = (1 + s)\delta_{i,n+1},$

we may describe the set $\phi(\mathbf{b})$ as follows:

(11.7) $\quad \phi(\mathbf{b}) = \{\mathbf{d} \mid \mathbf{d} = M_1 \mathbf{r}_1 + \cdots + M_{n+1} \mathbf{r}_{n+1}, \mathbf{r}_1 + \cdots + \mathbf{r}_{n+1} = \mathbf{b},$
$\quad\quad\quad\quad\quad\quad \mathbf{r}_j \geq 0, j = 1, \cdots, n + 1\}.$

We will also make use of certain standard set-theoretical notions and notations. If E and F are sets of vectors, we write $E \subseteq F$ or $F \supseteq E$ if E is included in F; we write $\mathbf{a} \in E$ if $\mathbf{a}$ is a member of the set E, write $\phi(E)$ for the set

(11.8) $\quad\quad\quad\quad\quad\quad \phi(E) = \{\phi(\mathbf{b}) \mid \mathbf{b} \in E\},$

and write $E + F$ and tE for the sets

(11.9) $\quad\quad\quad\quad\quad\quad E + F = \{\mathbf{b}_1 + \mathbf{b}_2 \mid \mathbf{b}_1 \in E, \mathbf{b}_2 \in F\}$

and

(11.10) $\quad\quad\quad\quad\quad\quad tE = \{t\mathbf{b} \mid \mathbf{b} \in E\},$

respectively. The union of E and F will be denoted by $E \cup F$; more generally, if $\{E_\alpha\}$ is an arbitrary collection of sets, indexed by an index α, then the union of all the sets E_α, i.e., the collection of all elements which lie in at least one of the sets E_α, will be written $\cup_\alpha E_\alpha$.

The following rather trivial lemmas will be quite useful.

LEMMA 11.2.   *Let $E \geqq F$.   Then $\phi(E) \geqq \phi(F)$.*

Proof: Let $c \in \phi(F)$, so that there exist $r_1, \cdots, r_{n+1} \geq 0$ such that

$$(11.11) \qquad r_1 + \cdots + r_{n+1} \in F, \; M_1 r_1 + \cdots + M_{n+1} r_{n+1} = c.$$

Then, since $E \geq F$, there exists, by Definition 1, a vector $b \in E$ such that $b \geqq r_1 + \cdots + r_{n+1}$. Put $q_{n+1} = b - r_1 - \cdots - r_n$. Then plainly $q_{n+1} \geqq 0$, $r_1 + \cdots + r_n + q_{n+1} = b \in E$, and $d = M_1 r_1 + \cdots + M_n r_n + M_{n+1} q_{n+1} \geq c$. Since $d \in \phi(E)$, our lemma is proved. Q.E.D.

LEMMA 11.3.   *Let $t \geq 0$ be a number.   Then $\phi(tE) = t\phi(E)$.*

Proof: Obvious.   Q.E.D.

We may now make our fundamental definition.

DEFINITION 11.4: *Let b and c be two nonnegative vectors. Then we write $b \succeq c$ (or $c \preceq b$) if for each $\epsilon > 0$ there exists an $n = n(\epsilon)$ such that $(1 + \epsilon)\phi^n(b) \geqq \phi^n(c)$. If both $b \succeq c$ and $c \succeq b$ are true, we write $b \sim c$. If $b \succeq c$ but $b \sim c$ is false, we write $b \succ c$.*

Note that, by Lemmas 2 and 3, the inequality $(1 + \epsilon)\phi^n(b) \geqq \phi^n(c)$ implies that $(1 + \epsilon)\phi^m(b) \geqq \phi^m(c)$ for all $m \geq n$. In particular, $b \geqq c$ implies $b \succeq c$.

The relationship $b \succeq c$ has the following heuristic significance. The set $\phi(b)$ is the collection of all inventory-positions attainable after the lapse of one day by an entrepreneur whose initial holdings are b; similarly, $\phi^n(b)$ is the collection of all inventory-positions attainable after the lapse of n days by an entrepreneur whose initial holdings are b. Thus $b \succeq c$ signifies that the inventory-position b is preferable to the inventory-position c in the sense that after the lapse of a certain number of days any position which could have been attained starting with c could have been bettered by a position attainable with the start b (at any rate, if c is diminished by any arbitrarily small percentage ϵ). Thus, any long-term inventory target attainable from c can be bettered if one's start is b. Hence, $b \succeq c$ means that "b is preferable to c in the long run."

It is heuristically plain that the relationship $b \succeq c$ is transitive. The following lemma states this simple fact formally.

LEMMA 11.5.   *If* $b \succeq c$ *and* $c \succeq b$, *then* $b \succeq c$.

Proof: By hypothesis, and by Definition 4 and the remark which follows it, there exists a finite number $n(\epsilon)$ such that $n \geq n(\epsilon)$ implies that $(1 + \epsilon)\phi^n(b) \geq \phi^n(c)$ and $(1 + \epsilon)\phi^n(c) \geq \phi^n(d)$. Thus $(1 + \epsilon)^2\phi^n(b) \geq \phi^n(c)$ for $n \geq n(\epsilon)$. Q.E.D.

COROLLARY.   *The relationship* $b \sim c$ *is reflexive, transitive, and symmetric. If* $b \sim c$, *then* $b \succeq d$ *and* $c \succeq d$ *are equivalent.*

Lemma 5 shows that the relationship $b \succeq c$ establishes an ordering between vectors; the central fact which we now wish to establish is that *this ordering is a linear ordering,* i.e., that it enables us to compare any two nonnegative vectors with the result that exactly one of $b \succ c$, $b \sim c$, $c \succ b$ holds in every case. Heuristically, this means that of two inventory positions b and c, either one is distinctly better (in the heuristic sense explained above) or both are equally good. This fact and somewhat more are stated in the following main theorem.

THEOREM 11.6.   *There exists a positive vector* v'_0 *such that the statement* $b \succeq c$ *is equivalent to the statement* $v'_0 \cdot b \geq v'_0 \cdot c$. *Thus, for any pair* $\overline{b}$ *and* c *of nonnegative vectors, exactly one of the statements* $b \succ c$, $b \sim c$, $c \succ b$ *is true.*

The proof of Theorem 6 will be given in what is to follow.

Theorem 6 may be taken as establishing the existence of an exhaustive ranking of inventory positions as more or less favorable. Making the heuristically plausible assumption that an entrepreneur always strives to attain the most favorable position open to him, we arrive at a description of his optimal plan. Formal statements and results are contained in the following definition and in Theorem 9 below.

DEFINITION 11.7.   *A sequence of vectors* $b_1, b_2, \cdots$ *is an optimal path beginning at* b *if and only if* $b_1 = b$; $b_{n+1} \in \phi^n(b)$, $n \geq 1$ *and* $b_n \geq \phi^n(b)$ *for arbitrarily large integers* n.

Our second main result will characterize the set of all optimal paths beginning at b. In order to do this, we need a number of preliminary definitions. The following definition extends the definition of dom (A) to arbitrary matrices.

DEFINITION 11.8a.   *Let A be a matrix.   Then* dom (A) *is the maximum of the absolute value of all the (real or complex) eigenvalues of A.*

DEFINITION 11.8b.   *Let $M_1 \cdots M_{n+1}$ be the matrices of (11.5)– (11.7).   Then the optimal matrices are those M_j for which the quantity* dom (M_j) *attains the value $K = \max_{1 \leq j \leq n+1}$* dom (M_i).

We may now state the second main result.

THEOREM 11.9.   *The sequence of vectors $\mathbf{b}_1, \mathbf{b}_2, \cdots$ is an optimal path beginning at $\mathbf{b}$ if and only if $\mathbf{b}_1 = \mathbf{b}$ and $\mathbf{b}_{k+1}$ has the form*

$$(11.12) \qquad \mathbf{b}_{k+1} = M_1 \mathbf{r}_1 + \cdots + M_{k+1} \mathbf{r}_{n+1}$$

where

$$(11.13) \qquad \mathbf{r}_j \geq 0, j = 1, \cdots, n+1; \quad \mathbf{r}_1 + \cdots + \mathbf{r}_{n+1} = \mathbf{b}_k$$

and where in addition we require that all components of $\mathbf{r}_j$ but the jth and $(n+1)$st vanish if M_j is optimal, all components of $\mathbf{r}_j$ but the jth vanish if M_j is nonoptimal, and $\mathbf{r}_{n+1} = 0$ if M_{n+1} is nonoptimal.

COROLLARY.   *Any finite sequence $\mathbf{b}_1, \cdots, \mathbf{b}_m$ satisfying the conditions of the previous theorem for $k + 1 \leq m$ may be extended to an optimal sequence.*

If we examine the definition of the matrices M_j as given by formulae (11.5)–(11.6) in the light of Theorem 9, making use of the fact that $\mathbf{b} \succeq \mathbf{c}$ means that $\mathbf{b}$ is bound to be preferable to $\mathbf{c}$ in the long run, we recognize the heuristic significance of Theorem 9 to be as follows: the only sound procedure for an entrepreneur whose holdings are $\mathbf{b}$ is to

(*1*) offer the whole of each of his commodity stocks for sale;

(*2*) use the whole of his cash holdings for the expansion of those stocks whose sale yields the greatest rate of profit; here, the money commodity C_{n+1} is to be considered as yielding the rate of profit s.

Theorem 9 then merely states a principle of investment practice so familiar as to be cliché.   What is somewhat new is the derivation of this principle from the rather general definition of preference given by Definitions 1 and 4.   We should emphasize that in (*2*) of the preceding paragraph, the "rate of profit" yielded by sale of a commodity C_j is to be defined as the dominant of the 2×2 matrix

$$(11.14) \qquad \begin{bmatrix} 0 & \eta_j \\ \sigma_j & \tau_j(1 - \sigma_j) \end{bmatrix}.$$

The dominant is the unique positive root of the equation

$$(11.15) \qquad \lambda_j{}^2 - \lambda_j\tau_j(1 - \sigma_j) - \sigma_j\eta_j = 0;$$

from this it is plain that λ increases with η and τ. Moreover, if $\eta \geq 1$, then since

$$\eta^2 - \eta\tau(1 - \sigma) - \sigma\eta \geq \eta(1 - \tau(1 - \sigma) - \sigma) > 0,$$

we have $\lambda < \eta$: similarly $\lambda > \tau(1 - \sigma)$ and hence

$$(11.16) \qquad \partial\lambda/\partial\sigma = (\eta - \lambda\tau)/(2\lambda - \tau(1 - \sigma)) > 0.$$

Thus if $\eta \geq 1$, λ increases with σ also. If $\sigma = 0$ then $\lambda = \tau$; hence, as $\sigma \to 0$, $\eta \to \tau$. Consequently, Theorem 9 tells us that if (heuristically speaking) the stocks in every line of industry are sufficiently large so that each parameter σ_j is distinctly reduced from 1, and if in addition the rate $\tau_j{}^{-1}$ of obsolescence in each line of industry is sufficiently large so that the eigenvalues λ_j of (11.15) are all less than $(1 + s)$, the only prudent action may be to sell off stocks and hold the bond-money commodity C_{n+1}; *this can be the case even if the rate s of interest is zero, provided that the rates $\tau_j{}^{-1}$ of obsolescence are sufficiently high.* Theorem 9 thus gives a basis in efficiency economics to the decision to reduce stocks which played an important but unanalyzed role in the theory of Lectures 5–10.

We now intend to give the proof of Theorems 6 and 9; unfortunately, the proof involves a surprising mass of technical detail. We shall begin the proof in the present lecture, but shall only be able to conclude it in the following lecture.

3. Proof of Theorem 6. Initial Part

In proving Theorem 6, we shall have use for some results from the theory of convex sets, which we shall now state, referring the reader to the monograph of Bonessen-Fenchel, *Konvexe Körper*, for proofs. The condition that a set E be convex may be written as $tE + (1 - t)E \subseteq E$, $0 \leq t \leq 1$. Let us recall that the closure of a set E of vectors is the set of all vectors $\mathbf{b}$ such that $\mathbf{b}$ is the limit of a sequence of vectors $\mathbf{b}_n$ in E. The closure of an arbitrary set is easily seen to be a closed set.

LEMMA 11.10.   *Let E and F be convex sets.   Then*

(a)   *tE is convex for each $t \geq 0$*
(b)   *$E + F$ is convex*
(c)   *the closure of E is convex*
(d)   *if $\{E_n\}$ is a sequence of convex sets, and $E_n \subseteq E_{n+1}$ for all n, then $\cup_n E_n$ is a convex set.*

For (a) and (b), see Bonessen-Fenchel, pp. 29 and 30; for (c) note that if $\mathbf{b}$ and $\mathbf{c}$ are in the closure of E, then $\mathbf{b} = \lim_{n \to \infty} \mathbf{b}_n$ and $\mathbf{c} = \lim_{n \to \infty} \mathbf{c}_n$, where $\mathbf{b}_n$ and $\mathbf{c}_n$ belong to E.   Thus, if $0 \leq t \leq 1$, we have

$$t\mathbf{b} + (1 - t)\mathbf{c} = \lim_{n \to \infty} (t\mathbf{b}_n + (1 - t)\mathbf{c}_n).$$

Since E is convex, $t\mathbf{b}_n + (1 - t)\mathbf{c}_n$ lies in E, and hence $t\mathbf{b} + (1 - t)\mathbf{c}$ lies in the closure of E.   This proves (c).

To prove (d), note that if $\mathbf{b} \in \cup_n E_n$ and $\mathbf{c} \in \cup_n E_n$, then, since $E_n \subseteq E_{n+1}$, there exists an integer m such that $\mathbf{b} \in E_m$ and $\mathbf{c} \in E_m$. Thus, if $0 \leq t \leq 1$,

$$t\mathbf{b} + (1 - t)\mathbf{c} \in E_n \subseteq \cup_n E_n. \quad \text{Q.E.D.}$$

The following is a useful definition of convergence for closed convex sets.

DEFINITION 11.11.   *Let K_n, $n \geq 1$, and K be closed convex sets. Then we write $\lim_{n \to \infty} K_n = K$ or $K_n \to K$, and say that the sequence K_n approaches K, if for each $\epsilon > 0$ there exists an $n(\epsilon)$ such that for all $n \geq n(\epsilon)$ we have*

(11.17) $K_n \subseteq K + S_\epsilon$ and $K_n + S_\epsilon \supseteq K$,

S_ϵ denoting the sphere of radius ϵ.

LEMMA 11.12.   *Let K_n, K, E_n, E ($n \geq 1$) be bounded closed convex sets.   Then if $K_n \to K$ and $E_n \to E$, it follows that $tK_n \to tK$ for all real $t \geq 0$, and that $K_n + E_n \to K + E$.*

For a proof, see Bonessen-Fenchel, p. 35.

LEMMA 11.13.   *Let $E_n, n \geq 1$, be a sequence of bounded closed convex sets such that $E_n \subseteq E_{n+1}$.   Then, if $\cup_n E_n$ is bounded, and if E denotes the closure of $\cup_n E_n$, we have $E_n \to E$.*

Proof: Note first that it follows from Lemma 10 that the set E is convex (and, of course, closed and bounded). Since $E_n \subseteq E$ for all n, we have only to prove that for each ϵ there exists an n sufficiently large so that $E \subseteq E_n + S_\epsilon$. If this is false, then for each n there exists a vector $\mathbf{p}_n \in E$ whose minimum distance from the set E_n exceeds ϵ. Since E is bounded, we may find a subsequence $\mathbf{p}_{n_i}$ of $\mathbf{p}_n$ which converges to a vector $\mathbf{p}$; plainly, the minimum distance from $\mathbf{p}$ to E_{n_i} exceeds $\epsilon/2$ for all sufficiently large i. Since $E_{n+1} \supseteq E_n$, it follows that E, which is the closure of $\cup_n E_n$, is also the closure of $\cup_{i \geq j} E_{n_i}$ for each j no matter how large; thus the minimum distance from $\mathbf{p}$ to E is at least $\epsilon/2$. But, since $\mathbf{p}$ is the limit of a sequence of vectors in E, this is impossible. Q.E.D.

After these necessary generalities, we begin to build up the statements more directly required for the proof of Theorem 6, in a series of lemmas.

LEMMA 11.14. *The relationship $\succeq$ defined in Definition 4 depends upon the matrices $M_1, \cdots, M_{n+1}$, but remains invariant if $M_1, \cdots, M_{n+1}$ are all multiplied by a common positive factor.*

Proof: The first part of the statement is obvious from Definition 4 and the definition (11.7) of the map ϕ. Formula (11.7) also makes it plain that if $M_1, \cdots, M_{n+1}$ are all multiplied by a common factor t, then the map ϕ is changed into $t\phi$, and thus the set $\phi^n(\mathbf{b})$ is changed into the set $t^n\phi^n(\mathbf{b})$. The present lemma then follows at once from Definition 4. Q.E.D.

Lemma 14 shows that in proving Theorem 6 we may assume without loss of generality that $\max_j \mathrm{dom}\,(M_j) = 1$. This will be assumed throughout the remainder of the present section. A certain subset of the matrices M_j will have the distinguishing property $\mathrm{dom}\,(M_j) = 1$; these are the matrices which are *optimal* in the sense of Definition 8. By renumbering the commodities $C_1, \cdots, C_n$, we may suppose without loss of generality that set of optimal matrices is either the set $M_m, \cdots, M_n$ or the set $M_m, \cdots, M_{n+1}$. By examining the form (11.5) of the matrices M_j, remembering that the matrices M_j initially introduced are first to be multiplied by a common positive factor $t \leq (1+s)^{-1}$, we see at once that if $M_j, j \leq n$, is an optimal matrix we have $1 = \sigma_j(1 - \tau_j) + \sigma_j \eta_j$; if M_j is not optimal, we have $1 > \sigma_j(1 - \tau_j) + \sigma_j \eta_j$. Similarly, the matrix M_{n+1} is optimal if and only if $(M_{n+1})_{n+1,n+1} = 1$. The form (11.5) of the matrices M_j also makes evident the following lemma.

LEMMA 11.15.   *Each optimal matrix M_j has a unique fixed vector $\mathbf{u}_j$. All components of this vector except the jth and $(n + 1)$st vanish.*

Next we use the form (11.5) of the matrices M_j to prove

LEMMA 11.16.   (a) *There exists a positive vector ω' such that $\omega' M_j \leq \omega', j = 1, \cdots, n + 1$.* (b) *For any vector $\mathbf{b} \geq 0$, the set $\phi^n(\mathbf{b})$ remains bounded.*

Proof: Note first that (b) follows from (a). Indeed, if $\mathbf{c} \in \phi(\mathbf{b})$, then, by the definition (11.7) of $\phi(\mathbf{b})$ and by (a), we have $\omega' \cdot \mathbf{c} \leq \omega \cdot \mathbf{b}$. By induction, this same inequality must hold for each $\boldsymbol{\alpha} \in \phi^n(\mathbf{b})$, proving (b). To prove (a), we let $\omega_{n+1} = 1$, and then define ω_j for each j between 1 and n by requiring that $(1, \omega_j)$ be a dominant eigenvector of the transpose of the transformation $[a, b] \rightarrow [\sigma_j b, \eta_j a + \sigma_j (1 - \tau_j)b]$. Since the constants τ_k are all less than 1, it follows from the form (11.5) of the matrices M_j that if $[\omega_1, \cdots, \omega_n, 1] = \omega'$, we have $\omega' M_j \leq \omega'$. Q.E.D.

COROLLARY.   *We have $\omega' M_j \mathbf{u} < \omega' \cdot \mathbf{u}$ for a nonnegative vector $\mathbf{u}$ unless M_j is an optimal matrix and all components of $\mathbf{u}$ but the jth and $(n + 1)$st vanish.*

Proof: It is plain from our construction that if M_j is nonoptimal $\omega' M_j < \omega'$, and that even if M_j is optimal $(M_j \omega')_k < (\omega')_k$ unless $k = j$ or $n + 1$. Q.E.D.

Next we give a useful algebraic property of the mapping ϕ.

LEMMA 11.17.   *Let E_1 and E_2 be two sets of nonnegative vectors. Then $\phi(E_1) + \phi(E_2) = \phi(E_1 + E_2)$.*

Proof: First suppose that $\mathbf{r}_1 \in \phi(E_1)$, $\mathbf{r}_2 \in \phi(E_2)$. Then, by the definition (11.7) of the map ϕ, we may find nonnegative vectors $\mathbf{q}_1, \cdots, \mathbf{q}_{n+1}$ and $\mathbf{q}^*_1, \cdots, \mathbf{q}^*_{n+1}$ such that

(11.18) $\mathbf{r}_1 = M_1 \mathbf{q}_2 + \cdots + M_{n+1} \mathbf{q}_{n+1}; \quad \mathbf{r}_2 = M_1 \mathbf{q}^*_1 + \cdots + M_{n+1} \mathbf{q}^*_{n+1},$

while

$$\mathbf{q}_1 + \cdots + \mathbf{q}_{n+1} \in E_1, \quad \mathbf{q}^*_1 + \cdots + \mathbf{q}^*_{n+1} \in E_2.$$

Hence

$$(\mathbf{q}_1 + \mathbf{q}^*_1) + \cdots + (\mathbf{q}_{n+1} + \mathbf{q}^*_{n+1}) \in E_1 + E_2,$$

while

$$\mathbf{r}_1 + \mathbf{r}_2 = M_1(\mathbf{q}_1 + \mathbf{q}^*_1) + \cdots + M_{n+1}(\mathbf{q}_{n+1} + \mathbf{q}^*_{n+1}).$$

This shows that

$$\phi(E_1) + \phi(E_2) \subseteq \phi(E_1 + E_2).$$

Conversely, let $\mathbf{r} \in \phi(E_1 + E_2)$. Then there exist nonnegative vectors $\mathbf{s}_1, \cdots, \mathbf{s}_{n+1}$ such that $\mathbf{s}_1 + \cdots + \mathbf{s}_{n+1} = \mathbf{e}_1 + \mathbf{e}_2$, where $\mathbf{e}_1 \in E_1$ and $\mathbf{e}_2 \in E_2$, and such that $\mathbf{r} = M_1\mathbf{s}_1 + \cdots + M_{n+1}\mathbf{s}_{n+1}$. Define vectors $\mathbf{q}_k$ inductively by putting

$$(11.19) \quad (\mathbf{q}_1 + \cdots + \mathbf{q}_k)_j = \min((\mathbf{s}_1 + \cdots + \mathbf{s}_k)_j, (\mathbf{e}_1)_j),$$
$$j = 1, \cdots, n + 1, \; k = 1, \cdots, n + 1;$$

Then clearly $\mathbf{q}_k \geqq 0$, $1 \geq k \geq n + 1$, and $\mathbf{q}_1 + \cdots + \mathbf{q}_{n+1} = \mathbf{e}_1$. It is also clear from (11.19) that, for $k \geq 2$, $(\mathbf{q}_k)_j = 0$ unless $(\mathbf{s}_1 + \cdots + \mathbf{s}_k)_j > (\mathbf{s}_1 + \cdots + \mathbf{s}_{k-1})_j$, and that $(\mathbf{s}_k)_j \geq (\mathbf{q}_k)_j$. Since by (11.19) this last inequality also holds for $k = 1$, we have

$$(11.20) \qquad \mathbf{s}_k \geq \mathbf{q}_k, \quad k = 1, \cdots, n + 1.$$

Let vectors $\mathbf{q}^*_k$ be defined by $\mathbf{q}^*_k = \mathbf{s}_k - \mathbf{q}_k$; then it is clear from (11.20) that $\mathbf{q}^*_k \geq 0$. We have

$$(11.21) \qquad \sum_{k=1}^{n+1} \mathbf{q}^*_k = \sum_{k=1}^{n+1} \mathbf{s}_k - \sum_{k=1}^{n+1} \mathbf{q}_k = \mathbf{e}_1 + \mathbf{e}_2 - \mathbf{e}_1 = \mathbf{e}_2.$$

Thus

$$\mathbf{r}_1 = M_1\mathbf{q}_1 + \cdots + M_{n+1}\mathbf{q}^{n+1} \in \phi(E_1)$$

and

$$\mathbf{r}_2 = M_1\mathbf{q}^*_1 + \cdots + M_{n+1}\mathbf{q}^*_{n+1} \in \phi(E_2).$$

Since it is plain that $\mathbf{r} = \mathbf{r}_1 + \mathbf{r}_2$, we have

$$\phi(E_1 + E_2) \subseteq \phi(E_1) + \phi(E_2). \quad \text{Q.E.D.}$$

LEMMA 11.18.   *If E is convex, then $\phi(E)$ is convex.*

Proof: By the preceding lemma we have

$$t\phi(E) + (1 - t)\phi(E) = \phi(tE + (1 - t)E) \subseteq \phi(E)$$

for $0 \leq t \leq 1$ since E is convex; thus $\phi(E)$ is convex. Q.E.D.

We may now argue as follows. By Lemma 15, each optimal matrix M_j has a unique fixed vector $\mathbf{u}_j$. The definition (11.7) of ϕ makes it plain that $\phi(\mathbf{u}_j) \supseteq M_j\mathbf{u}_j = \mathbf{u}_j$. Thus, inductively, $\phi^n(\mathbf{u}_j) \supseteq \phi^{n-1}(\mathbf{u}_j)$. By the preceding lemma, all the sets $\phi^n(\mathbf{u}_j)$ are convex. By Lemmas 13 and 16(b), the sequence of sets $\phi^n(\mathbf{u}_j)$ converges to a bounded closed convex set K_j; K_j is the closure of $\cup_n\phi^n(\mathbf{u}_j)$. The next lemma contributes an essential bit of information by showing that all the sets K_j are substantially the same.

LEMMA 11.19. (a) *If ω' is the vector of Lemma 16, and the fixed vectors $\mathbf{u}_j$ of the optimal matrices M_j are normalized by the condition $\omega' \cdot \mathbf{u}_j = 1$, then all of the sets K_j are identical.* (b) $\phi(K_j) = K_j$. (c) *The set K_j contains the vector 0; thus $tK_j \subseteq K_j$ for $0 \leq t \leq 1$.*

Proof: We first put the definition (11.7) of the mapping ϕ into a more convenient form. Let μ denote an arbitrary nonnegative $(n + 1) \times (n + 1)$ matrix whose entries μ_{ij} satisfy the condition

$$(11.22) \qquad \sum_{i=1}^{n+1} \mu_{ij} = 1, \quad i = 1, \cdots, n + 1.$$

Let $\Sigma_j(\mu)$, $j = 1, \cdots, n + 1$, be the mapping which takes a vector $\mathbf{b}$ into the vector $\Sigma_j(\mu)\mathbf{b}$ whose components are

$$(11.23) \qquad [\mu_{1,j}b_1, \cdots, \mu_{n+1,j}b_{n+1}].$$

Then plainly $\sum_{j=1}^{n+1} \Sigma_j(\mu)\mathbf{b} = \mathbf{b}$, and (11.7) shows that $\phi(\mathbf{b})$ may be written in the form

$$(11.24) \qquad \phi(\mathbf{b}) = \bigcup_{\mu} \left\{ \sum_{j=1}^{n+1} M_j\Sigma_j(\mu)\mathbf{b} \right\}.$$

Thus, if we let

$$(11.25) \qquad M(\mu) = \sum_{j=1}^{n+1} M_j\Sigma_j(\mu),$$

we have

$$(11.26) \qquad \phi(\mathbf{b}) = \bigcup_{\mu} M(\mu)\mathbf{b}.$$

Since the mappings $M(\mu)$ are continuous, it follows from this last formula that

$$M(\mu)K_j = M(\mu) \lim_{n\to\infty} \phi^n(u_j) \subseteq \lim_{n\to\infty} M(\mu)\phi^n(u_j)$$
$$\subseteq \lim_{n\to\infty} \phi^{n+1}(u_j) \subseteq K_j;$$

thus
$$M(\mu)K_j \subseteq K_j,$$

and hence by (11.26) we have

(11.27) $$\phi(K_j) \subseteq K_j.$$

Since $u_j \in \phi(u_j) \subseteq \phi^2(u_j) \subseteq \cdots \to K_j$, it follows that $u_j \in K_j$, and thus $\phi(u_j) \subseteq \phi(K_j)$ and $u \in \phi(K_j)$. Inductively from (11.27) we have $\phi^n(K_j) \subseteq K_j$; thus $\phi^n(u_j) \subseteq \phi^{n+1}(K_j) \subseteq \phi(K_j)$. Letting $n \to \infty$ in this last inclusion, it follows that $K_j \subseteq \phi(K_j)$. Combining this with (11.27), statement (b) of the present lemma follows.

It is plain from the form (11.5) of the matrices M that $\phi(u_j)$ includes a vector of the form $[c_1, \cdots, c_n, 0]$. Thus $\phi^{n+1}(u_j)$ includes $[\tau_1{}^n c_1, \cdots, \tau_n{}^n c_n, 0]$. Since $\tau_j < 1$, it follows on letting $n \to \infty$ that $0 \in K_j$, proving (c) of the present lemma.

To prove (a) of the present lemma, we shall show that if M_j and M_k are optimal matrices and u_j and u_k the corresponding fixed vectors, then $u_j \subseteq K_k$. Using (b) it will then follow that $\phi^n(u_j) \subseteq K_k$, and, letting $n \to \infty$, that $K_j \subseteq K_k$. Statement (a) will then follow at once by symmetry. If we renumber the commodities $C_m, \cdots, C_n$, we may suppose without loss of generality that $k = n$ and $j = n + 1$ or $j = n - 1$. We shall treat only the case $j = n - 1$, leaving it to the reader to elaborate the very similar and somewhat simpler details of the case $j = n + 1$.

Let ω' be the vector of Lemma 16(a). If we examine the construction of the vector ω' as described in the first paragraph of the proof of Lemma 16, and note the structure (11.5) of the matrices M_j, we find that $\omega'_0 = \lfloor 0, \cdots, 0, \omega_n, 1 \rfloor$ is a fixed vector of M_n, i.e., that $\omega'_0 M_n = \omega'_0$. Similarly, $\omega'_{00} = [0, 0, \cdots, \omega_{n-1}, 0, 1]$ is a fixed vector of M_{n+1}. Thus, if $\mathbf{u}$ is a vector all of whose components except the nth and $n+1$st vanish, we have

$$\omega' M_n \mathbf{u} = \omega'_0 M_n \mathbf{u} = \omega'_0 \cdot \mathbf{u} = \omega' \cdot \mathbf{u}.$$

Similarly, if $\mathbf{u}$ is a vector all of whose components except the $(n-1)$st and $(n+1)$st vanish, $\omega' M_{n-1} \mathbf{u} = \omega' \cdot \mathbf{u}$. Let $M = M_{n-1}P_1 + M_n P_2$, where P_1 and P_2 are the projection operators defined by

(11.28) $$P_1[u_1, \cdots, u_{n+1}] = [u_1, \cdots, u_{n-1}, 0, 0]$$
$$P_2[u_1, \cdots, u_{n+1}] = [0, \cdots, 0, u_n, u_{n+1}].$$

It is then clear from (11.7) that $M\mathbf{u} \in \phi(\mathbf{u})$ for each nonnegative vector $\mathbf{u}$. Moreover, from what has been proved just above, $\omega'M\mathbf{u} = \omega' \cdot \mathbf{u}$ if all the components of $\mathbf{u}$ except the $(n-1)$st, nth, and $(n+1)$st vanish. It follows from this, from (11.28) and from (11.5), and from the property of the vector $\mathbf{u}_{n-1}$ given by Lemma 5 that $\omega'M^m\mathbf{u}_{n-1} = 1$ for each m. According to (11.28) and the form (11.5) of the matrices M_j, the $(n-1)$st component of $M^m\mathbf{u}_{n-1}$ converges to zero, while the components 1 through $n-2$ are identically zero. A subsequence of this bounded sequence of vectors necessarily converges to some vector $\mathbf{v}$; this vector $\mathbf{v}$ has all components but its nth and $(n+1)$st equal to zero, while $\omega' \cdot \mathbf{v} = 1$ and $\mathbf{v}$ lies in the closed convex set K_{n-1}.

Equation (11.15) for the eigenvalues of the 2×2 matrix (11.14) has clearly two distinct roots, one positive and one negative, the positive having the larger absolute value unless the square of the matrix is a constant. Since we have normalized our matrices M_j in such a way that dom $(M_j) = 1$ if M_j is an optimal matrix, it follows that (if M_j is an optimal matrix) the corresponding matrix (11.14) has either the two-by-two identity matrix as its square, or has two eigenvalues of which one is $+1$ and the other is less than 1 in modulus. If $\mathbf{x}$ and $\mathbf{y}$ are the two eigenvectors of this 2×2 matrix, which we shall call N, $\mathbf{x}$ being the fixed vector, it follows in consequence that

$$(11.29) \qquad \lim_{n \to \infty} n^{-1} \sum_{k=0}^{n-1} N^k(\alpha\mathbf{x} + \beta\mathbf{y}) = \alpha\mathbf{x}.$$

Thus, inspecting the form (11.5) of the matrix M_n, it follows that

$$(11.30) \qquad \lim_{m \to \infty} m^{-1} \sum_{k=0}^{m-1} (M_n)^k\mathbf{v}$$

exists, and is a fixed vector $\mathbf{u}$ of the matrix M_n. Moreover, since we have as above that $\omega'(M_n)^k\mathbf{v} = 1$ for all k, it follows that $\omega' \cdot \mathbf{u} = 1$. Thus, since the fixed vector $\mathbf{u}_n$ of M_n is unique by Lemma 15 except for normalization, it follows that $\mathbf{u} = \mathbf{u}_n$. Since we have shown above that $\mathbf{v} \in K_{n-1}$ and since $\phi(K_{n-1}) = K_{n-1}$ by (b) while $M_n\mathbf{c} \in \phi(\mathbf{c})$ by (11.7), it follows from (11.30) that $\mathbf{u}_n \in K_{n-1}$. As we have remarked above, this fact implies (a). Q.E.D.

We pause at this point. The proof of Theorems 6 and 9 will be completed in the next lecture.

$$LECTURE \ 12$$

A Model of Liquidity Preference
(Concluded)

1. Proof of Theorem 11.6

The mathematical analysis of the final section of the preceding lecture brings us close to the proof of our first target: Theorem 11.6. The proof of the theorem will be based on the following fundamental lemma, which gives detailed information on the behavior of the convex sets $\phi^n(\mathbf{b})$ as $n \to \infty$.

LEMMA 12.1. *Let* $K = K_j$ *be the set of Lemma* 11.19. *Then for each vector* $\mathbf{b} \geq 0$ *there exists a strictly positive constant* $C = C(\mathbf{b})$ *such that* $\phi^n(\mathbf{b}) \to CK$ *as* $n \to \infty$.

Before proving Lemma 12.1, we will show how a proof of Theorem 11.6 may be based upon it.

Proof of Theorem 11.6: Let $\mathbf{b} \geq 0$ and $\mathbf{d} \geq 0$. Then by Lemmas 11.12, 11.17 and 11.20 we have

$$(12.1) \quad C(\mathbf{b} + \mathbf{d})K = \lim_{n \to \infty} \phi^n(\mathbf{b} + \mathbf{d}) = \lim_{n \to \infty} \phi^n(\mathbf{b}) + \phi^n(\mathbf{d})$$
$$= C(\mathbf{b})K + C(\mathbf{d})K = (C(\mathbf{b}) + C(\mathbf{d}))K.$$

Thus, if $x = (C(\mathbf{b}) + C(\mathbf{d}))/C(\mathbf{b} + \mathbf{d})$, we have $xK = K$. If $x > 1$, it would follow that K is unbounded, which we know to be false; similarly $x < 1$ is impossible, and thus

$$(12.2) \qquad\qquad C(\mathbf{b} + \mathbf{d}) = C(\mathbf{b}) + C(\mathbf{d}).$$

If we define the vector $\mathbf{v}$ by letting its jth component be $C(\delta_j)$, δ_j being the vector whose ith component is δ_{ij}, then it follows from

Lemma 12.1 that $\mathbf{v}'_0 > 0$, and from (12.2) that $C(\mathbf{b}) = \mathbf{v}'_0 \cdot \mathbf{b}$. Thus we have

$$(12.3) \qquad \lim_{n \to \infty} \phi^n(\mathbf{b}) = (\mathbf{v}'_0 \cdot \mathbf{b})K$$

for each nonnegative vector $\mathbf{b}$.

Let ω' be the vector of Lemma 11.16(a), and let its components be $[\omega_1, \cdots, \omega_{n+1}]$; write

$$(12.4) \qquad \| \mathbf{u} \| = \sum_{i=1}^{n+1} \omega_i \, | \, u_i \, |$$

for each vector $\mathbf{u}$, thereby introducing a norm for the vectors $\mathbf{u}$. Lemma 11.16(a) shows that $\omega' M(\mu) \leq \omega'$ for each μ; thus it follows immediately that $\| M(\mu)\mathbf{u} \| \leq \| \mathbf{u} \|$ for each μ and each vector $\mathbf{u}$. If S_ϵ denotes the sphere of radius ϵ centered at the origin, distances being measured in terms of the norm (12.4), it follows that $M(\mu)S_\epsilon \subseteq S_\epsilon$ for each μ.

Now suppose that $\mathbf{b}$ and $\mathbf{c}$ are nonnegative vectors, and that $\mathbf{v}'_0 \cdot \mathbf{b} \geq \mathbf{v}'_0 \cdot \mathbf{c}$. Then, from (12.3) it follows that, for sufficiently large n,

$$(12.5) \qquad \begin{aligned} \phi^n(\mathbf{c}) &\subseteq (\mathbf{v}'_0 \cdot \mathbf{c})K + S_\epsilon \\ &\subseteq (\mathbf{v}'_0 \cdot \mathbf{b})K + S_\epsilon \\ &\subseteq \phi^n(\mathbf{b}) + S_\epsilon + S_\epsilon = \phi^n(\mathbf{b}) + S_{2\epsilon}; \end{aligned}$$

we have used statement (c) of Lemma 11.19. Since if $\mathbf{b}$ is a nonnegative nonzero vector it is plain from (11.7) and (11.5) that $\phi^2(\mathbf{b})$ contains a positive multiple of the invariant vector $\mathbf{u}_j$ of any of the optimal matrices M_j, it follows that $D\phi^n(\mathbf{b}) \supseteq \mathbf{u}_j$ for $n \geq 2$ and any sufficiently large constant D independent of n. It therefore follows immediately that $\epsilon D'\phi^n(\mathbf{b}) \geq S_\epsilon$ for a sufficiently large constant D' independent of n. Thus we conclude from (12.5) that

$$(12.6) \qquad \begin{aligned} \phi^n(\mathbf{c}) &\leqq \phi^n(\mathbf{b}) + 2\epsilon D'\phi^n(\mathbf{b}) \\ &\leqq (1 + 2\epsilon D')\phi^n(\mathbf{b}), \end{aligned}$$

proving that $\mathbf{b} \succ \mathbf{c}$.

Conversely, let $\mathbf{b} \underset{=}{\succ} \mathbf{c}$. Since by Lemma 11.2 and Definition 11.4 this implies that

$$(12.7) \qquad (1 + \epsilon)\phi^n(\mathbf{b}) \geqq \phi^n(\mathbf{c})$$

for any positive ϵ and all sufficiently large n, we find from (12.7) on letting $n \to \infty$ that

(12.8) $$(1 + \epsilon)(\mathbf{v'}_0 \cdot \mathbf{b})K \geqq (\mathbf{v'}_0 \cdot \mathbf{c})K.$$

It follows, as in the first paragraph of the present proof, that $(1 + \epsilon)(\mathbf{v'}_0 \cdot \mathbf{b}) \geq (\mathbf{v'}_0 \cdot \mathbf{c})$; since ϵ is arbitrary, we have $\mathbf{v'}_0 \cdot \mathbf{b} \geq \mathbf{v'}_0 \cdot \mathbf{c}$. Q.E.D.

Now, finally, we fill in a last gap by giving the proof of Lemma 12.1.

Proof of Lemma 12.1: Let $\mathbf{u}_j$, $m \leq j \leq n$ or $m \leq j \leq n+1$, be an enumeration of the fixed vectors of the optimal matrices M_j as in Lemma 11.19(a). We define a (nonlinear) transformation A by writing $A\mathbf{v} = \Sigma c_k \mathbf{u}_k$, the summation being extended over $m \leq k \leq n$ or $m \leq k \leq n+1$ depending on whether or not M_{n+1} is optimal, and the constants $c_k = c_k(\mathbf{v})$ being defined inductively by

(12.9) $$c_{m+1} = \sup \{c \mid c\mathbf{u}_m \leq \mathbf{v}\}$$
$$c_{k+1} = \sup \{c \mid c\mathbf{u}_{k+1} + c_m\mathbf{u}_m + \cdots + c_k\mathbf{u}_k \leq \mathbf{v}\};$$

here we use the symbol sup for the supremum or least upper bound of a set of real numbers. We also put $B\mathbf{v} = \mathbf{v} - A\mathbf{v}$, $A(\mu) = AM(\mu)$, $B(\mu) = BM(\mu)$. It is then plain from (11.26) that

(12.10) $$\phi(\mathbf{u}) = \bigcup_{\mu} (A(\mu)\mathbf{u} + B(\mu)\mathbf{u})$$

for each nonnegative vector $\mathbf{u}$. Using Lemma 11.17 it is then easily seen that

(12.11) $$\phi^2(\mathbf{u}) = \bigcup_{\mu} \{(A(\mu)\mathbf{u}) + \phi(B(\mu)\mathbf{u})\}$$
$$= \bigcup_{\mu_1,\mu_2} \{\phi(A(\mu_1)\mathbf{u}) + A(\mu_2)B(\mu_1)\mathbf{u} + B(\mu_2)B(\mu_1)\mathbf{u}\}.$$

Thus, inductively, we have

(12.12) $$\phi^k(\mathbf{u}) = \bigcup_{\mu_1,\ldots,\mu_k} \{\phi^{k-1}(A(\mu_1)\mathbf{u}) + \phi^{k-2}(A(\mu_2)B(\mu_1)\mathbf{u}) + \cdots$$
$$+ A(\mu_k)B(\mu_{k-1}) \cdots B(\mu_1)\mathbf{u} + B(\mu_k)B(\mu_{k-1}) \cdots B(\mu_1)\mathbf{u}\}.$$

Next we show that as $k \to \infty$,

(12.13) $$\omega'B(\mu_k) \cdots B(\mu_1)\mathbf{u} \to 0$$

uniformly in $\mu_1 \cdots \mu_k$. To accomplish this, we shall prove that

(12.14) $$\omega'B(\mu_2)B(\mu_1)\mathbf{u} < \omega' \cdot \mathbf{u}$$

for each nonnegative nonzero vector $\mathbf{u}$; since $B(\mu)$ is continuous in μ, it will follow immediately from this last inequality that there exists a constant $\delta < 1$ such that

$$(12.15) \qquad \omega' B(\mu_2) B(\mu_1) \mathbf{u} \leq \delta(\omega' \cdot \mathbf{u}).$$

Thus the expression (12.13) will converge to zero not only uniformly but even as fast as the powers $\delta^{k/2}$. To prove (12.14), note that since $A(\mu) + B(\mu) = M(\mu)$, since $A(\mu)\mathbf{u}$ and $B(\mu)\mathbf{u}$ are evidently non-negative if $\mathbf{u}$ is a nonnegative matrix, and since $\omega' \cdot M(\mu) \leq \omega'$ by (11.22), (11.23), (11.25) and Lemma 11.16(a), we have $A(\mu_1)\mathbf{u} = 0$ if $\omega' B(\mu_2) B(\mu_1)\mathbf{u} = \omega' \cdot \mathbf{u}$. But, if $A(\mu_1)\mathbf{u} = 0$, then the definition (12.9) of the transformation A shows that $\mathbf{v} = B(\mu_1)\mathbf{u} = M(\mu_1)\mathbf{u}$ is a vector which does not exceed a positive multiple of any of the vectors $\mathbf{u}_j$. Thus, if M_{n+1} is an optimal matrix, it follows that all the components u_l of $\mathbf{u}$ with $m \leq l \leq n + 1$ are zero; similarly, if M_{n+1} is not an optimal matrix all the components u_l with $m \leq l \leq n$ are zero. The corollary of Lemma 11.16 now shows that, in the first case, $\omega' B(\mu_2) B(\mu_1)\mathbf{u} = \omega' M(\mu_2) M(\mu_1)\mathbf{u} \leq \omega' \cdot M(\mu_1)\mathbf{u} < \omega' \cdot \mathbf{u}$, contradicting the statement $\omega \cdot B(\mu_2) B(\mu_1)\mathbf{u} = \omega' \cdot \mathbf{u}$ and establishing (11.14). In the second case (that in which M_{n+1} is nonoptimal), we come in the same way to the contradiction $\omega' B(\mu_2) B(\mu_1)\mathbf{u} < \omega' \cdot \mathbf{u}$ unless all components of $\mathbf{u}$ but its last vanish; repeating our argument, we see that the same contradiction must arise unless all components of $B(\mu_1)\mathbf{u} = M(\mu_1)\mathbf{u}$ but its last component vanish also. The definition (11.22), (11.23), (11.25) of the matrix $M(\mu_1)$, and the form (11.5) of the matrices M_j, then shows that we must have $M(\mu_1)\mathbf{u} = M_{n+1}\mathbf{u}$; since M_{n+1} is nonoptimal we have then $\omega' M_{n+1}\mathbf{u} < \omega' \cdot \mathbf{u}$, and we are led to the same contradiction. Thus (12.14) is established in every case; as we have seen, (12.13) follows.

Let $\mathbf{u}$ be a definite nonnegative nonzero vector. The definition (12.9) of the transformation A shows that the vector $A(\sigma_k)B(\sigma_{k-1}) \cdots B(\sigma_1)\mathbf{u}$ may be written in the form

$$(12.16) \qquad A(\sigma_k)B(\sigma_{k-1}) \cdots B(\sigma_1)\mathbf{b} = \sum_j c_j(\sigma_k, \cdots, \sigma_1)\mathbf{u}_j,$$

the real constants $c_j(\sigma_k, \cdots, \sigma_1)$ being nonnegative and the summation being extended over all $m \leq j \leq n$ if M_{n+1} is not optimal, and over all $m \leq j \leq n + 1$ if M_{n+1} is optimal. (In the remainder of the present proof, we shall suppose for the sake of definiteness that

M_{n+1} is nonoptimal; the details in this case differ only trivially from the details in the other case.) Then, using (12.12) and Lemma 11.7, we may write

$$(12.17) \quad \phi^k(\mathbf{b}) = \bigcup_{\mu_1, \ldots, \mu_k} \left(\sum_{j=m}^n \phi^{k-1}(\mathbf{u}_j) \cdot c_j(\mu_1) + \sum_{j=m}^n \phi^{k-2}(\mathbf{u}_j) c_j(\mu_2, \mu_1) \right.$$
$$\left. + \cdots + \sum_{j=m}^n \mathbf{u}_j c_j(\mu_k, \cdots, \mu_1) + B(\mu_k) \cdots B(\mu_1)\mathbf{b} \right).$$

Let S_ϵ denote the sphere of radius ϵ, defined, as in the preceding proof, relative to the norm (12.4).

Let

$$(12.18) \quad C = \sup \left(\sum_{j=m}^n c_j(\mu_1) + \sum_{j=m}^n c_j(\mu_2, \mu_1) + \cdots + \sum_{j=m}^n c_j(\mu_k, \cdots, \mu_1) \right).$$

Then it follows from (12.17), since $tK \subseteq K$ for $0 \leq t \leq 1$ and since $\phi^l(u_j) \subset K$ by Lemma 11.19, that

$$(12.19) \quad \phi^k(\mathbf{b}) \subseteq CK + \bigcup_{\mu_1, \ldots, \mu_k} B(\mu_k), \cdots, B(\mu_1)\mathbf{b}.$$

Thus, by (12.13), for each positive ϵ we have for $k \geq k(\epsilon)$

$$(12.20) \quad \phi^k(\mathbf{b}) \subseteq CK + S_\epsilon^2.$$

On the other hand, since by (12.13) we have

$$0 \in B(\mu_k) \cdots B(\mu_1)\mathbf{b} + S_\epsilon$$

for each positive ϵ and each $k \geq k(\epsilon)$ it follows from (12.17) that

$$(12.21) \quad \phi^k(\mathbf{b}) + S_\epsilon' \supseteq \sum_{j=m}^n c_j(\mu_1)\phi^{k-1}(\mathbf{u}_j) + \sum_{j=m}^n c_j(\mu_2, \mu_1)\phi^{k-2}(\mathbf{u}_j)$$
$$+ \cdots + \sum_{j=m}^n c_j(\mu_k, \cdots, \mu_1)\mathbf{u}_j$$

for each $\mu_1, \cdots, \mu_k$ and each sufficiently large k. A fortiori, we have

$$(12.22) \quad \phi^k(\mathbf{b}) + S_\epsilon \supseteq \sum_{j=m}^n (c_j(\mu_1) + \cdots + c_j(\mu_k, \cdots, \mu_1))\mathbf{u}_j$$

for each sufficiently large k, so that since $\phi^k(\mathbf{b})$ remains bounded, the supremum C must be finite.

Thus, if $\epsilon > 0$ is given, we may choose $\mu_1, \cdots, \mu_k$ so that

$$(12.23) \quad C \geq \sum_{j=m}^{n} (c_j(\mu_1) + \cdots + c_j(\mu_k, \cdots, \mu_1)) \geq C - \epsilon.$$

Then, for any additional $\mu_{k+1}, \cdots, \mu_{k_0}$ we must have

$$(12.24) \quad \sum_{=m}^{n} \{c_j(\mu_{k+1}, \cdots, \mu_1) + \cdots + c_j(\mu_{k_0}, \cdots, \mu_1)\} < \epsilon.$$

Since, as we have remarked immediately following formula (12.4), $\| M(\mu)\mathbf{u} \| \leq \| \mathbf{u} \|$, it follows inductively from (11.26) and from $\| \mathbf{u}_j \| = \boldsymbol{\omega} \cdot \mathbf{u}_j = 1$ that $\phi^l(\mathbf{u}_j) \subseteq S_1$. Thus, by (12.24),

$$(12.25) \quad \sum_{j=m}^{n} \phi^{k_0-k-1}(\mathbf{u}_j)c_j(\mu_{k+1}, \cdots, \mu_1)$$

$$+ \sum_{j=m}^{n} \phi^{k_0-k-2}(\mathbf{u}_j)c_j(\mu_{k+2}, \cdots, \mu_1)$$

$$+ \cdots + \sum_{j=m}^{n} \mathbf{u}_j c_j(\mu_{k_0}, \cdots, \mu_1) \subseteq S_\epsilon.$$

Hence, by (12.21), we have

$$(12.26) \quad \phi^{k_0}(\mathbf{b}) + S_{2\epsilon} \supseteq \sum_{j=m}^{n} c_j(\mu_1)\phi^{k_0-1}(\mathbf{u}_j)$$

$$+ \cdots + \sum_{j=m}^{n} \phi^{k_0-k}(\mathbf{u}_j)c_j(\mu_k, \cdots, \mu_1)$$

for each sufficiently large k_0. By Lemma 11.19, we have also

$$(12.27) \quad \phi^{k_0-l}(\mathbf{u}_j) + S_\epsilon \supseteq K$$

for $1 \leq l \leq k$ and each sufficiently large k_0. Thus, by (12.26),

$$(12.28) \quad \phi^{k_0}(\mathbf{b}) + S_{2\epsilon} + \sum_{j=m}^{n} \{c_j(\mu_1) + \cdots + c_j(\mu_k, \cdots, \mu_1)\}S_\epsilon$$

$$\supseteq \sum_{j=m}^{n} (c_j(\mu_1) + \cdots + c_j(\mu_k, \cdots, \mu_1))K,$$

for all sufficiently large k_0, which by (12.23), implies

$$(12.29) \quad \phi^{k_0}(\mathbf{b}) + S_{(C+2)\epsilon} \supseteq (C - \epsilon)K.$$

Since K is bounded, this implies the existence of a finite constant D such that

$$(12.30) \qquad \phi^{k_0}(\mathbf{b}) + S_{(C+D+2)\epsilon} \supseteq CK$$

for all sufficiently large k_0. Formulas (12.20) and (12.30) together show that

$$(12.31) \qquad \phi^k(\mathbf{b}) \to CK \quad \text{as} \quad k \to \infty,$$

proving Lemma 20. Q.E.D.

2. Proof of Theorem 11.9

We now apply Theorem 11.6 and the ideas developed in its proof to prove our second main result, Theorem 11.9.

Let us first note that Definitions 11.7 and 11.8 depend on the matrices $M_1, \cdots, M_{n+1}$, but that if we multiply each of these matrices by a common factor $t > 0$, and, simultaneously, multiply the vectors $\mathbf{b}_n$ of Definition 11.7 by the factor t^n, then, by Lemma 11.14, optimal paths (relative to $M_1, \cdots, M_{n+1}$) are mapped into optimal paths (relative to $tM_1, \cdots, tM_{n+1}$); optimal matrices into optimal matrices, and the relationship $\succ$ is unchanged. We may consequently assume without loss of generality, just as in the preceding lecture, that $\mathrm{dom}\,(M_j) = 1$ if and only if M_j is optimal, and that the optimal matrices are either $M_m, \cdots, M_n$ or $M_m, \cdots, M_{n+1}$. This assumption will be made throughout the present section.

LEMMA 12.2. *Let* $\mathbf{b} \geq 0$. *Then if* $\mathbf{c} \in \phi(\mathbf{b})$ *we have* $\mathbf{b} \succ \mathbf{c}$; *on the other hand, there exists some vector* $\mathbf{c} \in \phi(\mathbf{b})$ *such that* $\mathbf{c} \succ \mathbf{b}$.

Proof: If $\mathbf{c} \in \phi(\mathbf{b})$, then $\phi^n(\mathbf{c}) \subseteq \phi^{n+1}(\mathbf{b})$. By Theorem 11.6 and by (12.3) of the proof of Theorem 11.6 it follows from this on letting $n \to \infty$ that $(\mathbf{v}'_0 \cdot \mathbf{c})K \subseteq (\mathbf{v}'_0 \cdot \mathbf{b})K$. Thus we conclude as in the first paragraph of the proof of Theorem 11.6 that $\mathbf{v}'_0 \cdot \mathbf{c} \leq \mathbf{v}'_0 \cdot \mathbf{b}$, so that, by Theorem 11.6, $\mathbf{b} \succeq \mathbf{c}$.

On the other hand, suppose that there exists no $\mathbf{c} \in \phi(\mathbf{b})$ such that $\mathbf{c} \succ \mathbf{b}$, i.e., no $\mathbf{c}$ such that $\mathbf{v}'_0 \cdot \mathbf{c} \geq \mathbf{v}'_0 \cdot \mathbf{b}$. Since it follows readily from (11.7) that the set $\phi(\mathbf{b})$ is bounded and closed, there must then exist a constant $\delta < 1$ such that $\mathbf{v}'_0 \cdot \mathbf{c} \leq \delta(\mathbf{v}'_0 \cdot \mathbf{b})$ for all $\mathbf{c} \in \phi(\mathbf{b})$. By what has been proved immediately above, we must then have $\mathbf{v}'_0 \cdot \mathbf{c} \leq \delta \mathbf{v}'_0 \cdot \mathbf{b}$ for all $\mathbf{c} \in \phi^m(\mathbf{b})$. Letting $m \to \infty$ and using (12.3) of the proof of Theorem 11.6, it follows that $(\mathbf{v}'_0 \cdot \mathbf{b})(\mathbf{v}'_0 \cdot \mathbf{c}) \le \delta(\mathbf{v}'_0 \cdot \mathbf{b})$ for each $\mathbf{c} \in K$, i.e., that $\mathbf{v}'_0 \cdot \mathbf{c} \le \delta$ for each $\mathbf{c} \in K$. Let $\mathbf{u}_j$ be one of the fixed vectors of Lemma 11.19. Then, since $\phi^m(\mathbf{u}_j) \to K$, it follows from (12.3) that $\mathbf{v}'_0 \cdot \mathbf{u}_j = 1$. On the other hand, since as was observed following Lemma 11.18, $\mathbf{u}_j \in \phi(\mathbf{u}_j) \subseteq \phi^2(\mathbf{u}_j) \subseteq \cdots \subseteq K$, we have $\mathbf{u}_j \in K$ and have hence a contradiction completing the proof of the present lemma. Q.E.D.

COROLLARY. *Let $\mathbf{v}'_0$ be the vector of Theorem 11.6. The maximum $\mathbf{v}'_0 \cdot \mathbf{c}$ as $\mathbf{c}$ ranges over $\phi(\mathbf{b})$ is $\mathbf{v}'_0 \cdot \mathbf{b}$.*

We may now show that $\mathbf{b}_1 = \mathbf{b}, \mathbf{b}_2, \mathbf{b}_3, \cdots$ is an optimal path beginning at $\mathbf{b}$ if and only if $\mathbf{b}_{n+1} \in \phi(\mathbf{b}_n)$ and $\mathbf{v}'_0 \cdot \mathbf{b}_n = \mathbf{v}'_0 \cdot \mathbf{b}$. Indeed, if $\mathbf{b}_n \succeq \phi^n(\mathbf{b})$ for arbitrarily large n, then, by Theorem 11.6 and by the preceding corollary, $\mathbf{v}'_0 \cdot \mathbf{b}_n \ge \mathbf{v}'_0 \cdot \mathbf{b}$, for arbitrarily large n. Thus, since $\mathbf{b}_{n+1} \in \phi(\mathbf{b}_n)$ for all n, it follows by the preceding corollary that $\mathbf{v}'_0 \cdot \mathbf{b}_n \ge \mathbf{v}'_0 \cdot \mathbf{b}$ for all n; on the other hand, $\mathbf{v}'_0 \cdot \mathbf{b} \ge \mathbf{v}'_0 \cdot \mathbf{b}_n$ is even more obvious from the preceding corollary. Conversely, if $\mathbf{v}'_0 \cdot \mathbf{b}_n \ge \mathbf{v}'_0 \cdot \mathbf{b}$ for all n, then $\mathbf{b}_n \succeq \phi^n(\mathbf{b})$ follows at once from the preceding corollary and from Theorem 11.6.

Next we prove the following lemma.

LEMMA 12.3. *If M_j is an optimal matrix and $\mathbf{u} \ge 0$, then $\mathbf{v}'_0 \cdot M_j\mathbf{u} \le \mathbf{v}'_0 \cdot \mathbf{u}$ with equality if and only if all components of $\mathbf{u}$ except the jth and $(n+1)$st vanish; if M_j is a nonoptimal matrix, we have this same inequality with equality if and only if all components of $\mathbf{u}$ except the jth vanishes and $j \ne n+1$.*

Proof: The inequality results immediately from the above corollary. The form (11.5) and (11.6) of the matrices M_j (and the fact that the constants τ_j are less than 1) makes it plain that, if the jth and $(n+1)$st components of $\mathbf{u}_0$ are zero but $\mathbf{u}_0$ is nonzero, we have $M_j\mathbf{u}_0 \le \mathbf{u}_0$ and thus $\mathbf{v}'_0 M_j\mathbf{u}_0 < \mathbf{v}'_0 M_j\mathbf{u}_0$. A vector $\mathbf{u} \ge 0$ which has any components but the jth and $(n+1)$st different from zero may be decomposed into the sum of two nonnegative vectors $\mathbf{u} = \mathbf{u}_0 + \mathbf{u}_1$, with $\mathbf{u}_0$ as above; thus $\mathbf{v}'_0 \cdot M_j\mathbf{u} < \mathbf{v}'_0\mathbf{u}$ follows.

Let M_j be optimal: if $j = n+1$, then, using (11.6) and recollecting that each of the matrices has been multiplied by a factor t equal to the reciprocal of the largest dom (M_k), we have $(M_{n+1})_{n+1,n+1} = 1$, and the first statement of the present lemma follows in this case. If M_j is optimal and $j \ne n+1$, then, for notational convenience and without loss of generality, we may assume $j = n$. Let $\mathbf{v}'_0$ $= [v_1, \cdots, v_{n+1}]$. If we apply the inequality $\mathbf{v}'_0 \cdot M_n \mathbf{u} \leq \mathbf{v}'_0 \cdot \mathbf{u}$ to an arbitrary vector $\mathbf{u} \geq 0$ of the form $[0, \cdots, 0, u_n, u_{n+1}]$, and use the form (11.5) of the matrix M_n, it follows that the two-dimensional vector $\mathbf{v}' = [v_n, v_{r+1}]$ and the transformation M:

$$[u_n, u_{n+1}] \rightarrow [\eta_n u_{n+1} + \tau_n(1 - \sigma_n)u_n, \sigma_n u_n]$$

stand in the relationship $\mathbf{v}'M \leq \mathbf{v}'$. Since, as was observed following the statement of Theorem 11.9, M_n is optimal only if dom (M) $= 1$, it follows from Lemma 2.4 of Lecture 2 that $\mathbf{v}'M = \mathbf{v}'$. Thus $\mathbf{v}'_0 M_n \mathbf{u} = \mathbf{v}'_0 \mathbf{u}$ if $\mathbf{u} = [0, \cdots, 0, u_n, u_{n+1}]$, completing the proof of the first assertion of the present lemma.

If M_{n+1} is not dominant, then using (11.6) as above we see that $\mathbf{v}'_0 M_{n+1} \mathbf{u} < \mathbf{v}'_0 \mathbf{u}$ if $\mathbf{u} \geq 0$. If M_j is not dominant and $j = n + 1$, then, for notational convenience and without loss of generality, we may assume $j = n$. Introducing $\mathbf{v}'$ and M as in the preceding paragraph we find just as in the preceding paragraph that $\mathbf{v}'M \leq \mathbf{v}'$; since dom $(M) < 1$ we find by the second corollary of Theorem 2.1 that $\mathbf{v}'M \leq \mathbf{v}'$. Thus we have $\mathbf{v}'_0 M_n \mathbf{u} < \mathbf{v}'_0 \cdot \mathbf{u}$ either for a vector $\mathbf{u} \geq 0$ of the form $[0, \cdots, 0, u_{n+1}]$ or for a vector $\mathbf{u} \geq 0$ of the form $[0, \cdots, 0, u_n, 0]$. Since by the Corollary of Lemma 2, by the definition (11.7) of the mapping ϕ, and by the parts of the present lemma already established we must have $\mathbf{v}'_0 M_n \mathbf{u} = \mathbf{v}'_0 \cdot \mathbf{u}$ for a vector of the second form, it follows that $\mathbf{v}'_0 M_n \mathbf{u} < \mathbf{v}'_0 \cdot \mathbf{u}$ for a vector of the first form. Arguing now as in the first paragraph of the present proof, we find that $\mathbf{v}'_0 M_n \mathbf{u} = \mathbf{v}'_0 \mathbf{u}$ if and only if all components of $\mathbf{u}$ except its nth component vanish. Q.E.D.

Theorem 11.6, Lemma 3 and the characterization of optimal paths given in the paragraph immediately preceding Lemma 3, plainly imply Theorem 11.9. Similarly, Theorem 11.6, Lemma 3, the characterization of optimal paths given in the paragraph immediately preceding Lemma 3, and the Corollary of Lemma 2 plainly imply the Corollary of Theorem 11.9.

Thus we have proved all the results stated in the present and in the preceding lecture.

3. Implications for the Theory of the Preceding Lectures

If the rate of interest is s, then we have seen that in the model just presented investment in a given line of production can only appear reasonable to an entrepreneur if the positive eigenvalue of the matrix

$$(12.32) \qquad \begin{bmatrix} 0 & \eta \\ \sigma & \tau(1-\sigma) \end{bmatrix}$$

formed with the coefficients η, σ, and τ relevant for that line of enterprise exceeds $1 + s$. This condition is evidently equivalent to the condition

$$(12.33) \qquad (1+s)^2 - \tau(1-\sigma)(1+s) - \sigma\eta \leq 0,$$

or

$$(12.34) \qquad (1+s)^2 \leq \tau(1-\sigma)(1+s) + \sigma\eta.$$

How will the various coefficients in this equation vary over the dynamic path of an economy? The rate s will vary, but $(1 + s)$ will of course vary only slightly; similarly, the coefficient η will vary slightly, as prices vary. The coefficient τ is essentially invariant and less than 1, its nearness to 1 being a measure of the extent to which the given commodity is an imperishable staple. The coefficient σ however is the ratio of sales to stocks, and the accumulation of stocks is in principle capable of driving this coefficient down to zero. Since condition (12.34) will always fail for sufficiently small σ, we see that if stocks are sufficiently high relative to sales it is inevitably unwise to continue a given line of production. Thus we may expect each form of production, or even all together, to be suspended when stock-sales ratios reach a certain level. As we have seen in our earlier lecture, if the set of permissible stock-sales ratios has a sufficiently low average over the whole economy, we may expect the motion of the economy to be subject to the Keynes relation, production adjusting to consumption on the average, and occasional periods occurring in which production is reduced while consumption reduces inventories.

Critique of the Neoclassical Equilibrium Theory.   Keynesian Equilibria

The Neoclassical or
Walrasian Equilibrium—Introduction

Our discussion of cycle theory and our preliminary discussion of Keynesian equilibrium has now given us sufficient perspective so that we may profitably return to price theory, taking up the study of general "neoclassical" or "Walrasian" price equilibrium of an economy. The history of this topic, as well as an interpretation of its significance, is given by Karlin.

The main advances to date in the study of equilibrium models are associated with the names of Walras, Wald, McKenzie and Arrow and Debreu. To Walras we owe the first sophisticated formulation of the equilibrium phenomenon. Wald later carried out a comprehensive mathematical analysis of Walras's equations and established the existence and uniqueness of solutions to these equations under a wide variety of conditions. Finally, McKenzie, and Arrow and Debreu independently formulated general models of equilibrium and proved the existence of a competitive equilibrium. None of the three models (Walras-Wald, McKenzie, Arrow-Debreu) subsumes any of the others as a special case; rather, all three should be viewed as variant descriptions of equilibrium in a competitive economy. Alternative analyses of the same models or other versions of equilibrium have been proposed independently by Gale, McKenzie and Uzawa.

It will soon be seen that we regard this theory somewhat critically.

Our model will be like that of Arrow and Debreu, but with linear Leontief-like features as introduced in the first four lectures, differing only in an expanded treatment of consumer preference. Thus the equilibrium price theory will be strictly comparable to the price theory developed in the first four lectures: we will be able to see explicitly how much or how little is added to the conclusions we are able to draw, by the introduction of consumer preferences.

The elements of the model are to be as follows. In the first place, we will have a number of competing firms, each of which seeks to maximize its own profits; secondly, we will have a number of consumption units (families) each of which places a subjective "utility" upon each "bill of goods" that their labor and their dividends from ownership of industry will purchase. Each consumption unit then seeks to maximize this subjective utility, measured by an individual "utility function." A careful formulation of the law of supply and demand will then allow us to find the conditions under which there exist prices at which all of these maxima are simultaneously realized; continuing, we shall investigate the further properties of such a "competitive equilibrium."

1. The Model Explicitly Defined

Our model of the whole economy will consist first of a number m of "firms" or "investment syndicates" each of which is capable of producing (i.e., has the ability and the freedom to produce) any, several, or all of the n commodities $C_1, \cdots, C_n$ of the economy. Labor will first be considered (inessentially) as being homogeneous and regarded as commodity C_0; consequently we will generalize the model to include various distinct labor sectors. The kth firm in the first instance is described by a set of numbers $\pi_{ij}^{(k)}$, which represent the amount of C_j required by firm k for the production of one unit of C_i. We shall take these numbers as being the same for all firms, however, and write π_{ij} for each of them. Thus we assume that no firm can have a clear technological advantage over another firm. We measure the wealth of each firm by assuming that firm k has an initial ownership inventory of $q_i^{(k)}$ units of commodity C_i, $(i = 1, \cdots, n)$ and that this inventory is economically liquid, i.e., could be freely sold or traded for equal value (under prices yet to be determined). In this model, then, the only distinction between different firms is their total capitalization as reflected in their ownership inventories. In the same way we assume a fixed capital matrix with elements ϕ_{ij}, taking $\phi_{oi} = \phi_{io} = 0$ for all i.

The model consists next of a number f of consumption units, or families. The νth family's fractional title to the ownership of the kth firm is $h_{\nu k}$, where

(13.1) $\sum_{\nu=1}^{f} h_{\nu k} = 1$ for all $k = 1, \cdots, m$.

The νth family's satisfaction as derived from consumption of commodities $C_1, \cdots, C_n$, as well as the negative consumption of commodity C_0 (the amount of labor which is supplied by the consumption unit) is described by a *utility function:*

(13.2) $u_\nu(s_0, s_1, \cdots, s_n)$ $s_0 \leq 0;$ $s_1, \cdots, s_n \geq 0;$

this is subjective value placed by the νth family on the "bill of goods," or "commodity bundle," or "labor-consumption plan" consisting of (consumption of) commodities of the various kinds in amounts $s_1, \cdots, s_n$ and (expenditure of) labor in the amount $-s_0$. It clearly would not be realistic to assume linearity here, for ten cars cannot have ten times the subjective value of one for most families. Fortunately, it is not necessary to delve deeply into the form of the utility functions.

It is canonical to remark here that these utility functions play a role in the determination of equilibrium only through being maximized; thus each of these functions may be indifferently replaced by any monotone-increasing function of itself. Putting this differently, it is not the functions u_ν themselves, but only the "indifference surfaces" $u_\nu = $ constant that are strictly necessary for the model. Another perfectly equivalent way of putting this same circumstance is to state that what we require is a linear ordering of bills of goods, some being rated as preferable to others. The utility function is then a mere shorthand for expressing these somewhat more subtle facts.

We assume about our utility functions that for each $\mathbf{x}^{(1)}$ and ν there exists an $\mathbf{x}^{(2)}$ for which

(13.3) $\mathbf{x}^{(2)} \geq \mathbf{x}^{(1)}$ and $u_\nu(\mathbf{x}^{(2)}) > u_\nu(\mathbf{x}^{(1)}).$

Since the signs of the parameters s_0 have been taken as negative, this says that, given any family and any bill of goods, either a decrease in the amount of labor expended, or an increase in the amount of some commodity, consumed, or both, will always be considered desirable. Our assumption says in consequence that there is no "saturation point," i.e., given any commodity bundle $\mathbf{x}^{(1)}$, there is always another commodity bundle $\mathbf{x}^{(2)}$ which the νth family will regard as strictly preferable.

A rather opposite fact was emphasized in the preceding Keynesian discussions; that *consumption* did not always rise to meet income, but that in certain circumstances inventories of *producer goods* or *trade inventories* would be purchased *if the possibility of using these producer goods or trade inventories profitably was real*. Thus, in making the assumption expressed by (13.3), which is a mathematical form of the oft-repeated economic dictum "appetite is boundless," we implicitly assume away all Keynesian difficulties. We shall see that without the assumption expressed by (13.3), our model does *not necessarily admit any equilibrium;* if we admit accumulation of producer inventories as an auxiliary term in the consumer utility functions, then our whole notion of "equilibrium" comes into question, since our equilibrium corresponds to a continual (and *continually unobstructed*) growth of the wealth of firms. It follows that notions derived from the Walrasian equilibrium cannot legitimately be used to criticize the Keynesian analysis; to bring these two approaches to a direct confrontation, a common model generalizing them both is required. Holding all these difficulties in abeyance for the moment, we shall continue to investigate price equilibrium in the neoclassical model as we have it.

We shall introduce a few more assumptions as the discussion proceeds, but the model defined in the last few paragraphs is basically the model we shall analyze.

We now wish to study the following question. With each of the firms attempting to maximize its own profits, and with each of the consumption units attempting to maximize its individual utility functions, is there a price vector (i.e., a set of prices $p_0, p_1, \cdots, p_n$) which leads to a production and exchange equilibrium? The answer is yes, as we shall see. In obtaining this positive answer, we shall also explore the properties of the "equilibrium price vector"; this exploration will put us in a position to criticize the theory under examination.

2. Price Equilibrium

We must now give the rather lengthy definition of "price equilibrium," thereby giving, in the sense of Walras, a complete and general definition of the more fragmentary concept ordinarily called the "law of supply and demand."

By a "price equilibrium," we shall mean a set of prices $p_0, \cdots, p_n$, a set of production figures $a_1^{(k)}, \cdots, a_n^{(k)}$, and a set of consumption figures $s_0^{(\nu)}, \cdots, s_n^{(\nu)}$, which satisfy the following four conditions.

Condition (a).   The prices are nonnegative, i.e.,

$$(13.4) \qquad\qquad p_j \geq 0 \quad \text{for} \quad j = 0, \cdots, n;$$

and at least one price is not zero.

The significance of this condition is evident.

Condition (b).   For each firm $k = 1, \cdots, m$ the number (profit)

$$(13.5) \qquad\qquad \sum_{i=1}^{n} \sum_{j=0}^{n} a_i^{(k)} (\delta_{ij} - \pi_{ij}) p_j$$

is a maximum over all sets $\tilde{a}_i$ which satisfy

$$(13.6) \qquad\qquad \sum_{i=1}^{n} \sum_{j=0}^{n} \tilde{a}_i \phi_{ij} p_j \leq \sum_{j=1}^{n} q_j^{(k)} p_j.$$

This condition states that, whatever the equilibrium prices of the various commodities (including labor) may be, each firm will choose to manufacture a list of products (in amounts $a_1^{(k)}, \cdots, a_n^{(k)}$) for which the profit is greater than (or at least not less than) the profit obtainable by production of any other list of products which could be produced, subject to the budgetary condition (13.6). The left-hand side of (13.6) is the amount of capital which must be laid out to assemble the elements necessary for production of commodities in the amounts $\tilde{a}_i$, while the right-hand side is the value of the total assets of the firm. We are therefore neglecting the possibility of borrowing, but since the amount of money a firm can borrow is approximately proportional to its total assets, this should not introduce overwhelming errors.

Condition (c).   For each consumer unit $\nu = 1, \cdots, f$, the number

$$(13.7) \qquad\qquad u_\nu(s_0^{(\nu)}, \cdots, s_n^{(\nu)})$$

is a maximum over all $\tilde{s}_i$ which satisfy

$$(13.8) \qquad -\sum_{j=0}^{n} \tilde{s}_j p_j + \sum_{j=0}^{n} \sum_{i=1}^{n} \sum_{k=1}^{n} a_i^{(k)} (\delta_{ij} - \pi_{ij}) p_j h_{\nu k} \geq 0.$$

This condition states that, whatever the equilibrium prices may be, each consumption unit will choose to consume that list of commodities whose subjective value is the greatest among all lists of commodities which could be consumed subject to the budgetary condition (13.8). The first term in (13.8) is the excess of expenditure over wages, while the second term is dividend income. Borrowing is therefore ruled out again.

Condition (d). Everything that is consumed must be produced, i.e.,

$$(13.9) \qquad \sum_{i,k} a_i^{(k)}(\delta_{ij} - \pi_{ij}) - \sum_{\nu} s_j^{(\nu)} \geq 0 \quad j = 0, \cdots, n.$$

We assume in addition that if there is an excess at equilibrium of production over consumption for some commodity C_i, then at equilibrium the price of this commodity must drop to zero, so that *equality holds in* (13.9) *whenever* $p_i > 0$.

Conditions (a) through (d) are then the conditions to be satisfied by the p, the a, and the s, for a Walrasian price equilibrium to subsist.

We intend in what follows to prove the existence of a price equilibrium. However, let us, for the moment, assume the existence of such a price equilibrium, and develop its properties. To establish the consequences of condition (b), we shall use the following lemma.

LEMMA. *Let it be required to find that solution* $x_1, \cdots, x_m$ *of the inequalities*

$$(13.10) \qquad \sum_{j=1}^{m} \alpha_j x_j \leq \beta; \quad x_j \geq 0$$

(*where* $\alpha_1, \cdots, \alpha_j$, *are nonnegative constants not all zero*) *for which*

$$(13.11) \qquad \phi = \sum_{j=1}^{m} \gamma_j x_j$$

(*where* $\gamma_1, \cdots, \gamma_j$ *are nonnegative constants*) *is a maximum. Let* S *be the set of indices* s *for which*

$$(13.12) \qquad \gamma_s/\alpha_s = \max_j (\gamma_j/\alpha_j).$$

Then the most general solution of our maximum problem is at the same time the most general vector $\mathbf{x}$ *for which* $x_j = 0$ *if* $j \notin S$ *and for which* $\sum_{j=1}^{m} \alpha_j x_j = \beta$ *is satisfied as an equality.*

This principle is useful in various branches of mathematics, particularly in statistics, where it is known as the fundamental lemma of Neyman and Pearson. We shall give a heuristic rather than a formal proof; the former is at once more convincing and more transparent than the latter.

Suppose that various types of sand from various sacks are available for purchase at various fixed amounts per pound and that, subject to the requirement that one not exceed a given budget (condition (13.10)) one wishes to acquire as much sand as possible (maximize (13.11)). How to proceed? Evidently the answer is to buy sand only from those sacks which are cheapest per pound of sand; it is, however, a matter of complete indifference from which of these sacks one purchases sand. But this is the conclusion which we have expressed more formally in our lemma. Q.E.D.

This lemma shows that condition (b) requires that each firm produce only those commodities C_i for which

$$(13.13) \qquad \left[\sum_j (\delta_{ij} - \pi_{ij})p_j\right] / \left[\sum_j \phi_{ij}p_j\right]$$

is a maximum over i. Let this maximum be ρ. Then we have

$$(13.14) \qquad \sum_{j=0}^{n} (\delta_{ij} - \pi_{ij} - \rho\phi_{ij})p_j = 0$$

for each commodity C_i which is produced in nonzero quantities. We have encountered this equation before—it tells us that all commodities produced are produced at the same profit per unit investment, i.e., the *same rate of profit*. Thus, in the present model we recover in a more formal way the fundamental principle for equilibrium which we derived heuristically in our earlier discussion of prices: the *rate of profit on each commodity produced is the same for all firms*. Further, since only those commodities for which the rate of profit is maximum will be produced, we can conclude that the *rate of profit is the same for all commodities which are produced in positive amounts*. Unless all firms are to refrain from producing nonzero amounts of any commodity, ρ *must* of course be *nonnegative*. If $\rho = 0$, so that no profit is obtained in any case, then expression (13.5) has the "maximum" zero identically for all activity levels satisfying the inequality (13.6). However, if $\rho > 0$ then the preceding lemma shows that the expression (13.5) only attains its maximum if the inequality (13.6) degenerates into an equality; i.e., *if $\rho > 0$ condition* (b) *implies that*

$$(13.15) \qquad \sum_{i=1}^{n} \sum_{j=1}^{n} a_i^{(k)} \phi_{ij} p_j = \sum_{j=0}^{n} q_j^{(k)} p_j.$$

That is, *if equilibrium occurs at a positive rate of profit, each firm will insist upon utilizing all its capital.*

If the elements π_{ij} (not including the zero row) form a connected matrix, we find that we have returned to the price theory of the first four lectures. Making reference to the results established there, we find that (13.11) *alone determines the price ratios as a function of ρ.*

Thus *the only possible effect that the consumer utility functions can have upon prices is through the determination of the rate of profit.* We emphasize: as far as equilibrium price theory in our model goes, the generalization of our model (as compared to the simpler model discussed in the first four lectures) to include consumer preferences can *at best* only determine the rate of profit; we shall find even this much cannot be very securely attained.

Walrasian Equilibrium in the Case
of a Single Labor Sector

1. Significance of the Quantity $\rho_{\max}$

We continue to develop the consequences of the definition of a price equilibrium. In the previous lecture we saw that condition (b)— the condition that each firm of the model optimize its own profit —implies the existence of a number ρ, the same for all firms, defined by

$$(14.1) \qquad \rho = \left[\sum_{j=0}^{n} (\delta_{ij} - \pi_{ij}) p_j \right] \Big/ \left[\sum_{j=0}^{n} \phi_{ij} p_j \right]$$

for all values of $i = 1, \cdots, n$. If these equations are written

$$(14.2) \qquad \sum_{j=0}^{n} (\delta_{ij} - \pi_{ij}) p_j = \rho \sum_{i=0}^{n} \phi_{ij} p_j, \quad i = 1, \cdots, n,$$

we see that we have merely returned to the price theory of the third lecture. If, as in Lecture 3, we define the number $\rho_{\max}$ to be dominant of the matrix π_{ij} with the $j = 0$ column removed, so that

$$(14.3) \qquad \sum_{j=1}^{n} (\delta_{ij} - \pi_{ij}) p_j = \rho_{\max} \sum_{j=1}^{n} \phi_{ij} p_j, \quad i = 1, \cdots, n,$$

the results established in the first four lectures show that $\rho_{\max}$ is a certain number, which is a supremum of the set of numbers ρ for which (14.2) has a solution $\mathbf{p}$ with all $p_j \geq 0$. The number ρ we call, as previously, the rate of profit. We saw in these earlier lectures

189

that (14.2) determines the price ratios as a function of ρ; we may consequently write $p_j(\rho), j = 0, \cdots, n$, for the solution (unique up to a common factor depending on ρ) of the equations (14.2). The functions $p_j(\rho)$ are, of course, defined only for $\rho \leq \rho_{\max}$.

If the number $\rho_{\max}$ is negative, it therefore follows at once that ρ is negative. Hence, at equilibrium each firm must sustain a loss on every item it produces, so that the firm attains its maximum profit by producing nothing at all; all the production levels $a_j^{(k)}$ are zero, and the case is devoid of interest. We will consequently confine our attention to cases in which $\rho \geq 0$, and hence to cases in which $\rho_{\max} \geq 0$ and to the range $0 \leq \rho \leq \rho_{\max}$. Since we know from the results established in the first four lectures that if $\rho_{\max} \leq 0$ then no arrangement of production levels can produce a nonzero surplus, we see that this restriction is not in the least unnatural.

It follows from the results established in Lecture 3 that $p_i(\rho) > 0$ for $0 \leq \rho \leq \rho_{\max}$ and $i = 1, \cdots, n$, while $p_0(\rho) > 0$ for $0 \leq \rho < \rho_{\max}$.

2. Necessary Conditions for Equilibrium

Let us now try to analyze the interesting case—that in which $\rho_{\max}$ is positive. We assume the existence of a price equilibrium and develop the properties of such an equilibrium. Condition (b) implies, as was shown in the preceding lecture, that unless $\rho = 0$, every firm must utilize all its capital in production. Thus its profit must be exactly ρ times its total capital, i.e., $\rho \sum_{i=1}^{n} q_i^{(k)} p_j(\rho)$. The profit of each firm is then evidently a function of ρ only, because the price ratios are functions of ρ only. Now since the profit of each firm is a function of ρ alone, and since the share in ownership of each firm held by each family is a given quantity, the dividend income of each consumption unit (family) is also a function of ρ alone. Accordingly, we may write the expression

$$(14.4) \qquad \Delta^{(\nu)}(\rho) = \rho \sum_{j=1}^{n} \sum_{k=1}^{m} q_j^{(k)} p_j(\rho) h_{\nu k}$$

for the dividend income of the νth family. If $\rho = 0$, this expression degenerates to zero, and thus remains correct.

The utility function $u^{(\nu)}(s_0, \cdots, s_n)$, (remember that s_0 is negative while $s_1, \cdots, s_n$ are positive) is assumed, in the manner explained in the preceding lecture, always to increase if a suitable one of its arguments is increased; therefore, in maximizing the $u^{(\nu)}$ subject to the budgetary condition (c), i.e., subject to the condition

$$(14.5) \qquad \sum_{j=0}^{n} p_j(\rho)s_j^{(\nu)} \leq \Delta^{(\nu)}(\rho),$$

equality is always attained, i.e., we always have

$$(14.5a) \qquad \sum_{j=0}^{n} p_j(\rho)s_j^{(\nu)} = \Delta^{(\nu)}(\rho)$$

at the maximum of utility. (To maximize utility, all income from wages and dividends must be spent.)

If, as we shall henceforth assume, the maximizing $[s_0^{(\nu)}, \cdots, s_n^{(\nu)}]$ is unique, it is then clear that from the preceding equation and from (14.4) that the quantities $s_j^{(\nu)}$ depend only upon ρ; thus each family's demand for commodities is a function of ρ alone. We will indicate this fact in what follows by writing these quantities as $s_0^{(\nu)}(\rho)$, $s_1^{(\nu)}(\rho), \cdots, s_n^{(\nu)}(\rho)$. (It is possible and even customary to introduce geometric conditions under which the above maximum will be unique, but they are rather artificial. Therefore we introduce uniqueness of the maximum explicitly as an additional assumption.)

Next we define

$$(14.6) \qquad s_i(\rho) = \sum_{\nu=1} s_i^{(\nu)}(\rho);$$

then $s_i(\rho)$ is the total demand for commodity C_i, while $s_0(\rho)$ is the total amount of labor offered by all the families. As the notation suggests, the $s_i(\rho)$ are functions of ρ alone.

Let $a_i = \sum_{k=1}^{m} a_i^{(k)}$ so that a_i is the total amount of the commodity C_i produced. Since all of the prices, excepting possibly p_0, are positive, condition (d) yields

$$(14.7) \qquad \sum_{i=0}^{n} a_i(\delta_{ij} - \pi_{ij}) - s_i(\rho) = 0, \quad j = 1, \cdots, n$$

which determines the total production levels a_i as a function of ρ. Moreover, again by condition (d), equation (14.7) holds for $j = 0$ as well, unless $p_0(\rho) = 0$, i.e., unless $\rho = \rho_{\max}$.

Let $d_0(\rho)$ be the total demand for labor, i.e., let

$$(14.8) \qquad d_0(\rho) = \sum_{i=0}^{n} a_i(\rho)\pi_{i0}.$$

Then for $\rho < \rho_{max}$, equation (14.7) says

(14.9) $d_0(\rho) = -s_0(\rho)$

while if $\rho = \rho_{max}$, condition (d) gives directly

(14.10) $d_0(\rho) \leq -s_0(\rho)$.

We now have sufficiently many equations in hand. What do they mean? Let us review: we start with the fact that at equilibrium prices are determined competitively, and hence by the rate of profit ρ. From this we deduce that dividend income, hence consumption and total production levels, are all determined by ρ. All that remains is the determination of this one number ρ. This is determined as follows: the supply of labor is determined by ρ (through the utility functions). The demand for labor is also determined by ρ (through the utility functions and the demand for other commodities). Thus, unless $\rho = \rho_{max}$, the rate of profit is determined by equation (14.9): demand = supply, for labor. This familiar conclusion remains banal unless we have some information on the form of the schedules of demand and supply for labor. We now turn to the elucidation of those schedules.

3. Supply and Demand of Labor

We first investigate the form of the function $-s_0(\rho)$. Unthinking economic habit might lead us to assume that $-s_0(\rho)$ must be a monotone decreasing function of ρ, since we may argue that labor, like any other commodity, is subject to the "law of supply," which normally would require that as the wages paid to labor go down (as a result of increasing ρ) the amount of labor which people are willing to supply must also go down. The supply of labor is governed differently, however, as many authors have observed. When wages fall low enough, people must work more in order to get by; second members of families, women, children, etc., all enter the market in this range of wages; thus there is a minimum in the plot of $s_0(\rho)$ against ρ. This fact has been consciously used in determining the wage level in many parts of the world. If, however, wages fall to the point where the labor force can no longer subsist, then the labor offered must fall rapidly to zero. This "subsistence effect" would take place for a value of ρ close to ρ_{max}. The qualitative form of the labor supply schedule, i.e., the graph of $-s_0(\rho)$ against ρ, must then be as shown in Fig. 19.

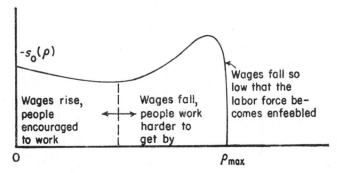

Fig. 19. Supply of labor plotted against the profit rate.

The demand $d_0(\rho)$ arises, as equation (14.8) shows, from the demand for commodities. This latter demand is generated, as equation (14.5a) shows, by income from two sources: by wage income and by dividend income. The demand for labor may therefore be approximately regarded as a sum of two terms: the demand for labor generated by wages and the demand for labor generated by dividends. The demand $d^{(1)}$ for labor generated by wages depends, of course, upon wages; it may be obtained approximately by multiplying the actual labor offered (for a given ρ) by the wage rate. Thus it has a nonzero value for $\rho = 0$, and falls to zero when $\rho = \rho_{max}$

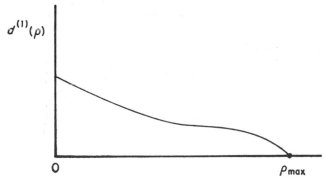

Fig. 20. Demand for labor generated by wages as a function of the rate of profit.

If we multiply the schedule $s_0(\rho)$ in Fig. 19 by the wage rate, we will obtain a schedule which is qualitatively like the schedule drawn in Fig. 20; knowing little about its detailed form, we may still be confident that it is not grossly misrepresented by an approximately straight line. A plot of $d^{(1)}(\rho)$ against ρ, obtained by multiplying $s_0(\rho)$ by the wage rate is shown in Fig. 20. The demand $d^{(2)}$ for labor generated by dividends is, of course, to a good approximation a linear function of the rate of profit, since, at full utilization of

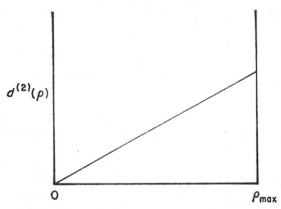

Fig. 21.   Dividend-generated demand for labor and rate of profit.

capital, profits depend linearly on rate of profit. This is shown in Fig. 21. The total demand for labor $d_0(\rho) = d^{(1)}(\rho) + d^{(2)}(\rho)$ must then be quantitatively as shown in Fig. 22; though which of cases (a), (b), and (c) subsist, our rough arguments do not tell us.

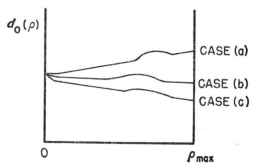

Fig. 22.   Total demand for labor against rate of profit.

The rate of profit must now satisfy the relation

$$-s_0(\rho) = d_0(\rho)$$

(unless $\rho = \rho_{\max}$). To see what this means, let us superimpose the curves of Fig. 19 and Fig. 22 in a single plot as shown in Figure 23.

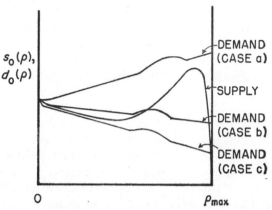

Fig. 23. Supply and demand for labor. Three hypothetical cases.

(In drawing this figure, we have made use of the fact, to be established in the next lecture, that $s_0(0) = d_0(0)$. We will show in the next lecture that in spite of this identity, $\rho = 0$ is an equilibrium point only if $(d/d\rho)(d_0(\rho) + s_0(\rho))|_{\rho=0} > 0$.)

Three cases arise, according to the slope of the curve of demand for labor. In case (a) the only solution for ρ is $\rho = 0$. This is the case in which an incorrigibly lazy populace refuses to work except to an amount so small that not all capital is utilized. In this case, ρ falls to zero and everything which is produced is turned back to the populace to be consumed. In case (b) people are "lazy" in this sense unless wages are sufficiently small. This means that, if wages rose from their equilibrium value, so many people would decide not to work, or decide to work only sporadically, that a labor shortage would develop. While this theoretical situation has often been taken as descriptive of the woes of management in establishing, say, rubber plantations among primitive populations not accustomed to regular industrial labor, it is hard to believe that it is descriptive of an economy like that of the United States. The United States, we must hence rather assume, falls into our case (c).[1] We are then led in-exorably by the present neoclassical theory to the unpalatable con-clusion that the supply of labor exceeds the demand up to that point where wages are so low that the labor force becomes enfeebled.

Why is this not the case? To escape from our dilemma we must note that the demand for labor rises with its price: If the demand for labor fell as its price rose, we would necessarily be either in case (a) or in case (b) (cf. Fig. 23!). How can this apparently paradoxical behavior be understood? A full answer must await our subsequent development of a more general equilibrium model incorporating the Keynesian features which the present model neglects. Nevertheless we may give part of the answer without difficulty. There is in our model no substitute for labor, so that even ordinary supply-demand considerations would tell us that demand should be insensitive to price; whether demand for labor increases or decreases with its price, the present theory does not suggest. This fact is often missed, in consequence of the fact that equilibrium analysis is normally "par-tial" rather than "general." Realizing this, we must next realize that such a situation—demand rising with or insensitive to price—is a ready-made temptation to monopoly (a similar remark may be made about any essential commodity, i.e., any commodity with price-inelastic demand). The role of trade unions is then quite clear. Unions have a product to sell for which the demand is much the same or even greater the higher the price. If, by one or another method, to be graphic, say by the hiring of thugs to murder anyone offering to work below a certain wage, the labor supply curve is made to fall to zero at that wage, then the aforesaid wage (and corresponding profit rate) will be the equilibrium.

The proper conclusion at this point is that the rate of profit ρ is not successfully determined by the Walrasian theories from con-sideration of production coefficients, utility functions, and so forth. What our analysis shows, in fact, is that the determination of the

---

[1] This implies that the demand for labor schedule slopes downward with increasing ρ, cf. Fig. 23. This empirical conclusion corresponds to the fact, to be emphasized below in our discussion of the propensity to consume, that the transfer of income from the low-income to the high-income range re-duces total consumption. Of course, as was pointed out in the previous lecture, the present Walrasian and the Keynesian models which lead to such conclusions are not entirely comparable.

rate of profit is not purely a question of economics at all, but is rather a social-political question involving, among other things, union-management relations, pressures and counterpressures, etc. Thus an initial skepticism about classical equilibrium analysis is justified. What this analysis aims to give us is a set of prices. But all the price-ratios are already determined by a small part of the theory, to wit by the competitive equality of profit rates. All that remains to be determined on the score of prices, is the rate of profit— but, as we have just seen, the Walrasian determination of this rate is questionable. (If taken seriously, it justifies the most pessimistic views on the wage of labor, to which views there has been much objection!) What are determined more successfully are the amounts of production—but this is more a humble matter of consumption habits at given prices than a highly recondite matter of consumption schedules at a variety of hypothetical prices.

It is interesting to compare our conclusions with the views expressed by Mr. Henry Hazlitt in a passage which we have already cited once:

> If I were put to it to name the most confused and fantastic chapter in the whole of the *General Theory*, the choice would be difficult. But I doubt that anyone could successfully challenge me if I named Chapter 19 on "Changes in Money-Wages."
>
> Its badness is after all not surprising. For it is here that Keynes sets out to challenge and deny what has become in the last two centuries the most strongly established principle in economics—to wit, that if the price of any commodity or service is kept too high, (i.e., above the point of equilibrium) some of that commodity or service will remain unsold. This is true of eggs, cheese, cotton, Cadillacs, or labor. When wage rates are too high there will be unemployment. Reducing the myriad wage rates to their respective equilibrium points may not in itself be a sufficient step to the restoration of full employment (for there are other possible disequilibriums to be considered), but it is an absolutely necessary step.
>
> This is the elementary and inescapable truth that Keynes, with an incredible display of sophistry, irrelevance, and complicated obfuscation, tries to refute.

Proof of the Existence of Walrasian Equilibrium

1. Case of a Single Labor Sector

In the previous lecture we derived a set of conditions necessarily satisfied at any price equilibrium. In the present lecture, we shall show that these conditions are also sufficient, and that they may all be satisfied simultaneously. In this way we shall establish the existence of a price equilibrium for the model introduced in Lecture 13, i.e., we shall show the existence of prices p_j such that the following conditions are satisfied

(a) $p_j \geq 0, j = 0, \cdots, N$; moreover, for some k, $p_k > 0$

(b) $\sum \sum a_i{}^{(k)}(\delta_{ij} - \pi_{ij})p_j = \max$ subject to

$$\sum \sum a_i{}^{(k)}\phi_{ij}p_j \leq \sum q_j{}^{(k)}p_j.$$

(See Lecture 13 for a more precise statement.)

(c) $u^{(\nu)}(s_j{}^{(\nu)}) = \max$ subject to

$$\sum_j p_j s_j{}^{(\nu)} \leq \sum_k \sum_j \sum_i a_i{}^{(k)}(\delta_{ij} - \pi_{ij})p_j h_{\nu k}.$$

(See Lecture 13 for a more precise statement.)

(d) $\sum_{i,k} a_i{}^{(k)}(\delta_{ij} - \pi_{ij}) - \sum_l s_j{}^{(l)} \geq 0$, for all j and

$$\sum_i \sum_k a_i{}^{(k)}(\delta_{ij} - \pi_{ij}) + \sum_k s_j{}^{(k)} = 0 \text{ for all } j \text{ for which } p_j > 0.$$

We recall that these conditions have the following briefly stated heuristic significance:

(a) the price of each commodity is nonnegative;

(b) each firm operates so as to maximize its profits subject to its capital limitations;

(c) each consumption unit optimizes its own utility function subject to its own budgetary constraints, and

(d) whatever is consumed must be produced, and overproduction cannot occur for a commodity whose price is positive.

Having established the existence of a set of prices, production schemes, and consumption schemes satisfying (a)–(d) above, we shall formulate a more general model, in which not one but several kinds of labor will be included, and show the existence of a general price equilibrium in that case also.

2. A Preliminary Existence Theorem

We shall proceed by setting up an *ansatz* giving prices, production, consumption, etc., as functions of a rate-of-profit parameter ρ, and then choosing ρ so as to obtain a price equilibrium. In determining the form of our *ansatz*, we will of course be guided by the analysis carried out in the preceding lecture. Let us begin by assuming prices $p_j(\rho)$ as solutions of the equation

$$(15.1) \qquad \sum_{j=0}^{n} (\delta_{ij} - \pi_{ij}) p_j(\rho) = \rho \sum_{j=0}^{n} \phi_{ij} p_j(\rho); \quad i = 1, \cdots, n$$

where ρ is a parameter; we know from Lecture 3 that a nonnegative (and nontrivial) solution of these equations exists for all values of ρ satisfying $0 \leq \rho \leq \rho_{\max}$ and that these prices satisfy condition (a), provided only that $\overset{\circ}{\Pi}$ is a connected matrix. The matrix $\overset{\circ}{\Pi}$ will be assumed to be connected throughout the present lecture. Note that this implies that the prices $p_j(\rho), j = 1, \cdots, n$, are strictly positive for all ρ, $0 \leq \rho \leq \rho_{\max}$. The price $p_0(\rho)$ is positive if and only if $\rho \neq \rho_{\max}$, while $p_0(\rho_{\max}) = 0$.

Next we choose the consumption levels $s_j^{(\nu)}$ so as to maximize each of the utility functions $u^{(\nu)}$ subject to the constraint

$$(15.2) \qquad \sum_j p_j(\rho) s_j^{(\nu)} = \Delta^{(\nu)}(\rho)$$

where, as in the preceding lecture, we put

$$(15.3) \qquad \Delta^{(\nu)}(\rho) = \rho \sum_{j,k} q_j^{(k)} p_j(\rho) h_{\nu k}.$$

As we saw in the preceding lecture, this condition determines the quantities $s_j{}^{(\nu)}$ as functions of the rate of profit ρ. We define the total consumption $s_i(\rho)$ of the ith commodity as

$$(15.4) \qquad s_i(\rho) = \sum_{k=1}^{f} s_i{}^{(\nu)}(\rho).$$

Finally, we determine the total production $a_i = \sum_{k=1}^{m} a_i{}^{(k)}$ of the ith commodity by the equation

$$(15.5) \qquad \sum_{i=1}^{n} a_i(\rho)(\delta_{ij} - \pi_{ij}) = -s_j(\rho), \quad j = 1, \cdots, n.$$

We put $q_j = \sum_{k=1}^{m} q_j{}^{(k)}$, $j = 1, \cdots, n$ for convenience.

The following lemma then reduces the problem of establishing the existence of a price equilibrium to a more tractable form.

LEMMA 15.1.   *Let the prices, consumption, and total production be determined from ρ as above. Then there will exist a determination of the production levels $a_j{}^{(k)}$ for the various firms satisfying*

$$(15.6) \qquad \sum_{k=1}^{m} a_j{}^{(k)} = a_j(\rho)$$

which, together with the prices and consumption schemes determined above, will satisfy the conditions (a)–(d), i.e., will define a price equilibrium, provided that

(1) either $\sum_{i,j} a_i(\rho)\phi_{ij}p_j(\rho) = \sum_{j} q_j p_j(\rho)$

or $\rho = 0$ *and* $\sum_{i,j} a_j(0)\phi_{ij}p_j(0) \leq \sum q_j p_j(0)$

and provided also that

(2) either $\sum_{i=1}^{m} a_i(\rho)\pi_{i0} = -s_0(\rho)$

or $\rho = \rho_{\max}$ *and* $\sum_{i=1}^{n} a_i(\rho)\pi_{i0} \leq -s_0(\rho).$

Proof: If the prices satisfy (15.1), they are nonnegative and not all zero so that (a) is satisfied. If in condition *(1)* we have $\rho > 0$, it is plain that we may divide the total production levels $a_j(\rho)$ into individual-firm contributions $a_j^{(k)}$ as in (15.5), in such a way that

$$\sum_{i,j} a_j^{(k)} \phi_{ji} p_i(\rho) = \sum_j q_j^{(k)} p_j(\rho)$$

for each k, $k = 1, \cdots, m$. Similarly, if in condition (1) we have $\rho = 0$, we may divide the total levels into individual-firm contributions $a_j^{(k)}$ in such a way that

$$\sum_{i,j} a_j^{(k)} \phi_{ji} p_i(0) \leq \sum_j q_j^{(k)} p_j(0)$$

for each k, $k = 1, \cdots, m$. Thus, if condition (1) is satisfied, we may in any case divide the total production levels $a_j(\rho)$ into individual-firm contributions in such a way that no firm's production plans will require the outlay of more capital than it possesses; moreover, unless $\rho = 0$, each firm will make use of the whole of its capital. As we have seen in the previous lecture, this, coupled with (15.1), is just the condition that each firm's profits be maximized. Thus (b) of our conditions, defining a price equilibrium, is satisfied. We have determined the consumption schemes $s_i^{(\nu)}(\rho)$ in such a way that (c) is automatically satisfied. Finally, since all the relations in (d) except the first, i.e., the $j = 0$ relations, are satisfied in consequence of the way the $a_i^{(k)}$ have been defined, and since condition (2) is the condition that the $j = 0$ relation be satisfied also (recall that $\rho = \rho_{\max}$ means that the price of labor is zero), condition (d) is also satisfied. Q.E.D.

In the trivial case $\rho_{\max} = 0$, we have $p_0 = 0$ and $\rho = 0$, so that $s_j^{(\nu)} = 0$ for $j \geq 1$ by (15.2) and (15.3); thus $s_j = 0$ for $j \geq 1$ by (15.4) and $a_j = 0$ by (15.5), so that the above lemma tells us that a price equilibrium exists and is to be determined by our formulas (15.1)–(15.5). We consequently may, and shall unless the contrary is explicitly indicated, assume in what follows that $\rho_{\max} > 0$.

Let us define the demand for labor $d_0(\rho)$ by

(15.7) $$d_0(\rho) \equiv \sum_i a_i(\rho) \pi_{i0}$$

and recall that we have already defined the supply of labor $-s_0(\rho)$ by (14.5). The following useful identity reduces the conditions of Lemma 1 to a more manageable form.

LEMMA 15.2.   Let $a_i(\rho)$, $p_i(\rho)$, $s_0(\rho)$, and $d_0(\rho)$ be as above.   Then

$$(-s_0(\rho) - d_0(\rho))p_0(\rho) = \rho \left(\sum_{j=1}^{n} a_i(\rho)\phi_{ij}p_i(\rho) - \sum_{j=1}^{n} q_j p_j(\rho) \right).$$

Proof: Consider the expression

(15.8) $$\sum_{j=0}^{n} \left(\sum_{i=1}^{n} a_i(\rho)(\delta_{ij} - \pi_{ij})p_j(\rho) - s_j(\rho)p_j(\rho) \right).$$

All terms in this expression, except possibly the $j = 0$ term, are zero by (15.5).   Therefore (15.8) is just

$$- \sum_{i=1}^{n} a_i(\rho)\pi_{i0}p_0(\rho) - s_0(\rho)p_0(\rho)$$

or, equivalently,

$$(-s_0(\rho) - d_0(\rho))p_0(\rho).$$

But (15.8) can be written (using (15.1), (15.2), and (15.3)) as

(15.9) $$\rho \sum_{j=0}^{n} \sum_{i=1}^{n} a_i(\rho)\phi_{ij}p_j(\rho) - \rho \sum_{j=0}^{n} q_j p_j(0).$$

Therefore

(15.10) $(-s_0(\rho) - d_0(\rho))p_0(\rho) = \rho \left[\sum\sum a_i(\rho)\phi_{ij}p_j(\rho) - \sum q_j p_j(\rho) \right].$

Q.E.D.

Putting together Lemmas 1 and 2 yields the following corollary:

COROLLARY 15.3.   *Let prices and total production be determined from ρ as above.   Then there will exist a determination of the production levels for the various firms satisfying (15.6), which, together with the prices and consumption schemes determined above, will define a price equilibrium, provided that*

either	(a) $0 < \rho < \rho_{\max}$	*and*	$d_0(\rho) + s_0(\rho) = 0$
or	(b) $\rho = \rho_{\max}$	*and*	$d_0(\rho) + s_0(\rho) \leq 0$
or	(c) $\rho = 0$	*and*	$\sum_{i,j} a_i(0)\phi_{ij}(0) \leq \sum_{j} q_j p_j(0).$

Lemma 2 also yields trivially the following corollary, which states a fact used in the construction of the diagrams of the previous lecture and also gives an equivalent alternate version of the condition under (c) of the preceding corollary.

COROLLARY 15.4.

(i) $d_0(0) + s_0(0) = 0$

(ii) $(d/d\rho)(d_0(\rho) + s_0(\rho))|_{\rho=0} = \sum_j q_j p_j(0) - \sum_{i,j} a_i(0)\phi_{ij}(0)p_j(0).$

Proof: Statement (i) follows from Lemma 2, and statement (ii) follows from statement (i) and Lemma 2. Q.E.D.

We have supposed that $\rho_{max} > 0$. Using what we have proved we may distinguish three possibilities for $s_0(\rho) + d_0(\rho)$. The first is that for some ρ, $0 < \rho \le \rho_{max}$, supply and demand for labor are equal, i.e., $s_0(\rho) + d_0(\rho) = 0$. The second is that for all ρ, $0 < \rho \le \rho_{max}$, $-s_0(\rho) < d_0(\rho)$. The third possibility is that for all ρ, $0 < \rho \le \rho_{max}$, it is the case that $-s_0(\rho) > d_0(\rho)$. Note that in any case, by Corollary 4, $s_0(0) + d_0(0) = 0$.

In the first case, condition (a) of Corollary 3 is satisfied. In the second case, since $s_0(\rho) + d_0(\rho)$ is positive for $\rho > 0$ and zero for $\rho = 0$, the derivative of $s_0(\rho) + d_0(\rho)$ is nonnegative at $\rho = 0$, so that by Corollary 4, condition (c) of Corollary 3 is satisfied. If $s_0(\rho) + d_0(\rho)$ is negative for $\rho > 0$, the condition (b) of Corollary 2 is satisfied. This establishes the existence of a price equilibrium in every case.

The following theorem summarizes the necessary conditions for equilibrium derived in the preceding lecture and the sufficient conditions derived in the present section.

THEOREM 15.5.   *Let* $\phi_0(\rho) = s_0(\rho) + d_0(\rho)$, *where* $s_0(\rho), d_0(\rho)$ *are defined as above. Then price equilibria correspond to those values* $0 < \rho < \rho_{max}$ *for which* $\phi_0(\rho) = 0$; *and also to the value* $\rho = \rho_{max}$ *if and only if* $(d/d\rho)[\phi_0(\rho)]_{\rho=0} \ge 0$; *and also to the value* $\rho = \rho_{max}$ *if and only if* $\phi_0(\rho_{max}) \le 0$. *At each such equilibrium the prices are unique; the total activity levels are also unique, and these totals may be divided among the firms in any way consistent with the requirement*

$$\sum_{i,j} a_j{}^{(k)} \pi_{ji} p_j(\rho) \le \sum_j q_j{}^{(k)} p_j(\rho), \quad k = 1, \cdots, m.$$

3. Price Equilibrium for a Nonhomogeneous Labor Force

We now extend our price-equilibrium model to include several labor sectors, considered as originating labor commodities $C_0, C_{-1}, \cdots, C_{-L}$.

If $\rho_{\max} = 0$, no wages can be paid; hence the distinction between labor sectors is entirely irrelevant, and we return to the model of the preceding section. Hence we may and shall assume without loss of generality that $\rho_{\max} > 0$.

In the present more general context, we shall reestablish results much like those of the two preceding lectures. We will find, in particular, that price equilibria exist whenever supply and demand for labor are simultaneously in balance in all of the labor sectors.

As we have seen in Lecture 3, prices may be determined by the basic relation (15.1) (the range of summation of j being extended from $-L$ to N) as functions of ρ and of the ratios θ_j ($j = 0, \cdots, L$) of the wages, where we normalize these ratios by demanding that $\sum_{j=0}^{L} \theta_j = 1$. Thus, letting $p_j(\rho, \theta)$ be the prices so determined, we can write

$$(15.11) \qquad \sum_{j=-L}^{n} (\delta_{ij} - \pi_{ij}) p_j(\rho, \theta) = \rho \sum_{j=-L}^{n} \phi_{ij} p_j(\rho, \theta).$$

We shall assume throughout the present section that each form of labor is required as input to the production of at least one commodity, and shall also assume that the $n \times n$ matrix $\mathring{\Pi}$, obtained by deleting all elements of π_{ij} but those with both i and j between 1 and n, is connected.

To construct a price equilibrium, we imitate the procedure of the preceding sections, as follows. The consumption levels $s_j^{(\nu)}$ are again chosen so as to maximize

$$(15.12) \qquad\qquad u^{(\nu)}(s_j)$$

over all s_j such that

$$(15.13) \qquad \sum_{j=-L}^{n} p_j(\rho, \theta) s_j = \rho \sum_{i,k} q_i^{(k)} p_i(\rho, \theta) h_{k\nu}.$$

This determines total consumption, defined by

$$(15.14) \qquad\qquad s_i(\rho, \theta) \equiv \sum_j s_i^{(\nu)}(\rho, \theta).$$

Total activity levels are then defined by the equations

$$(15.15) \qquad \sum_{i=1}^{n} a_i(\rho, \theta)(\delta_{ij} - \pi_{ij}) = s_j(\rho, \theta), \quad j = 1, \cdots, n,$$

and we define the demand for labor in the various sectors by

$$(15.16) \qquad d_{-j}(\rho, \theta) = \sum_{i=0}^{n} a_i(\rho, \theta) \pi_{i,-j}, \quad j = 0, \cdots, L.$$

The above formulae define individual-family consumption schemes, prices, and total production as functions of ρ and θ, but not the division of total production among the individual firms. It will be convenient in what follows to speak of those values of ρ and θ for which the total production levels a_j may be divided into the sum of individual-firm contributions $a_j{}^{(k)}$ to yield a set of individual-firm production levels, family consumption and labor schemes, and prices satisfying the conditions (a)–(d) defining a price equilibrium as *values ρ, θ corresponding to a price equilibrium*. This terminology will be employed in stating a number of the theorems and lemmas which are to follow. Put

$$\phi_{-j}(\rho, \theta) = d_{-j}(\rho, \theta) + s_{-j}(\rho, \theta).$$

We aim to obtain the following result.

THEOREM 15.6. A. *A price equilibrium will correspond to each of those and only those points $0 < \rho \le \rho_{\max}$, $\theta_0, \cdots, \theta_L$, for which $\phi_{-j}(\rho, \theta) \le 0$ for all $j = 0, \cdots, L$ with equality whenever $p_{-j}(\rho, \theta) \ne 0$; and also to those and only those points $\rho = 0$, $\theta_1, \cdots, \theta_n$ for which $\phi_{-j}(0, \theta)$ is nonnegative for $j = 0, \cdots, L$ and*

$$(15.17) \qquad d/d\rho \left[\sum_{j=0}^{L} p_{-j}(\rho, \theta)\phi_{-j}(\rho, \theta) \right]_{\rho=0} \ge 0.$$

B. *Furthermore, there always exists at least one equilibrium point.*

The remainder of this lecture will be devoted to proving the above theorem. The proof of part A follows the development in Section 2 of this lecture quite closely, but to prove part B we must employ some deeper topological theorems, since we cannot make use of the basically one-dimensional division into three collectively exhaustive cases $\phi > 0$, $\phi = 0$, $\phi < 0$ as in the last part of Section 2.

Since equation (15.11) is homogeneous in the prices p_j, it only determines these prices up to a scalar factor. In the arguments which are to follow, it is important to make this factor definite and convenient to choose it in an appropriate way. For this reason, we preface our proof by a lemma characterizing a manner of normalizing the solutions $p_j(\rho, \theta)$ of (15.11), to which normalization we shall adhere in the remainder of the present section.

LEMMA 15.7.   *The solution $p_j(\rho, \theta)$ of equations (15.11) may be made definite by imposing the additional requirement*

$$(15.18) \qquad \rho + \sum_{j=0}^{L} p_{-j}(\rho, \theta) \equiv \rho_{\max}.$$

The solutions determined in this way depend continuously on ρ and θ; moreover, they satisfy the condition

$$(15.19) \qquad p_j(\rho, \theta) > 0, \quad j = 1, \cdots, n.$$

Proof: The factors θ_j have been chosen to satisfy $\sum_{j=0}^{L} \theta_j = 1$. Thus, a solution of (15.11) will satisfy (15.18) if and only if $p_{-j}(\rho, \theta) = (\rho_{\max} - \rho)\theta_j$; hence what we must do is prove the continuity and positivity of the solutions $p_j(\rho, \theta)$ of the equation

$$(15.20) \quad \sum_{j=1}^{L} (\delta_{ij} - (1 + \rho)\pi_{ij})p_j(\rho, \theta) = (1 + \rho)(\rho_{\max} - \rho) \sum_{j=0}^{L} \pi_{i,-j}\theta_j;$$
$$i = 1, \cdots, n.$$

If we let $\mathbf{v}(\rho, \theta)$ be the vector whose ith component is

$$(1 + \rho) \sum_{j=0}^{L} \pi_{i,-j}\theta_j$$

and let $\mathbf{p}_1(\rho, \theta)$ be the vector of length n whose components are $p_j(\rho, \theta), j = 1, \cdots, n$, we may write the solution of (15.20) in vectorial form as

$$(15.21) \qquad \mathbf{p}_1(\rho, \theta) = (\rho_{\max} - \rho)(I - (1 + \rho)\mathring{\Pi})^{-1}\mathbf{v}(\rho, \theta).$$

This formula makes it evident that the proof of the present lemma will result immediately once we establish the following lemma.

LEMMA 15.8.   *Let A be a connected positive matrix with $\mathrm{dom}\,(A) < 1$, and let α be determined by the equation $\mathrm{dom}\,((1 + \alpha)A) = 1$, i.e., $\alpha = (\mathrm{dom}\,(A))^{-1} - 1$. Then the matrix*

$$(15.22) \qquad (\alpha - \rho)(1 - (1 + \rho)A)^{-1} = J(\rho)$$

is continuous and strictly positive in the whole closed interval $0 \leq \rho \leq \alpha$.

Proof: The correctness of our statement in the interval $0 \leq \rho < \alpha$ follows at once from Lemmas 3.3, 3.5, and 3.6. Thus we have only to show that the matrix (15.22) has a limit as ρ approaches α from below, and that this limiting matrix is positive.

Let $\mathbf{v}$ be the dominant eigenvector of A, so that $(1 + \alpha)A\mathbf{v} = \mathbf{v}$. Then

$$(15.23) \quad (\alpha - \rho)(I - (1 + \rho)A)^{-1}\mathbf{v} = \{(\alpha + \rho)/1 - [(1 + \rho)/(1 + \alpha)]\}\mathbf{v}$$
$$= (1 + \alpha)\mathbf{v},$$

so that $J(\rho)\mathbf{v}$ is bounded. Since every component of $\mathbf{v}$ is positive, and since all the entries of $J(\rho)$ are positive for $\rho < \alpha$, it follows at once that $J(\rho)$ remains bounded as $\rho \to \alpha$. Thus we may extract a convergent subsequence from the family of matrices $J(\rho)$; i.e., we may find a sequence $\rho_n \to \alpha$ such that the sequence of matrices has a limit: $\lim_{n \to \infty} J(\rho_n) = J$. Since the limit of a sequence of non-negative matrices is nonnegative, it follows from (15.23) that J is nonnegative and $J\mathbf{v} = (1 + \alpha)\mathbf{v}$.

Since $(I - (1 + \rho)A)J(\rho) = (\alpha - \rho)$, it follows on letting ρ approach α that $(1 + \alpha)AJ = J$; thus every column of the matrix J must be proportional to the column vector $\mathbf{v}$; similarly, we may show that every row of the matrix J must be proportional to the uniquely defined adjoint vector $\mathbf{u}'$ which satisfies $\mathbf{u}(1 + \alpha)A = \mathbf{u}'$. Hence the elements J_{ik} of J must have the form $J_{ik} = cv_iu_k$. Since $(1 + \alpha)J\mathbf{v} = (1 + \alpha)\mathbf{v}$, we must have $c\mathbf{u}'\mathbf{v} = 1 + \alpha$, so that $c = (\mathbf{u}'\mathbf{v})^{-1}(1 + \alpha)$ is positive, and thus J is positive and uniquely defined.

Let ρ'_n be any other sequence of numbers approaching α from below for which $\lim_{n \to \infty} J(\rho'_n) = J'$ exists. Then, by the argument of the preceding paragraph, we must have $J' = J$. This shows that $\lim_{\rho \to \alpha} J(\rho) = J$ exists, establishing the continuity and positivity of $J(\rho)$ in the closed interval $0 \leq \rho \leq \alpha$, and completing the proof of the present lemma and of Lemma 7. Q.E.D.

Next we give a lemma generalizing the key Lemma 2 of the preceding section.

LEMMA 15.9. *Let $\phi_{-j}(\rho, \theta) = -d_{-j}(\rho, \theta) - s_{-j}(\rho, \theta), j = 0, \cdots, L$ as above, and put*

$$(15.24) \quad \phi_{-L-1}(\rho, \theta) = \sum_j q_j p_j(\rho, \theta) - \sum_{i,j} a_i(\rho, \theta)\pi_{ij}p_j(\rho, \theta),$$

where $q_j = \Sigma q_j{}^{(k)}$.   *Moreover, put*

(15.25) $\theta^*{}_j = [1 - (\rho/\rho_{\max})]\theta_j$, $i = 0, \cdots, L$

and

(15.26) $\theta^*{}_{L+1} = \rho/\rho_{\max}$.

Then

(15.27) $\displaystyle\sum_{j=0}^{L+1} \phi_{-j}(\rho, \theta)\theta^*{}_j = 0.$

Moreover,

(15.28) $\theta^*{}_j{}' \geq 0$ *and* $\displaystyle\sum_{j=0}^{L+1} \theta^*{}_j = 1.$

Proof: By (15.11), (15.13), (15.14), and (15.15) we have

$$(15.29) \quad \rho \left[\sum_{i,j} a_i(\rho, \theta)\phi_{ij}p_j(\rho, \theta) - \sum q_j p_j(\rho, \theta) \right]$$

$$= \sum_{i,j} a_i(\rho, \theta)(\delta_{ij} - \pi_{ij})p_j(\rho, \theta) - \sum_j s_j(\rho, \theta)p_j(\rho, \theta)$$

$$= \sum_{j=1}^{n} s_j(\rho, \theta)p_j(\rho, \theta) - \sum_i \sum_{j=-L}^{0} a_i(\rho, \theta)\pi_{ij}p_j(\rho, \theta)$$

$$- \sum_{j=1}^{n} s_j(\rho, \theta)p_j(\rho, \theta) - \sum_{j=-L}^{0} s_j(\rho, \theta)p_j(\rho, \theta)$$

$$= \sum_{j=0}^{L} (-s_{-j}(\rho, \theta) - d_{-j}(\rho, \theta))p_j(\rho, \theta)$$

$$= \sum_{j=0}^{L} \phi_{-j}(\rho, \theta)p_{-j}(\rho, \theta).$$

Our lemma follows immediately on using the definitions (15.25) and (15.26). Q.E.D.

We may now conveniently make use of a result from elementary topology.

To state this result, we have first to make a number of simple geometric definitions.

DEFINITION.   *The k-dimensional simplex is the subset σ of Euclidean k + 1-dimensional space defined by the formula*

$$\sigma = \left\{ \mathbf{x} \mid \mathbf{x} \geq 0, \ \sum_{i=1}^{k+1} x_i = 1 \right\}.$$

DEFINITION.   *The* vertices *of the k-dimensional simplex* σ *are the* $k + 1$ *points* $\mathbf{p}^{(j)}$ *defined by*

(15.30) $\mathbf{p}_i^{(j)} = \delta_{ji}, \quad i,j = 1, \cdots, k + 1.$

DEFINITION.   *Let* $\mathbf{p}^{(j_1)}, \cdots, \mathbf{p}^{(j_r)}$ *be a set of r distinct vertices of the simplex* σ. *Then the* side *determined by these vertices is the subset* σ_0 *of* σ *defined by the formula*

(15.31) $\sigma_0 = \{ \mathbf{x} \in \sigma \mid x_j = 0 \quad \text{unless} \quad j = j_1 \quad \text{or}$
$\qquad\qquad\qquad\qquad\qquad\qquad j = j_2 \quad \text{or} \quad j = j_r \}.$

In terms of these definitions we may state the following useful topological theorem.

THEOREM 15.10.   *Suppose an* $n - 1$*-dimensional simplex is covered by n closed sets* $\Sigma_1, \cdots, \Sigma_n$, *in such a way that for each r the* $r - 1$*-dimensional side determined by the vertices* $p_{i_1}, \cdots, p_{i_r}$ *is contained in the union of the m sets* $\Sigma_{i_1}, \cdots, \Sigma_{i_r}$. *Then the sets* Σ *have a common point, i.e.,*

$$\Sigma_1 \cap \Sigma_2 \cap \cdots \cap \Sigma_n \neq \phi.$$

(For an elementary proof, see L. Graves, *Theory of Functions of Real Variables* (1946 Edn., p. 148).)

We can use this theorem to establish the following.

LEMMA 15.11.   *Let* σ *be the simplex defined by*

$$\sigma = \left\{ x \ \middle| \ \sum_{j=1}^{k} x_j = 1; \ \ x_i \geq 0 \right\}.$$

Let $f_j(x_1, \cdots, x_k), j = 1, \cdots, k$ *be continuous functions defined on* σ *such that*

$$\sum_{i=1}^{k} x_j f_j(x_1, \cdots, x_n) = 0, \quad x \in \sigma.$$

Then there is a point $x_1^0, \cdots, x_n^0$ *such that for every j*

$$f_j(x_1^0, \cdots, x_n^0) \geq 0,$$

with equality wherever $x_j^0 \neq 0$.

Proof: For each $j = 1, \cdots, k$ define the closed set Σ_j by writing

(15.32) $$\Sigma_j = \{\mathbf{x} \mid f_j(\mathbf{x}) \geq 0\}.$$

We first show that the $r - 1$-dimensional side σ' of σ with vertices $p_{i_1}, \cdots, p_{i_r}$ is contained in the union of the sets $\Sigma_{i_1}, \cdots, \Sigma_{i_r}$. After permuting the variables x, we may assume without loss of generality that $i_1, \cdots, i_r = 1 \cdots r$. Our side is then the subset of (15.32) defined by the equations

$$x_{r+1} = x_{r+2} = \cdots = x_k = 0$$

so that

$$\sum_{j=1}^{k} x_j f_j(x) = 0$$

everywhere along the side σ'. Therefore for each $\mathbf{x}$ in σ', at least one function f_j must be nonnegative. Thus the side σ' is contained in $\Sigma_1 \cup \cdots \cup \Sigma_r$.

By Theorem 12, then, the intersection of all the sets Σ_j is not void. Any point in the intersection is a point $(x_1^0, \cdots, x_n^0)$ satisfying the conditions of the present lemma. Q.E.D.

We may use Lemma 9 and Theorem 10 to derive the following lemma, which practically contains the main Theorem 6 which we are in the course of proving.

LEMMA 15.12. *There exists a point* ρ, θ *such that*

(15.33) $$\phi_{-j}(\rho, \theta) \geq 0, \quad j = 0, \cdots, L + 1.$$

At this point we have $\phi_{-j}(\rho, \theta) = 0$ *if* $j \neq L + 1$ *and* $p_{-j}(\rho, \theta) \neq 0$, *while* $\phi_{-L-1}(\rho, \theta) = 0$ *if* $\rho \neq 0$.

Proof: Let θ^*_i, $i = 0, \cdots, L + 1$ be the quantities defined in the statement of Lemma 9. Since ρ may be varied arbitrarily between 0 and $\rho_{\max}$, and since the quantities θ_j may be varied arbitrarily subject only to the restrictions $\theta_j \geq 0$ and $\sum_{j=0}^{L} \theta_j = 1$, it is plain that by choosing ρ and θ, the quantities θ^*_j may be varied arbitrarily subject only to the restrictions (15.28). It is clear from (15.25) and (15.26) that as long as $\theta^*_{L+1} \neq 1$, i.e., as long as $\rho \neq \rho_{\max}$, we may write ρ and θ as continuous functions of θ^*:

(15.34) $$\rho = \rho(\theta)^*, \quad \theta = \theta(\theta^*).$$

Thus the functions $\phi_{-j}(\rho(\theta^*), \theta(\theta^*))$ depend continuously on θ^* except at the vertex $\theta^*_{L+1} = 1$. However, since (cf. Lemma 15.7) $p_{-j}(\rho, \theta) = \theta^*_j$ even in the vicinity of $\rho = \rho_{\max}$, it follows from (15.11), (15.12)–(15.14), (15.15), (15.16) and the formula following (15.16), and (15.24)–(15.26) that $\phi_{-j}(\rho(\theta^*), \theta(\theta^*))$ depends continuously on θ^* even near $\theta^*_{L+1} = 1$. Thus, by Lemma 11, there exists a ρ and θ such that $\phi_{-j}(\rho, \theta) \geq 0, j = 0, \cdots, L+1$, with equality if $\theta^*_j \neq 0$.

Using (15.25) and (15.26), the present lemma follows at once. Q.E.D.

LEMMA 15.13.   *A point $\rho = 0$ satisfies*

$$(15.35) \qquad\qquad \phi_{-L-1}(0, \theta) \geq 0$$

if and only if

$$(15.36) \qquad (d/d\rho) \sum_{j=0}^{L} \phi_{-j}(\rho, \theta)p_{-j}(\rho, \theta)\big|_{\rho=0} \leq 0.$$

Proof: Use the identity

$$(15.37) \qquad \sum_{j=0}^{L} \phi_{-j}(\rho, \theta)p_{-j}(\rho, \theta) + \phi_{-L-1}(\rho, \theta) = 0$$

given by Lemma 9; differentiate and put $\rho = 0$.   Q.E.D.

Now we shall prove part A of Theorem 6.

Proof of Part A of Theorem 6. Suppose first that $\rho > 0$. Let ρ, θ be a rate of profit and a set of wage ratios such that $\phi_{-j}(\rho, \theta) \geq 0$, $0 \leq j \leq L+1$ with equality whenever $\theta_j \neq 0$. It is clear from Lemma 10 that not all the prices $p_j(\rho, \theta)$ are zero; thus condition (a) is satisfied. Since the consumption schemes $s_j^{(\nu)}(\rho, \theta)$ are determined by (15.12)–(15.13), they satisfy condition (c). Since the total activity levels $a_i(\rho, \theta)$ are defined by (15.15) and since by hypothesis we have $\phi_{-j}(\rho, \theta) \geq 0$ with equality whenever $p_{-j}(\rho, \theta) \neq 0$, we see that condition (d) is also satisfied. It only remains to show that condition (b) is satisfied; since with prices giving a uniform positive rate of profit a firm makes maximum profits if and only if it employs all its capital it is sufficient to show that the total activity levels $a_i(\rho, \theta)$ can be divided into the sum of individual-firm contributions $a_i^{(k)}$ in such a way that

(15.38) $$\sum_k a_i{}^{(k)} = a_i(\rho, \theta),$$

and

(15.39) $$\sum_{k,i,j} a_i{}^{(k)}\phi_{ij}p_j(\rho, \theta) = \sum q_j{}^{(k)}p_j(\rho, \theta).$$

It is plain that (15.38) and (15.39) can be satisfied simultaneously if and only if

(15.40) $$\sum_{i,j} a_i(\rho, \theta)\phi_{ij}p_j(\rho, \theta) = \sum q_j p_j(\rho, \theta),$$

where $q_j = \sum_k q_j{}^{(k)}$. Formula (15.24) shows that (15.40) holds, since, by hypothesis, $\phi_{-j}(\rho, \theta) = 0$ unless $p_{-j}(\rho, \theta) = 0$.

Conversely, suppose that we have a price equilibrium corresponding to the rate of profit $\rho > 0$ and the wage ratios θ. We know that condition (b) implies that the equilibrium prices are (proportional to) $p_j(\rho, \theta)$, $j = -L, \cdots, n$. Since we have seen that all the prices $p_j(\rho, \theta)$, $j - 1, \cdots, n$ are then strictly positive, it follows from condition (d) that the total activity levels $a_i = \sum_k a_i{}^{(k)}$, $i = 1, \cdots, n$ must satisfy (15.15). Moreover, by condition (b), each firm must employ its total capital; thus, the dividend income of the νth family is necessarily given by

(15.41) $$\rho \sum_{i,k} q_i{}^{(k)}p_i h_{\nu k},$$

which by condition (c) implies that the family's labor-consumption scheme must satisfy (15.12)–(15.13). Next we observe that condition (d) implies that at equilibrium we have $\phi_{-j}(\rho, \theta) \geq 0$, with equality if $p_{-j}(\rho, \theta) \neq 0$. Thus part Λ of Theorem 6 is proved in case $\rho > 0$.

If $\rho = 0$, we may argue in almost the same way, making use however of the information given by Lemma 13. We have only to amend the sixth sentence of the first paragraph of the present proof to state that if $\rho = 0$, a firm makes no profit in any case, so that condition (e) degenerates by the further argument of the present proof to the condition

(15.42) $$\sum_{i,j} a_i(0, \theta)\phi_{ij}p_j(\rho, \theta) \leq \sum q_j p_j(0, \theta),$$

i.e., to the condition $\phi_{-L-1}(0, \theta) \geq 0$. The converse argument in case $\rho = 0$ is again much like the converse argument in case $\rho > 0$;

we have only to amend the preceding paragraph with the remark that if profits are all zero, dividend income for each family is zero also. Thus part A of Theorem 6 is fully proved.

Proof of Part B *of Theorem* 6: This follows at once from Part A and from Lemmas 12 and 13. Q.E.D.

4. A Summary Remark

The analysis presented in the present lecture shows the Walrasian theory to be quite satisfactory from the purely mathematical point of view. On the other hand, we have seen above that its mathematical formulations are based upon unrealistically drastic assumptions, which artificially assume away all the Keynesian phenomena studied in Lectures 5–12. In order to incorporate the neoclassical ideas of the three preceding lectures into a less hopelessly unrealistic model, it is necessary for us to construct a generalized equilibrium model combining neoclassical and Keynesian features. We now turn to this task.

An Equilibrium Model Combining
Neoclassical and Keynesian Features

1. Savings and the Dynamical Background of the Walras Model

In the present lecture we wish to bring the Keynesian equilibrium theory of Lecture 8 and the Walrasian price-equilibrium theory of the preceding lectures to mutual confrontation, thereby casting some light on the traditional dispute between Keynesians and neoclassicists, which dispute normally if unfortunately involves considerable discussion at cross-purposes. Our method will be to construct a model which is a common generalization of the two equilibrium models that are to be compared; we will then see which aspects of the generalization are reflected in each of the particular models, and which neglected.

A crucial and entirely questionable assumption of the Walrasian equilibrium theory presented in the preceding lectures is the assumption introduced in the text immediately preceding and following formula (13.3). This assumption states that for each $\mathbf{x}^{(1)}$ and for each ν there exists an $\mathbf{x}^{(2)}$ for which

$$(16.1) \qquad \mathbf{x}^{(2)} \geq \mathbf{x}^{(1)} \quad \text{and} \quad \mathbf{u}_\nu(\mathbf{x}^{(2)}) > \mathbf{u}_\nu(\mathbf{x}^{(1)}).$$

Heuristically, this signifies that each family can always increase its satisfaction by *consuming* more of some commodity. As we saw in Lecture 14, this implies that if $u_\nu(\mathbf{x})$ is maximized over all labor-consumption schedules $\mathbf{x}$ lying in a region $\mathbf{x} \cdot \mathbf{p} \leq c$, the maximizing point will always lie on the boundary $\mathbf{x} \cdot \mathbf{p} = c$. Thus, we have assumed that to maximize its utility function, a family will always consume the whole of its (wage and dividend) income. In Keynesian terms, we have assumed a propensity to save of zero. We must then recognize that such an assumption is an impossibly bad description of any actual economy, and ask how the model of Walrasian equilibrium can be adjusted to include the phenomenon of saving.

Let us first consider the situation qualitatively and generally. An equilibrium model is, almost by definition, a model descriptive of a situation which may be taken to persist unchanged in time. Thus, to include saving in such an equilibrium model is bound to be problematical, since saving signifies an addition to productive stocks, and thus implies a change in the presumably invariant situation which an equilibrium theory is to describe. A dual question may be raised. Our model assigns to each consumption unit an income, out of which a certain optimal consumption is supported. We have assumed in assuming (16.1) that this optimal consumption includes the whole of income; this assumption is now to be removed. Consumption can then be less than income (leading to savings). Why can it not be more than income (leading to dissavings)? In our model, as presented in Lectures 13–14, we have simply assumed that consumption was bounded by current income; thus in our model, no consumption unit *could* draw on savings, and, because of (16.1), no consumption unit *would* add to savings. Thus, the model of Lectures 13–14 is seen to assign to each family a fixed and invariant mass of possessions, thereby begging the question of savings and investment which the Keynesian analysis in earlier lectures showed to be central. To improve this questionable procedure, we must have reference to the dynamic background of our equilibrium model.

Equilibrium models may be thought of as being derived from corresponding dynamic models by writing those equations which describe the fixed points (if any) of the dynamic motion. More generally, in dynamical situations in which a relatively rapid motion is coupled to a relatively slow motion (called in mechanics the "adiabatic case") we may build up a quasi-equilibrium model in which the slower motion is separated out as a constant external condition or constraint with which the rapid motion comes into equilibrium. What then are the principal dynamical aspects of the over-all economic motion which we must seek to build into our model? The elements of an answer to this question may be drawn from the cycle-theory of Lectures 5–12.

1. When total inventories of any commodity become excessive, production of that commodity will be cut back, resources being transferred to the production of alternate commodities, or even held idle if the rate of value-depreciation of new product is too large compared to the rate at which the product can be sold (cf. Lectures 11–12). Conversely, if the total inventory of any commodity is deficient, production of the commodity can be advanced rapidly.

2. In periods of recession, as described under *1*, the continuation of personal consumption at a high rate brings about a general reduction of inventories. Another factor reducing inventories in a period of recession is the stability, even after sales and production have fallen, of a variety of overhead costs, both of capital and of labor, and of depreciation charges attaching both to producers' equipment and to finished goods. These processes of consumption and decay are capable of reducing inventories by several billion dollars in the course of half a year.

3. The cyclical economic movement also involves shifts in the relative economic position of families, as systematic individual-family differences between expenditure and income (as well as a host of other individual circumstances) cause certain families to rise and others to fall in economic position, leading to a secular concentration or diffusion of wealth. This process, however, is slower than the motions of over-all inventory equilibration involved in the business cycle as described under *1* and *2* above. Assuming that the cyclical movement affects the total wealth of all families and firms equally should therefore not distort our view of the over-all tendencies of equilibration.

To a first approximation, then, we shall take the business cycle to impose equal gains or losses on all families, and hence take equilibrium to involve:

(a) zero rates of addition to or subtraction from aggregate inventories;

(b) fixed proportions between the wealth of the various firms and families.

To embed these heuristic conclusions in a more rigorous framework, we must construct an equilibrium model which in its initial formulation allows saving and dissaving. The condition saving = dissaving = 0 will then enter as a *condition of equilibrium*, not as an *implicit assumption of the model*. Moreover, it will be impossible to prescribe family and firm possessions arbitrarily: these holdings will themselves come into equilibrium (through the process of saving and dissaving). This fact, that besides an equilibrium price-level there exists an equilibrium inventory-level, was, as we recall, a notable property of the Keynesian cycle models studied earlier, bound to play an important role in permitting the construction of a model combining Keynesian and neoclassical features.

It will be nearly evident from the formulation of the model which is to follow that it must lead to results closely related to the results obtained from the more restricted model of the preceding chapters; our view of the foundations upon which these results rest will be considerably changed, however.

2. A Modified Equilibrium Model Described

The model which is now to be established will have many features in common with the model of Walras-Arrow-Debreu type introduced in Section 1 of Lecture 13; some of the key equations, however, will be revised. Again we will have m "firms"; a single homogeneous labor force producing the labor-commodity C_0; an input-output matrix π_{ij} and a fixed capital matrix ϕ_{ij}. We suppose as previously that $\phi_{jo} = 0$. We will again have f consumption units or families; each family will own a fixed share $h_{\nu k}$ of the kth firm. We now assume in addition that each firm has a fixed share ψ_k of the total value of all capital inventory. We have, of course, $\sum_{\nu} h_{\nu k} \equiv 1$, $\sum_k \psi_k \equiv 1$. The coefficients $\sum_{k=1}^{m} h_{\nu k} \psi_k = \psi_\nu$ give the νth family's share of the total value of capital inventory, as computed from its share in the ownership of each firm. The fact that we take the coefficients ψ as fixed reflects our heuristic assumption that gains or losses of property in booms and recessions are spread over firms and families in proportion to their wealth.

Each firm will have an inventory of $q_i^{(k)}$ units of the commodity C_i; now, however, we take these parameters not as fixed constants describing the model, but as quantities which will come into an equilibrium which our model is to describe. As in our previous model, we wish to characterize the system of preferences of the νth family by a consumption function u_ν. This function will, in the first place, depend, as previously, upon numbers $s_0, \cdots, s_n$ describing an amount of labor expended and a bill of commodities consumed. Since the possessions of a given family and firm are no longer to be taken invariant, however, we shall now take these functions to depend as well on the numbers

$$(16.2) \qquad q_{l\nu} = \sum_k h_{\nu k} q_l^{(k)}$$

which give the νth family's possessions as computed from its ownership share in each firm and the possessions of the firm. Since the decisions to consume or not to consume made by the owner of certain possessions depend upon the economic value of these possessions, our utility function must also depend on the price levels $p_0, \cdots, p_n$. Thus, finally, we will have, for each family, a utility function

$$(16.3) \qquad u_\nu(s_0, \cdots, s_n; \ q_1, \cdots, q_n; \ p_0, \cdots, p_n)$$

of the indicated variables. As previously, we take $s_0 \leq 0, s_1, \cdots,$ $s_n \geq 0$, and in addition $q_1, \cdots, q_n \geq 0, p_0, \cdots, p_n \geq 0$. We abandon the assumption (16.1).

A price equilibrium is now to be defined as a set of prices $p_0, \cdots, p_n$, production figures $u_1^{(k)}, \cdots, u_n^{(k)}$ for the kth firm, consumption figures $s_0^{(\nu)}, \cdots, s_n^{(\nu)}$ for the νth family, and inventory levels $q_j^{(k)}$ for the kth firm, satisfying the following conditions:

Condition (a). The prices are all nonnegative and at least one is different from zero.

Condition (b). For each firm $k = 1, \cdots, m$ the profit

$$(16.4) \qquad \sum_{i=1}^{n} \sum_{j=0}^{n} a_i^{(k)}(\delta_{ij} - \pi_{ij})p_j$$

is a maximum over all sets $\tilde{a}_i$ which satisfy

$$(16.5) \qquad \sum_{i=1}^{n} \sum_{j=0}^{n} \tilde{a}_i \phi_{ij} p_i \leq \sum_{j=1}^{n} q_j^{(k)} p_j.$$

(See (13.5)–(13.6) and *ff.* for a discussion of the heuristic significance of this condition.)

Condition (c). For each consumer unit $\nu = 1, \cdots, f$, the number

$$(16.6) \qquad u_\nu(s_0^{(\nu)}, \cdots, s_n^{(\nu)}; \ q_{1\nu}, \cdots, q_{n\nu}; \ p_0, \cdots, p_n)$$

is a maximum over all $\tilde{s}_0, \cdots, \tilde{s}_n$ which satisfy

$$(16.7) \quad -\sum_{j=0}^{n} \tilde{s}_j p_j + \sum_{j=0}^{n} \sum_{i=1}^{n} \sum_{k=1}^{n} a_i^{(k)}(\delta_{ij} - \pi_{ij})p_j h_{\nu k} \geq -\sum_{k=1}^{n} q_{k\nu} p_k;$$

here, $q_{k\nu}$ is defined by (16.2).

This condition states that, whatever the equilibrium prices may be, each family will consume that list of commodities, depending upon its possessions, whose subjective value is the greatest among all lists of commodities that can be consumed subject to the budgetary condition (16.7) that wage income + dividend income + value of saleable possessions exceeds expenditure.

Condition (d).   Total production must exactly balance total consumption, i.e.,

$$(16.8) \quad \sum_{k=1}^{m} \sum_{i=1}^{n} a_i{}^{(k)}(\delta_{ij} - \pi_{ij}) - \sum_{\nu=1}^{f} s_j{}^{(\nu)} = 0, \quad j = 0, \cdots, n.$$

This condition simultaneously forbids the accumulation of inventories, and requires that supply and demand of labor be in balance.

Condition (e).   No item of capital can be in short supply, i.e.,

$$(16.9) \quad \sum_{k=1}^{m} \sum_{i=1}^{n} a_i{}^{(k)}\phi_{ij} \leq \sum_{k=1}^{m} q_j{}^{(k)}, \quad j = 1, \cdots, n.$$

Condition (f).   Firms' relative position must remain unchanged, i.e.,

$$(16.10) \quad \psi_k \left\{ \sum_{k=1}^{m} \sum_{j=1}^{n} q_j{}^{(k)}p_j \right\} = \sum_{j=1}^{n} q_j{}^{(k)}p_j.$$

Condition (f) defines the class of equilibria attainable by the rapid business-cycle motions, as explained in Section 1 above; it is a "constraint" in terms of the analogy with mechanics drawn in Section 1.

Our model differs from the model introduced in Lecture 13

(a) in its formulation of Condition (c);

(b) in including the sharp Condition (e) on production, which we (rather harmlessly) omitted from our model in its previous presentation, so as not to introduce too many complications into an initial formulation;

(c) in replacing the earlier condition that each firm's and each family's mass of possessions remain invariant by the condition (16.10) that each firm's (and hence each family's) holdings *relative* to those of other firms (resp. families) remain invariant.

We may remark that Condition (d) makes what would otherwise be a model of continual growth into an equilibrium model.   Such an assumption might appear hopelessly pessimistic did not the empirical experience of recessions indicate that an economy can fall behind its technological possibilities of growth, and did not the theoretical analysis which we have carried out in Lectures 7–12 indicate clearly that an economic mechanism exists assuring that the unbounded growth of inventories will meet with obstacles.

We shall proceed in the first sections of the present lecture to analyze the consequences of Condition (d) in the strict form it has here been given, i.e., the consequences of an assumption that we have a strict equilibrium with a zero rate of stock increase. In the final section of the present lecture, we will relax this assumption to admit an amount of investment which we still take to be restricted for the reasons just stated, and analyze the consequences of this modification of our model.

3. Preliminary Analysis of the Modified Equilibrium Model

An analysis equivalent in all details to that presented in the final part of Lecture 13 shows that Condition (b) implies that the prices p_j are determined in terms of a nonnegative rate of profit parameter ρ through the equation

$$(16.11) \qquad p_i - \sum_{j=0}^{n} \pi_{ij} p_j = \rho \sum_{j=0}^{n} \phi_{ij} p_j.$$

Using the arguments of Lecture 13, we may also show just as in that lecture that Condition (b) is equivalent to the conjunction of this equation and the condition that if $\rho > 0$ each firm uses the whole of its capital in production, i.e., that

$$(16.12) \qquad \sum_{i=0}^{n} \sum_{j=1}^{n} a_j^{(k)} \phi_{ji} p_i = \sum_{i=1}^{n} q_i^{(k)} p_i,$$

the right side merely dominating the left if $\rho = 0$. As we saw in Lecture 13, (16.11) determines a set of prices all of which are positive unless $\rho = \rho_{\max}$, and all of which except p_0 are positive even if $\rho = \rho_{\max}$.

As in Lecture 14 we shall assume that the values $s_0^{(\nu)}, \cdots, s_n^{(\nu)}$ maximizing (16.6) subject to the conditions

$$(16.13) \qquad \sum_{j=0}^{n} s_j p_j \leq (1 + \rho) \sum_{k=1}^{n} q_{k\nu} p_k$$

are uniquely determined. Thus we may write the maximizing values as $s_j^{(\nu)}(q_{1\nu}, \cdots, q_{n\nu};\ p_0, \cdots, p_n)$.

We may emphasize here a point valid generally. The utility function (16.6) and the derived functions $s_j^{(\nu)}$ describe the consumption and spending-saving preferences of a given family, in dependence on savings and prices. These preferences are taken to be individually formed, and without dependence on the position of equilibrium which they will collectively imply. In any given situation a family will have certain spending and saving preferences; of the fact that the total pattern of savings preferences may in certain economic circumstances bring about inventory accumulations leading to recessions or other unwanted economic effects, we take the family to be innocent. Like players in the majority game analyzed in Lecture 5, the families make individual decisions based upon individual circumstances leading to a collective result; the result may be different from that desired, in any sense but the narrow sense in which one "desires" that adjustment to an unsatisfactory external reality which one actually makes, by any family.

Proceeding as in Lecture 14, we may next define total consumption of the jth commodity by

$$(16.14) \qquad s_j = s_j(q_{11}, \cdots, q_{nf};\ \rho)$$

$$= \sum_{\nu=1}^{f} s_j^{(\nu)}(q_{1j}, \cdots, q_{nj};\ p_0(\rho), \cdots, p_n(\rho)).$$

The last n equations of Condition (d) are then collectively equivalent to the restriction

$$(16.15) \qquad \sum_i a_i(\delta_{ij} - \pi_{ij}) = s_j(q_{11}, \cdots, q_{nf};\ \rho);$$

here, a_i is total production of the ith commodity, determined as previously by the equation

$$(16.16) \qquad \sum_{k=1}^{m} a_i^{(k)} = a_i.$$

Equations (16.15) may be solved for a_i, and determine a_i as functions of $q_{11}, \cdots, q_{nf}$ and ρ. Arguing as in Lectures 14 and 15, we may next assert that the separate conditions (16.12) upon the individual firms can be satisfied by a suitable division of total production into individual firm contributions if and only if total production and inventory satisfy the relationship corresponding to (16.12), i.e., if and only if

$$(16.17) \qquad \sum_{i=0}^{n} \sum_{j=1}^{n} a_j \phi_{ji} p_i = \sum_{i=1}^{n} q_i p_i$$

if $\rho > 0$, the right side merely dominating the left if $\rho = 0$. Here,

$$q_i = \sum_{k=1}^{m} q_i^{(k)} = \sum_{\nu=1}^{f} q_{i\nu}$$

is the total inventory of q_i. It is even more evident that Conditions (e) are conditions on total consumption, production, and inventory; indeed (16.9) states that

$$(16.18) \qquad \sum_{i=1}^{n} a_i \phi_{ij} \leq q_j, \quad j = 1, \cdots, n.$$

Thus, an equilibrium satisfying Conditions (a)–(f) may be obtained by finding inventories $q_{11}, \cdots, q_{nf}$ and a rate of profit ρ such that the corresponding $p_j(\rho)$, $a_i(q_{11}, \cdots, q_{nf}; \rho)$, $s_j^{(\nu)}(q_{1\nu}, \cdots, q_{n\nu}; \rho)$ and q_j simultaneously satisfy (16.10), (16.18), (16.17), the condition

$$(16.19) \qquad \sum_{\nu=1}^{f} \left\{ \sum_{j=0}^{n} s_j^{(\nu)} p_j - \rho \sum_{i=1}^{n} q_{i\nu} p_i \right\} = 0$$

derived from Condition (d) by use of (16.11) and (16.12), and the final condition

$$(16.20) \qquad -s_0(q_{11}, \cdots, q_{nf}; \rho) = \sum_{i=1}^{n} a_i(q_{11}, \cdots, q_{nf}; \rho) \pi_{i0},$$

unless $\rho = \rho_{\max}$, when the left side of (16.20) is merely required to dominate the right side. This last condition, of course, states that supply of labor and demand for labor are in balance.

4. Analysis of the Modified Equilibrium Model (Continued)

Our problem is then to satisfy equations (16.10) and (16.17)–(16.20) simultaneously. We first discuss the conditions (16.10) and (16.19). With nothing said about the form of the utility functions (16.6) there is of course no reason to expect that the conditions (16.19) have any solution.   Indeed, that without some additional assumption on the form of the utility functions our conditions of equilibrium may imply that consumption and inventories are all zero is already revealed by the analysis carried out in Lecture 10, Section 2, of cycle theory in a case where consumption is allowed to depend on income.   If consumption is strictly proportional to income, we saw in that lecture that in a typical depressive case production decreased at least as fast as the powers of a constant smaller than 1; hence, production in such a situation can converge to zero and remain indefinitely at zero.   More generally, our cycle theory discussion has emphasized the fact that the mechanism of recovery involves inventory reduction through a temporary excess of consumption over production, i.e., through dissaving.   A similar circumstance must, of course, play a role at equilibrium if any nontrivial equilibrium is to exist.   What is then needed is an additional assumption about the utility functions u_ν, or, what amounts to the same thing, an assumption about the form of the functions $s_j^{(\nu)}(q_{1\nu}, \cdots, q_{n\nu}; \rho)$, guaranteeing that in some cases desired consumption can exceed income.

The central empirical fact which this assumption must embody mathematically is the fact that if its income is sufficiently small, a family will spend its savings to support its living standard (dissave), rather than attempt to accumulate additional savings.   On the other hand, as income increases to a sufficiently large value, consumption will not keep pace, and saving will occur.   This means that there will exist a positive ϵ such that if

$$(16.21) \qquad \sum_{j=1}^{n} s_j^{(\nu)}(q_{1\nu}, \cdots, q_{n\nu}; \rho) < \epsilon$$

(so that consumption is small), we will have

$$(16.22) \qquad -\sum_{j=0}^{n} s_j^{(\nu)}(q_{1\nu}, \cdots, q_{n\nu}; \rho)p_j(\rho) + \rho \sum_{j=0}^{n} \sum_{i=1}^{n} q_{j\nu}p_j(\rho) < 0$$

unless $q_{1\nu} = \cdots = q_{n\nu} = 0$.   That is, a family with any nonzero savings would elect to consume at least a portion of its savings in order to avoid reducing its consumption below a certain level.

Now, if ρ is sufficiently close to $\rho_{\max}$ (so that wage income is small) the conditions (16.13) upon $s_j^{(\nu)}$ show that (16.21) must be satisfied for all sufficiently small $q_{1\nu}, \cdots, q_{n\nu}$. Let the numbers $\eta_1, \cdots, \eta_n$ be the numbers $q_1, \cdots, q_n$ divided by their sum q. Then the inequality (16.22) must hold for every family with positive savings if q is sufficiently small and ρ sufficiently close to $\rho_{\max}$. On the other hand, for a family with $q_{1\nu} = \cdots = q_{n\nu} = 0$, the inequality (16.22) and the condition (16.13) imply that the left-hand side of (16.22) must vanish; while, as we remarked above, it is reasonable to assume that if $\sum_{j=1}^{n} q_{j\nu} p_j$ is sufficiently large, the left-hand side of (16.22) is positive. Thus the expression

$$(16.23) \quad -\sum_{\nu=1}^{f} \sum_{j=0}^{n} s_j{}^{(\nu)}(q\psi_\nu \eta_1, \cdots, q\psi_\nu \eta_n; \ \rho) + \rho q \sum_{\nu=1}^{f} \sum_{j=1}^{n} \psi_\nu \eta_j p_j(\rho)$$

is negative for sufficiently small q and positive for sufficiently large q, provided that ρ is not too far below $\rho_{\max}$. The continuity of the functions involved then implies the existence of a positive value of q for which the expression (16.23) is zero. Such being the case, we shall also assume that this value of q is unique, and depends continuously on ρ and $\eta_1, \cdots, \eta_n$. All this is summarized formally in the following assumption.

ASSUMPTION. *There exists a $\rho_0 < \rho_{\max}$ such that for each set $\eta_1, \cdots, \eta_n$ of nonnegative numbers with sum 1 and each ρ between ρ_0 and $\rho_{\max}$, a unique positive number $q = q(\eta_1, \cdots, \eta_n; \ \rho)$ may be found for which the expression (16.23) is zero. The value $q(\eta_1, \cdots, \eta_n; \ \rho)$ depends continuously on $\eta_1, \cdots, \eta_n$ and ρ.*

Making this assumption on the reasonable grounds explained just above, we may proceed with the mathematical construction of an equilibrium for our model.

It will be helpful in what is to follow, however, if we remark that the profit rate ρ_0 of the above assumption is that rate of profit which corresponds to a wage scale sufficiently high so that the average family with zero dividend income will just begin to save consistently and appreciably out of wages. It is heuristically plain that for $\rho < \rho_0$ the condition (16.19) may have no solution; thus, in searching for an equilibrium, we confine ourselves to an examination of the range $\rho_0 \leq \rho \leq \rho_{\max}$.

For what follows, it is convenient to introduce certain notations. Let $q(\eta_1, \cdots, \eta_n; \ \rho)$ be as in the above assumption; put

$$q_j(\eta_1, \cdots, \eta_n; \ \rho) = \eta_j q(\eta_1, \cdots, \eta_n; \ \rho);$$
$$q_j^{(k)}(\eta_1, \cdots, \eta_n; \ \rho) = \psi_k \eta_j q(\eta_1, \cdots, \eta_n; \ \rho);$$

and

$$q_{j\nu} = q_{j\nu}(\eta_1, \cdots, \eta_n; \ \rho) = \psi_\nu \eta_j q(\eta_1, \cdots, \eta_n; \ \rho).$$

By our assumption, all these functions are uniquely defined and continuous, at least in a range $\rho_0 \leq \rho \leq \rho_{\max}$.

The functions $q_{j\nu}(\eta_1, \cdots, \eta_n; \ \rho)$ then satisfy equations (16.19); the functions $q_{jk}(\eta_1, \cdots, \eta_n; \ \rho)$ satisfy equation (16.10); and we have plainly

$$q_{j\nu} = \sum_{k=1}^{m} h_{\nu k} q_j^{(k)}.$$

We define a supply-of-labor function $s_0(\eta_1, \cdots, \eta_n; \ \rho)$ and a demand-for-labor function $d_0(\eta_1, \cdots, \eta_n; \ \rho)$ by putting

(16.24) $s_0(\eta_1, \cdots, \eta_n; \ \rho)$
$$= s_0(q_{11}(\eta_1, \cdots, \eta_n; \ \rho), \cdots, q_{nf}(\eta_1, \cdots, \eta_n; \ \rho); \ \rho)$$

and

(16.25) $d_0(\eta_1, \cdots, \eta_n; \ \rho)$
$$= \sum_{i=1}^{n} a_i(q_{11}(\eta_1, \cdots, \eta_n; \ \rho), \cdots, q_{nf}(\eta_1, \cdots, \eta_r; \ \rho); \ \rho)\pi_{io}.$$

To construct a price equilibrium, i.e., to satisfy equations (16.10) and (16.17)–(16.20), we must then find $\eta_1, \cdots, \eta_n$ and ρ such that

(16.26) $$-s_0(\eta_1, \cdots, \eta_n; \ \rho) = d_0(\eta_1, \cdots, \eta_n; \ \rho),$$

and such that

(16.27) $\displaystyle\sum_{i=1}^{n} a_i(q_{11}(\eta_1, \cdots, \eta_n; \ \rho), \cdots, q_{nf}(\eta_1, \cdots, \eta_n; \ \rho); \ \rho)\phi_{ij}$
$$\leq q_j(\eta_1, \cdots, \eta_n; \ \rho), \quad j = 1, \cdots, n.$$

Indeed, if (16.26) is satisfied and $\rho > 0$, then, using (16.23), the arguments of the first part of Lecture 15 tell us that (16.17) is necessarily satisfied also. To show that (16.27) can be satisfied, we may reason as follows. Call the expression on the left of (16.27) $\Gamma_j(\eta_1, \cdots, \eta_n; \ \rho)$. Let ρ be found as a function of $\eta_1, \cdots, \eta_n$ from the equation (16.26); we shall assume that the shape of the labor supply and demand schedules $-s_0$ and d_0 are such as to determine a unique solution $\rho = \rho(\eta_1, \cdots, \eta_n)$ of (16.26). A more detailed discussion of the form of these schedules will be found below. We also assume that the solution ρ depends continuously on the parameters $\eta_1, \cdots, \eta_n$. Let

$$(16.28) \quad \gamma_j(\eta_1, \cdots, \eta_n) = \left(\sum_{k=1}^{n} \Gamma_k(\eta_1, \cdots, \eta_n; \ \rho(\eta_1, \cdots, \eta_n)) \right)^{-1}$$
$$\times \Gamma_j(\eta_1, \cdots, \eta_n; \ \rho(\eta_1, \cdots, \eta_n)).$$

Then, for given ρ, the map $[\eta_1, \cdots, \eta_n] \to [\gamma_1, \cdots, \gamma_n]$ is a continuous transformation of the $(n-1)$-dimensional simplex defined by

$$(16.29) \qquad \sum_{j=1}^{n} \eta_j = 1; \ \ \eta_j \geq 0, \ \ j = 1, \cdots, n$$

into itself. By the theorem of Brouwer (cf. the statement of this theorem given in the eighth paragraph of Section 1, Lecture 2), there exists a point $\tilde{\eta}_1, \cdots, \tilde{\eta}_n$ of the simplex which is fixed under this transformation. Since $q_j = q\eta_j$, this means that

$$(16.30) \quad \sum_{i=1}^{n} a_i(q_{11}(\tilde{\eta}_1, \cdots, \tilde{\eta}_n; \ \rho), \cdots, q_{nf}(\tilde{\eta}_1, \cdots, \tilde{\eta}_n; \ \rho); \ \rho)\phi_{ij}$$
$$= Cq_j(\tilde{\eta}_1, \cdots, \tilde{\eta}_n; \ \rho), \ \ j = 1, \cdots, n,$$

with some constant C. If we multiply these equations by p_j, use (16.17), and recall also that $\phi_{i0} = 0$ for all i, it follows immediately that the constant C of equation (16.30) is 1. Thus (16.27) is satisfied, and even as an equality rather than as an inequality. The upshot of our analysis then is that if the single equation

$$(16.31) \qquad -s_0(\eta_1, \cdots, \eta_n; \ \rho) = d_0(\eta_1, \cdots, \eta_n; \ \rho)$$

can be solved for given $\eta_1, \cdots, \eta_n$ by a proper choice of the parameter ρ, then an equilibrium satisfying all the foregoing Conditions (a)–(e) will be determined.

The possibility of solving this equation depends on the shape of the schedules $-s_0$ and d_0 of supply of labor and demand for labor. We may in discussing these schedules extend the rough considerations of Lecture 14 to apply to the present case. The schedule of labor-supply should not look very different in the present case than in the case studied in Lecture 14. This assertion may be justified by the reflection that in any existing economy the great bulk of labor will be provided by families whose dividend income is so small as to have an almost negligible influence on decisions as to the amount of labor to be offered. On the other hand, the demand of labor is, as in Lecture 14, derived from the demand for commodities, which, again as in Lecture 14, we may divide approximately into the sum of two terms: demand for commodities based upon wage-generated income, and demand for commodities based upon dividend-generated income. The first of these demand contributions will increase with the wage rate, and hence fall with rising ρ, falling to zero at $\rho = \rho_{max}$. The second of these demand contributions will vary less with ρ, since as ρ rises the equilibrium amount q of savings which will yield a total of dividend income at which there will be no net addition to savings must fall. Thus total demand for labor must rise with decreasing ρ, confirming the less distinct but similar impression formed in Lecture 14. The configuration of the two schedules $-s_0$ and d_0 must then be much as in Lecture 14; we may represent them as in Fig. 24.

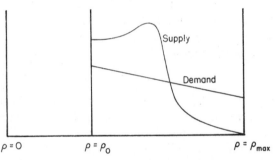

Fig. 24.   Supply and demand for labor.

We have drawn the schedules only in the range $\rho_0 \le \rho \le \rho_{max}$, ρ_0 being the profit-rate corresponding to a wage rate high enough so that appreciable savings out of a purely wage income begin to occur, for the reasons indicated in the paragraph following formula (16.23). The supply curve has been represented in a form showing what might be the effects of unionization. To the left of the intersection of supply and demand, demand must lie below supply, since the opposite case would involve regions in which the working-population requires the spur of reduced wages in order to overcome a lazy reluctance to work made possible by high wages, which situation we have rejected in Lecture 14 as implausible. An equilibrium will then exist as long as the supply of labor does not begin to diminish except for rates of pay corresponding to values of ρ rather larger than ρ_0; i.e., heuristically speaking, as long as the minimum acceptable wage rates are not so large that a population drawing wages at these rates and having no other income will normally accumulate substantial savings. In the latter case, the considerations of Section 4 make it plain that no equilibrium can exist.

The attentive reader will be well aware that the mathematical perfection of the present model is less marked than that of the more conventional equilibrium model presented in the preceding chapters. We may assert, however, that its economic significance is greater. The difficulties of the present model are themselves related to an important economic fact: that the satisfactory operation of an economy is directly dependent on dynamic expansion through investment, and that any equilibrium model must in consequence be untrustworthy to a certain extent.

We may appropriately comment here on the notion of *unemployment*. Our approximate analysis of the supply and demand schedules for labor reveals that in a variety of not unrealistic cases the point of equilibrium will lie in a section of the labor-supply schedule in which supply is falling rapidly (as, for instance, at the level of a union-determined minimum wage) from a nearby peak. The difference between supply *at this peak* and demand may be taken as the definition within equilibrium models like the present model of unemployment. That this definition is reasonable appears most readily if we idealize slightly and assume that the labor-supply cutoff is *sharp*, as in Fig. 25. The supply schedule is then multi-

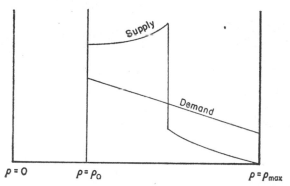

$\rho = 0$ $\rho = \rho_0$ $\rho = \rho_{max}$

Fig. 25. Idealized supply and demand for labor.

valued at the equilibrium rate of profit, and unemployment is the difference between the largest of its multiple values and the equilibrium value of demand. It is then plain from the form of our schedules that *unemployment ought to decrease with a rise in the wage rate,* contrary to the naïve presupposition which might be derived from a partial-equilibrium neoclassical analysis.

5. General Reflections on the Foregoing Model

Equilibrium models like the model of the present and preceding lectures give content to the classical notion of the "invisible hand" of economics, by describing the equilibrium point toward which this invisible hand is pushing. Enthusiasts of neoclassical policy have repeatedly emphasized the opinion that this equilibrium is satisfactory, and even optimal. After all, at equilibrium each family maximizes its satisfaction, and each firm maximizes its profits. The above analysis reveals the illusory character of this view. As we see from the above, motion toward equilibrium may very well involve a drastic reduction of capital inventory, i.e., empirically speaking, a protracted period of depression during which the national inventories of raw materials, traders' goods, and capital equipment can decay to suitable levels. Something of this sort began to take place during the depression of 1929–34, though, perhaps to the regret of the neoclassical purist, government action halted the process before capital and inventory levels, levels of technical skill, and even population, could fall very far. As to the universal optimization apparently involved in equilibrium: each family optimizes its subjective utility *subject to budgetary constraints;* each firm maximizes its profits *subject to its capital limitations.* As the above analysis shows, this may mean nothing more than that each family manages as best it can subject to a severe shortage of funds, and that each firm makes the largest possible profit on the small amounts of capital remaining to it after a severely depressive descent to equilibrium has brought about the evaporation of most of its capital. These reflections should make it evident that an external interference with the situation of equilibrium may very well improve the situation of every family and firm in our model. Thus, if, for instance, unions by cutting off the supply of labor at low wage rates are able to shift the position of equilibrium to a new, "artificial" point, one may expect to find on comparing this new equilibrium with the old equilibrium that the budgetary constraint on each family without significant dividend income had relaxed, that the consumption expenditure of families with significant dividend income was substantially the same as previously (these families having more savings), and that firms were making substantially the same total profit as before, or perhaps more, drawing a smaller rate of profit on a larger equilibrium mass of capital. Putting this last conclusion into a more realistic, dynamic rather than static, form, we may say that from the point of view of firms a higher general wage rate would mean not a diminution in average profits but an increased or unchanged average mass of profits, profits being drawn at a lower rate in periods of peak prosperity (though on a larger mass of capital), but periods of exceptionally low, recession-reduced profits being rarer and the general mass of capital being increased. Of course, it is the *general* wage rate that is controlling in the preceding statement: any firm which could individually escape from a general wage-rise, *while successfully insisting that all or most others comply*, would be able to achieve exceptional profits. (We may here make an analogy: any soldier who is able to evade participation in a general offensive, while ensuring that all others participate, will find his own chances of being on the victorious side only infinitesimally diminished, while his personal chance of enjoying the fruits of victory may be substantially increased.) It is, in the last analysis, this perplexing divergence between collective optimization and individual-firm optimization that makes it so difficult to organize a concerted attack on recessions. The difficulty would only be eliminated (short of centrally organized coercion) if wage-payments became indistinguishable from dividend-payments, i.e., if the body of stockholders in each firm were substantially identical with its body of employees.

6. Some Comments on the Role of Investment

Paradoxically, the preceding model reveals investment to be a crucial factor in the actual economy, but says nothing about investment. In the present section, therefore, we shall attempt to comment on this neglected topic, and to indicate how investment might be included in an essentially static model like the preceding models of equilibrium. Let us first remark, however, that certain very substantial categories of investment can be included in an equilibrium model without difficulty. *Housing investment* may without grave distortion be regarded as a form of personal consumption; *depreciation* may, indeed should, be included, as current input to production, in the π_{ij}-matrix; *defense expenditures*, which do not return as inputs to the economy, may be regarded as a form of consumption in which each family participates in appropriate proportion to its tax payments. The account of national dividend and its disposition given in Table XIA2. of Lecture 8 shows that approximately 65 of the 90 billions of U. S. national dividend would be accounted for in this way, leaving approximately 25 billions annually of "residual" investment still to be incorporated in our model.

The proper treatment, within a mathematical model, of this investment is bound to be difficult. A prime circumstance of which account must be taken is the circumstance, emphasized by various writers and especially by Schumpeter, that this investment depends significantly on the rate of technological change—"innovation"—and hence upon changes in the π_{ij} and ϕ_{ij} matrices which quantitative economic theory can hardly be expected to explain. The importance of this effect may be noted, for example, in the circumstance that expenditures for new plant and equipment in the steel industry rose in 1960 to the total of \$1.6 billion over a 1959 figure of \$1.0 billion, while utilization of existing capacity fell from 90 to 50 per cent in the same two years. We gain a similar impression from the fact that the introduction of jet service raised annual investment in civilian aircraft from an average of \$180 million in the years 1953–55 to a figure of \$480 million in 1958 and \$800 million in 1960.

Extra-rapid depreciation of capital owing to technological obsolescence might perhaps be included in our model simply by raising the coefficients π_{ij} to include an "average rate of obsolescence." A less Procrustean treatment of investment, however, can be established as follows. The period of adjustment to technological modifications and the period over which new equipment enters decisively into the pattern of production is normally rather larger than the period of the business cycle. Thus, as in the preceding sections, we may regard the volume of investment as being a given external datum relative to which the economy moves rapidly toward equilibrium. In our specific economic context, we may then take certain amounts I_j of our various commodities $C_1, \cdots, C_n$ to constitute given invest-

ment, and to assume that the resources for this investment are retained by firms instead of being paid out as dividends.

Our earlier model must then be modified as follows. Conditions
(a) and (b) remain the same as in the earlier model. The firms, however, retain the total amount $\sum_{j=1}^{n} I_j p_j$ of their profits, distributing
only the remaining amount. We will assume that the kth firm accounts for portions $I_i^{(k)}$ of the investment, the constants $I_j^{(k)}$ being
fixed. Then Condition (c) is to be modified by replacing the budget
constraint (16.7) by

$$(16.32) \quad -\sum_{j=0}^{n} s_j p_j + \sum_{j=0}^{n} \sum_{i=1}^{n} \sum_{k=1}^{m} a_i^{(k)}(\delta_{ij} - \pi_{ij})p_j h_{\nu k}$$

$$-\sum_{k=1}^{m} \sum_{j=1}^{n} I_j^{(k)} p_j h_{\nu k} \geq -\sum_{k=1}^{n} q_{k\nu} p_k.$$

Similarly, equation (16.8) of Condition (d) should be modified to

$$(16.33) \quad -\sum_{\nu=1}^{f} s_j^{(\nu)} + \sum_{k=1}^{m} \sum_{i=1}^{n} a_i^{(h)}(\delta_{ij} - \pi_{ij}) - \sum_{k=1}^{m} I_j^{(k)} = 0,$$

$$j = 1, \cdots, n.$$

Conditions (e) and (f) remain unchanged.

The analysis of the present modified equilibrium model may then
follow lines similar to the analysis of the unmodified equilibrium
model set forth in the earlier sections of the present lecture. The
prices again depend on a rate of profit parameter ρ as in (16.11);
Condition (b) is again equivalent to the conjunction of (16.11) and
(16.12). These conditions and Condition (c) require the νth family's
consumption plan to be described by the numbers $s_0^{(\nu)}, \cdots, s_n^{(\nu)}$
maximizing the utility function (16.6) subject to the condition

$$(16.34) \quad \sum_{j=0}^{n} s_j p_j \leq (1 + \rho) \sum_{k=1}^{n} q_{k\nu} p_k - \sum_{k=1}^{m} \sum_{j=1}^{n} I_j^{(k)} p_j h_{k\nu};$$

we may assume as above that this determines a set of maximizing
values $s_j^{(\nu)}(q_1, \cdots, q_n; p_0, \cdots, p_n)$. We may then determine total
production $a_i(q_{11}, \cdots, q_{nf}; \rho)$ as a function of the savings levels and
the rate of profit ρ as in (16.14)–(16.16), modifying the equation
(16.15), however, to

$$(16.35) \quad \sum_{i} a_i(\delta_{ij} - \pi_{ij}) = s_j(q_{11}, \cdots, q_{nf}; \rho) + I_j.$$

Note that the levels of activity in (16.35) increase with fixed s_j and increasing I_j, the dependence of $\mathbf{a}$ on $\mathbf{I}$ being given by a linear "multiplier" relation of the sort discussed in Lecture 8.

Next, we may show as above that an equilibrium can be obtained if we can simultaneously satisfy the equations (16.10), (16.17), (16.18), (16.20), and the equation

$$(16.36) \qquad \sum_{j=0}^{n} s_j(q_{11}, \cdots, q_{nf}; \; \rho)p_j = \rho \sum_{i=1}^{n} q_i p_i - \sum_{j=1}^{n} I_j p_j.$$

At this point, we may proceed as in Section 4 and on the basis of the assumption used there to find functions $q_{jv}(\eta_1, \cdots, \eta_n; \; \rho)$ $= \eta_j \psi_v q(\eta_1, \cdots, \eta_n; \; \rho)$, depending continuously on a set of non-negative parameters $\eta_1, \cdots, \eta_n$ satisfying $\Sigma_i \eta_i = 1$, which satisfy (16.36).

It then follows as in Section 4 that we find an equilibrium at any points $\eta_1, \cdots, \eta_n$ and ρ at which the supply and demand for labor as defined by (16.24)–(16.25) are equal and at which all the inequalities (16.27) are satisfied. Such points may now be found using the Brouwer fixed-point theorem and the form of the supply-demand schedules for labor, as in Section 4. Thus the mathematical treatment of the present model is hardly different from that of Sections 1–4.

It is interesting to see how the functions $s_j{}^{(v)}$ and q will vary with I. We shall show in fact that these functions should *all* increase with I, if the increase of I is "sufficiently general." Such a conclusion is entirely out of accord with neoclassical theory, which, as is appropriate for scarcity economics, would treat investment as a subtraction from consumption, and tend to insist that when one increases the other must decrease. Of course, it is plain from the outset that a person holding all his shares in a firm with investment plans which are exceptionally large relative to the investment plans of all other firms will find his equilibrium dividend income reduced and his consumption reduced in consequence. This is because the investment policy of a single firm can hardly change the location of over-all equilibrium by more than a few per cent, while on the other hand a firm by retaining a large part of its profits will reduce the dividends of its stockholders very greatly. We shall see, however, that if *all* the investment parameters $I_j{}^{(k)}$ are increased *in proportion*, equilibrium shifts to a new position at which not only investment by each firm but also consumption by each family is higher.

Our formal mathematical analysis is as follows. It is reasonable to assume that expenditure is, at given prices, an increasing function of savings and income, even though, of course, at high levels of savings we have assumed this increase to be moderate. This assumption may be formulated mathematically as follows: let $\hat{s}_j^{(\nu)}(k; q_1, \cdots, q_n; \rho)$ be the set of values s_j which maximize the utility function $u^{(\nu)}(s_0, \cdots, s_n; q_1, \cdots, q_n; p_1, \cdots, p_n)$ subject to the restriction $\sum_{j=0}^{n} s_j p_j \leq k$. Then if we assume that if $k \geq k'$, $q_1 \geq q'_1, \cdots, q_n \geq q'_n$, we have

$$(16.37) \quad \hat{s}_j^{(\nu)}(k; q_1, \cdots, q_n; \rho) \geq \hat{s}_j^{(\nu)}(k'; q'_1, \cdots, q'_n; \rho),$$
$$j = 0, \cdots, n.$$

Note that if

$$k = (1 + \rho) \sum_{l=1}^{n} q_{l\nu} p_l - \sum_{l=1}^{n} I_{l\nu} p_l,$$

where here and in what follows we shall write

$$I_{l\nu} = \sum_{j=1}^{m} I_l^{(j)} h_{j\nu},$$

then $\hat{s}_j^{(\nu)}(k; q_1, \cdots, q_n; \rho)$ reduces to $s_j^{(\nu)}(q_1, \cdots, q_n; \rho)$.

For given $\eta_1, \cdots, \eta_n$ and ρ, let $q(I_{11}, \cdots, I_{nf})$ be such that $q_{j\nu} = \eta_j \psi_\nu q$ satisfies (16.36). Let two different sets of numbers $I_{11}, \cdots, I_{nf}$ and $I'_{11}, \cdots, I'_{nf}$ be given, the numbers of the first set exceeding the corresponding numbers of the second set. Suppose, in addition, that

$$(16.38) \qquad \sum_{j=1}^{n} I_{j\nu} p_j = \psi_\nu \sum_{j=1}^{n} \sum_{\nu=1}^{f} I_{j\nu} p_j, \quad \nu = 1, \cdots, f,$$

and

$$(16.39) \qquad \sum_{j=1}^{n} I'_{j\nu} p_j = \psi_\nu \sum_{j=1}^{n} \sum_{\nu=1}^{f} I'_{j\nu} p_j, \quad \nu = 1, \cdots, f,$$

so that each family is assumed to participate in investment in proportion to its wealth; these equations give specific meaning to our earlier demand that the increase of investment (from I' to I) be "sufficiently general." Let q' be chosen so that

$$(16.40) \quad \rho q' \sum_{j=1}^{n} p_i \eta_i - \sum_{j=1}^{n} \sum_{\nu=1}^{f} I'_{j\nu} p_j$$

$$= \rho q(I_{11}, \cdots, I_{nf}) \sum_{i=1}^{n} p_i \eta_i - \sum_{j=1}^{n} \sum_{\nu=1}^{f} I_{j\nu} p_j.$$

Plainly $q' \leq q$. Putting $q'_{j\nu} = \eta_j \psi_\nu q'$ it follows from (16.38) and (16.39) that

$$(16.41) \quad \rho \sum_{i=1}^{n} q'_{i\nu} p_i - \sum_{j=1}^{n} I'_{j\nu} p_j = \rho \sum_{i=1}^{n} q_{i\nu} p_i - \sum_{j=1}^{n} I_{j\nu} p_j, \quad \nu = 1, \cdots, f$$

and hence

$$(16.42) \quad (1 + \rho) \sum_{i=1}^{n} q'_{i\nu} p_i - \sum_{j=1}^{n} I'_{j\nu} p_j$$

$$= k'_\nu \leq k_\nu = (1 + \rho) \sum_{i=1}^{n} q_{i\nu} p_i - \sum_{j=1}^{n} I_{j\nu} p_j, \quad \nu = 1, \cdots, f.$$

Thus, by the above assumption

$$(16.43) \quad \hat{s}_j^{(\nu)}(k'_\nu; \; q'_{1\nu}, \cdots, q'_{n\nu}; \; \rho) \leq \hat{s}_j^{(\nu)}(k_\nu; \; q_{1\nu}, \cdots, q_{n\nu}; \; \rho),$$
$$j = 0, \cdots, n; \quad \nu = 1, \cdots, f.$$

From this we may at once conclude, using (16.40) and (16.36), that

$$(16.44) \quad \sum_{j=0}^{n} \sum_{\nu=1}^{f} \hat{s}_j^{(\nu)}(q' \eta_1 \psi_1, \cdots, q' \eta_n \psi_f; \; \rho) p_j - \rho q' \sum_{j=1}^{n} \sum_{\nu=1}^{f} \eta_j \psi_\nu$$

$$+ \sum_{j=1}^{n} \sum_{\nu=1}^{f} I'_{j\nu} p_j \leq \sum_{j=0}^{n} \sum_{\nu=1}^{f} \hat{s}_j^{(\nu)}(q \eta_1 \psi_1, \cdots, q \eta_n \psi_f; \; \rho)$$

$$- \rho q \sum_{j=1}^{n} \sum_{\nu=1}^{f} \eta_j \psi_\nu + \sum_{j=1}^{n} \sum_{\nu=1}^{f} I_{j\nu} p_j = 0.$$

Since we are assuming, now, as in Section 4, that for sufficiently small q' the expression on the left of (16.44) will be nonnegative, it follows that the unique $q^* = q(I'_{11}, \cdots, I'_{nf})$ for which we have the equality

$$(16.45) \quad \sum_{j=0}^{n} \sum_{\nu=1}^{f} \hat{s}_j^{(\nu)}(q^* \eta_1 \psi_1, \cdots, q^* \eta_n \psi_f; \; \rho) p_j - \rho q^* \sum_{j=1}^{n} \sum_{\nu=1}^{f} \eta_j \psi_\nu$$

$$+ \sum_{j=1}^{n} \sum_{\nu=1}^{f} I'_{j\nu} p_j = 0$$

must satisfy $q^* \leq q' \leq q$. Moreover, since

$$(16.46) \quad (1 + \rho) \sum_{j=1}^{n} q^* \psi_\nu \eta_j p_j - \sum_{j=1}^{n} I'_{j\nu} p_j \leq (1 + \rho) \sum_{j=1}^{n} q_{j\nu} p_j$$

$$- \sum_{j=1}^{n} I_{j\nu} p_j$$

is then obvious from (16.42), it follows at once by the assumption made earlier in the present section that

$$(16.47) \quad s_j^{(\nu)}(q^* \psi_\nu \eta_1, \cdots, q^* \psi_\nu \eta_n; \; \rho) \leq s_j^{(\nu)}(q_{1\nu}, \cdots, q_{n\nu}; \; \rho),$$
$$j = 0, \cdots, n; \quad \nu = 1, \cdots, f.$$

Thus we have shown that for fixed $\eta_1, \cdots, \eta_n$, both sets of functions $q_{j\nu}(I_{11}, \cdots, I_{nf})$ and $s_j^{(\nu)}(I_{11}, \cdots, I_{nf})$ increase with a general increase in $I_{11}, \cdots, I_{nf}$.

As we saw in Section 4, to find an equilibrium once the functions $q_{j\nu}$ and $s_j^{(\nu)}$ are determined, we must

(a) determine ρ as a function of $\eta_1, \cdots, \eta_n$ from the condition that supply of labor balance demand for labor;

(b) determine $\eta_1, \cdots, \eta_n$, using the Brouwer fixed-point theorem and Condition (16.27).

We may expect the bulk of labor to be provided by families whose dividend income is so small as to have a negligible effect on their labor offerings; hence the supply-of-labor schedule should be relatively insensitive to the rate of investment parameters I. Since, as we have seen in Section 4, the rate of profit equilibrating supply and demand of labor tends to lie in the uniquely determined range of the parameter ρ in which s_0 changes rapidly, we may then conclude that ρ as determined from (a) changes very little if the parameters $I'_{j\nu}$ undergo a sufficiently general increase to new values $I_{j\nu}$. Determination of the parameters $\eta_1, \cdots, \eta_n$ from (16.27) as in (b) is then a mere adjustment of the *proportions* of the various components of capital, and ought not change the general levels of income or production. We may therefore expect that if the rate of investment parameters I undergoes a general increase, the equilibrium income and consumption of most families ought to increase also.

This Keynesian conclusion, while corresponding rather well with the common opinion of the effects of an investment boom, is, as we have remarked above, directly in conflict with neoclassical theory. Of course, our opposite conclusion is descriptive of the situation of eventual *equilibrium*. During a period in which investment is advancing more rapidly than production, i.e., in which the economy is moving along or toward a scarcity line like that of Lectures 6 and 7, investment may temporarily subtract from consumption. This temporary situation, however, ought to be characterized in the neoclassical terminology as a *frictional distortion*.

We may remark also that our conclusions are valid quite independently of the form of investment, be this investment in modernized capital equipment, in the latest military equipment, or, for that matter, in philanthropic gifts or donations. Since, from the economic point of view, such philanthropic donations are hardly distinguishable from increased wage-payments, we see that the present model reaffirms our earlier conclusion that an advance in the wage rate is capable of bettering the economic position (at equilibrium) of all dividend-drawing as well as all wage-drawing families, indeed, that this is its expected effect.

Analysis of a Neoclassical Contention

1. Production Functions and Parameter Families of Leontief Matrices

We have remarked in the first section of Lecture 8 that the difference as to whether the effect of wage cuts in a period of recession is to increase or decrease unemployment is a central point of dispute between the neoclassical and the Keynesian theories. As our analysis in Lecture 16 shows, as long as we assume a fixed scheme of production the Keynesian conclusion that wage cuts by lowering wage-generated commodity demand must lower demand for labor and hence raise unemployment is inescapable. The neoclassical contention thus depends on the possibility of shifts in the production scheme; a conclusion which the neoclassicist would be the first to emphasize, since the whole apparatus of neoclassical theory, revolving as it does about the notion of marginal product accruing to an increment of each input factor, does in fact center on an analysis of variations in the scheme of production. This means that the equilibrium analysis of Lecture 16 has come to such distinctly Keynesian conclusions as it has only by assuming away the basis for the neoclassicist's argument. At the present point, therefore, we shall attempt to generalize the analysis of Lecture 16 to include the possibility of shifts in the production scheme, hoping to estimate the extent to which such shifts are likely to affect our earlier conclusions.

In all of our earlier analyses we have taken the production of one unit of the commodity C_i to require π_{ij} units of each of the commodities C_j as input. This, of course, involves the assumption of a fixed scheme of production. Neoclassical analysis abandons this assumption by taking the productive combination of arbitrary amounts $\alpha_0, \cdots, \alpha_n$ of the commodities $C_0, \cdots, C_n$ to yield an output of $F_j(\alpha_0, \cdots, \alpha_n)$ units of the commodity C_j; the function F_j is the *production function* for the commodity C_j, and the surfaces $F_j(\alpha_0, \cdots, \alpha_n) = const.$ are the *indifference surfaces* for production of the commodity C_j. More generally, taking fixed as well as circulating capital into account, we may say that the input of $\alpha_0, \cdots, \alpha_n$ units of commodities $C_0, \cdots, C_n$, together with the utilization as fixed capital of $\beta_1, \cdots, \beta_n$ units of commodities $C_1, \cdots, C_n$ for one day, will yield $F_j(\alpha_0, \cdots, \alpha_n; \beta_1, \cdots, \beta_n)$ units of the commodity C_j. These new functions $F_j(\alpha_0, \cdots, \alpha_n; \beta_1, \cdots, \beta_n)$ will also be called production functions (including fixed capital), and the surfaces $F_j = const.$ called indifference surfaces. The assumption of constant returns to scale implicit in our earlier Leontief model of production may be made here explicitly as

$$(17.1) \quad tF_j(\alpha_0, \cdots, \alpha_n; \ \beta_1, \cdots, \beta_n) = F_j(t\alpha_0, \cdots, t\alpha_n; \ t\beta_1, \cdots, t\beta_n).$$

For the sake of simplicity and of comparability with our earlier models we will make the assumption of constant returns to scale in all that follows.

Let us next investigate the relation between the above description of production and the Leontief description by input-output matrices which we have used in all preceding lectures. First of all, the Leontief matrices may be described by neoclassical production functions of a particular form. We may convince ourselves of this as follows. In setting up the Leontief model of production, we state that the production of one unit of commodity C_j requires π_{ji} units of each commodity C_i as input and ϕ_{ji} units of each commodity C_i as fixed capital. In making this statement we mean to imply that additional units of C_i, out of the proper proportions π_{ji} or ϕ_{ji}, make a zero contribution to output. It is then evident that the corresponding neoclassical production function is

$$(17.2) \quad F_j(\alpha_0, \cdots, \alpha_n; \ \beta_1, \cdots, \beta_n) =$$
$$\max \{t \mid t\pi_{ji} \le \alpha_i, \ \ i = 0, \cdots, n \ \text{ and } \ t\phi_{ji} \le \beta_i, \ \ i = 1, \cdots, n\}.$$

Let us examine the geometrical form of the indifference surface for such a production function. In order to be able to draw a geometric figure, we take $n = 3$. Then (17.2) shows that the surface $F_j = 1$ has the form

(17.3) $\qquad \alpha_0 = \pi_{j0}$ and $\alpha_1 \geq \pi_{j1}$ and $\beta_1 \geq \phi_{j1}$;

$\quad$ or $\quad \alpha_0 \geq \pi_{j0}$ and $\alpha_1 = \pi_{j1}$ and $\beta_1 \geq \phi_{j1}$;

$\quad$ or $\quad \alpha_0 \geq \pi_{j0}$ and $\alpha_1 \geq \pi_{j1}$ and $\beta_1 = \phi_{j1}$.

Our surface is thus the union of 3 quarter-planes with the common corner π_{j0}, π_{j1}, ϕ_{j1}, as indicated by crosshatchings in Fig. 26.

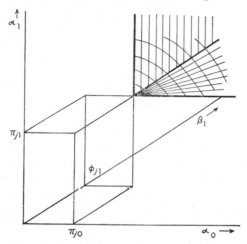

Fig. 26. Indifference surface for the Leontief model.

The form of the indifference surface of Fig. 26 shows plainly why all the "marginality" considerations of neoclassical economics are absent in analyses of models of the Leontief type. These considerations center about the study of the points at which a plane is tangent from below to the indifference surface of the production function. But Fig. 26 shows that for the Leontief model this tangency always occurs at the unique corner of the indifference surface. The marginal contribution of all factors of production but those found from the Leontief matrices to be in short supply is zero.

A more general production function would be represented by a curved indifference surface, as in Fig. 27 (again we take $n = 1$ so as to be able to draw a three-dimensional figure).

It is clear on comparing Figs. 26 and 27 that the Leontief input-output model with fixed production-scheme is appropriate for use in any situation in which the indifference surface has a very high curvature near an approximate "corner"; the coordinates of this "corner" will define the entries of the input-output matrices.

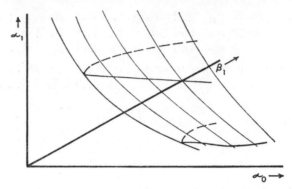

Fig. 27.   Indifference surface for general production function.

We have represented the indifference surface of Fig. 27 above as being convex downward. This representation is justified by the reflection that it is only those points of an indifference surface at which the surface is tangent from above to a plane which correspond to production schemes which can ever be optimal. Points lying in regions of the surface in which the surface is not convex downward consequently represent irrelevant even if conceivable production schemes; it is always possible to improve such production schemes, replacing them by a suitable convex combination or "mixture" of production schemes corresponding to points on the appropriately convex portion of the indifference surface. More generally, only the *extreme points* of an indifference surface like that of Fig. 27 correspond to essentially original production schemes: all other production schemes represented by points on the indifference surface may be regarded as "mixtures" of the production schemes represented by the extreme points. Every point of a smoothly curved indifference surface like that of Fig. 27 may, of course, be an extreme point; on the other hand, a polyhedral indifference surface will have only a finite collection of extreme points, and will thus represent the production of a commodity for which only a finite number of essentially distinct schemes are available. A corresponding "linear programming" approximation to the problem of optimal production may appropriately be used in any situation in which the general indifference surface of Fig. 27 has very high curvature near a finite collection of corners and edges.

In Fig. 28 we depict a polyhedral indifference surface representing a situation in which a commodity can be produced in two essentially distinct fashions.

The coordinates π_{j0}, π_{j1}, ϕ_{j1} of the extreme point P_1 in Fig. 28 correspond to one Leontief scheme for the production of the com-

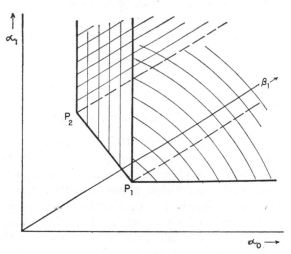

Fig. 28. Indifference surface with two extreme points.

modity C_j; the coordinates π'_{j0}, π'_{j1}, ϕ'_{j1} of the point P_2 in Fig. 28 correspond to an alternate Leontief scheme for producing C_j. Similarly, if σ is a parameter varying over the extreme points of the curved indifference surface of Fig. 27, then the coordinates $\pi_{j0}(\sigma)$, $\pi_{j1}(\sigma)$, $\phi_{j1}(\sigma)$ of σ describe a parameter family of Leontief schemes for producing the commodity C_j. In general, if σ is a parameter varying over the extreme points of the indifference surface

$$(17.4) \qquad F_j(\alpha_0, \cdots, \alpha_n; \beta_1, \cdots, \beta_n) = 1,$$

then the coordinates $\pi_{j0}(\sigma), \cdots, \pi_{jn}(\sigma)$; $\phi_{j1}(\sigma), \cdots, \phi_{jn}(\sigma)$ describe a parameter family of Leontief schemes for producing the commodity C_j. One unit of C_j may be produced with inputs $\pi_{j0}(\sigma), \cdots, \pi_{jn}(\sigma)$ of $C_0 \cdots C_n$, and with the use for a "day" of fixed capital consisting of $\phi_{j1}(\sigma), \cdots, \phi_{jn}(\sigma)$ units of the commodities $C_1 \cdots C_n$. The scheme σ is at our disposal. It should be noted, however, that a scheme σ_j of production is to be chosen independently for each commodity C_j; thus, a full set of n production functions $F_1 \cdots F_n$

correspond to n separate parameter-families of Leontief input-output and capital coefficients

$$(17.5) \qquad \begin{array}{l} \pi_{10}(\sigma_1), \cdots, \pi_{1n}(\sigma_1); \; \phi_{11}(\sigma_1), \cdots, \phi_{1n}(\sigma_1) \\ \pi_{20}(\sigma_2), \cdots, \pi_{2n}(\sigma_2); \; \phi_{21}(\sigma_2), \cdots, \phi_{2n}(\sigma_2) \\ \qquad\qquad \cdots\cdots \\ \pi_{n0}(\sigma_n), \cdots, \pi_{nn}(\sigma_n); \; \phi_{n1}(\sigma_n), \cdots, \phi_{nn}(\sigma_n). \end{array}$$

Thus a set of production-functions is equivalent to a parameter-family of Leontief matrices, and conversely.

2. Theory of Prices with Varying Leontief Matrices

The preceding analysis has served to indicate the manner in which the neoclassical and the Leontief descriptions of production are related to each other. To advance our analysis, we must now generalize the theory of competitive prices presented in Lecture 3 to apply to the situation in which a continuum of production schemes is available to the producer of each commodity. Let $p_0, p_1, \cdots, p_n$ be the prices of $C_0, C_1, \cdots, C_n$. To what restrictions must these prices be subject? In the first place, the hypothesis of perfect competition implies, just as in Lectures 2 and 3, that no manufacturer can better his rate of profit by going over to the production of another commodity. We conclude, just as in Lectures 2 and 3, that all lines of production must yield the same profit ρ. Thus, if $\sigma_1, \cdots, \sigma_n$ are parameters describing the production schemes which the manufacturers of commodities $C_1, \cdots, C_n$ will actually choose to employ, we must have

$$(17.6) \qquad p_i - \sum_{j=0}^{n} \pi_{ij}(\sigma_i)p_j = \rho \sum_{j=1}^{n} \phi_{ij}(\sigma_i)p_j$$

just as in Lecture 3. As in Lecture 3, we will normalize our prices by taking $p_0 = 1$. It then follows, just as in Lecture 3, that these equations determine the prices $p_1, \cdots, p_n$. We shall call the solutions of equations (17.6) $p_j(\sigma_1, \cdots, \sigma_n; \rho)$.

The next condition which prices must satisfy is the condition that no manufacturer can, by changing his scheme of production, improve his profit. That is, for $p_j(\sigma_1, \cdots, \sigma_n; \rho)$ to be equilibrium prices we must have

$$(17.7) \quad p_i(\sigma_1, \cdots, \sigma_n; \ \rho) - \sum_{j=0}^{n} \pi_{ij}(\sigma'_i) p_j(\sigma_1, \cdots, \sigma_n; \ \rho)$$

$$- \rho \sum_{j=1}^{n} \phi_{ij}(\sigma'_i) p_j(\sigma_1, \cdots, \sigma_n; \ \rho) \leq 0, \quad i = 1, \cdots, n,$$

$$\text{for all } \sigma'_1, \cdots, \sigma'_n.$$

Let us examine the condition (17.7) for a particular value of i, say for $i = 1$. Let M denote the $n \times n$ matrix whose elements M_{ij} are defined by the equations

$$(17.8) \qquad \begin{aligned} M_{1j} &= \pi_{1j}(\sigma'_1) + \rho\phi_{1j}(\sigma'_1) \\ M_{ij} &= \pi_{ij}(\sigma_i) + \rho\phi_{ij}(\sigma_i), \quad i = 2, \cdots, n. \end{aligned}$$

Similarly, let $\mathbf{v}$ denote the vector whose components v. are defined by

$$(17.9) \qquad \begin{aligned} v_1 &= \pi_{10}(\sigma'_1) \\ v_i &= \pi_{i0}(\sigma_i), \quad i = 2, \cdots, n. \end{aligned}$$

Then the first of the conditions (17.7), together with all but the first of equations (17.6), may be written in the form

$$(17.10) \qquad (1 - M)\mathbf{p}(\sigma_1, \cdots, \sigma_n; \ \rho) \leqq \mathbf{v}.$$

On the other hand, it is clear that we have

$$(17.11) \qquad (1 - M)\mathbf{p}(\sigma'_1, \sigma_2, \cdots, \sigma_n; \ \rho) = \mathbf{v}.$$

Thus

$$(17.12) \quad (1 - M)\{\mathbf{p}(\sigma_1, \cdots, \sigma_n; \ \rho) - \mathbf{p}(\sigma'_1, \sigma_2, \cdots, \sigma_n; \ \rho)\} \leqq 0.$$

Using Lemmas 3.3–3.6 it follows at once that

$$(17.13) \qquad \mathbf{p}(\sigma_1, \cdots, \sigma_n; \ \rho) \leqq \mathbf{p}(\sigma'_1, \sigma_2, \cdots, \sigma_n; \ \rho)$$

for all σ'_1. We may show in exactly the same way that the condition

$$(17.14) \quad p_1(\sigma_1, \cdots, \sigma_n; \ \rho) - \sum_{j=0}^{n} \pi_{1j}(\sigma'_1) p_j(\sigma_1, \cdots, \sigma_n; \ \rho)$$

$$- \rho \sum_{j=1}^{n} \phi_{1j}(\sigma'_1) p_j(\sigma_1, \cdots, \sigma_n; \ \rho) \geq 0$$

implies the statement

$$(17.15) \qquad \mathbf{p}(\sigma_1, \cdots, \sigma_n; \ \rho) \geqq \mathbf{p}(\sigma'_1, \sigma_2, \cdots, \sigma_n; \ \rho).$$

Thus, it follows at once that the first of the conditions (17.7), the condition (17.13), and the condition

$$(17.16) \qquad p_1(\sigma_1, \sigma_2, \cdots, \sigma_n; \ \rho) \geq p_1(\sigma'_1, \sigma_2, \cdots, \sigma_n; \ \rho)$$

are all equivalent. From this we see at once that the full set of conditions (17.7) are equivalent to the statement

$$(17.17) \quad p_j(\sigma_1, \cdots, \sigma_{j-1}, \sigma_j, \sigma_{j+1}, \cdots, \sigma_n; \ \rho)$$
$$\leq p_j(\sigma_1, \cdots, \sigma_{j-1}, \sigma'_j, \sigma_{j+1}, \cdots, \sigma_n; \ \rho), \quad j = 1, \cdots, n.$$

Let me now remind you that we have met conditions of precisely this mathematical form previously: in Lecture 5, Section 1, where we gave the definition of equilibrium points (in the sense of Nash) for an arbitrary game. Comparing the definition given there with the conditions (17.17), we see that our "game" now depends on an additional parameter ρ; in the "ρth game" the "payoff to the jth player" is $-p_j(\sigma_1, \cdots, \sigma_n; \ \rho)$. Let the game with these payoff functions be called $\Gamma(\rho)$. In order not to complicate the course of our analysis, we shall make the not unreasonable assumption that the equilibrium point of the game $\Gamma(\rho)$ is stable and unique, i.e. that conditions (17.17) determine a unique set of parameters $\sigma_1(\rho), \cdots, \sigma_n(\rho)$. We shall also assume that the functions $\sigma_j(\rho)$ so determined depend smoothly on the parameter ρ. Thus, for any given value of the parameter ρ, there exists a uniquely defined "optimal" scheme for production of the ith commodity, with input coefficients $\pi_{ij}(\sigma_i(\rho))$ and capital coefficients $\phi_{ij}(\sigma_i(\rho))$. By the symbols $\pi_{ij}(\rho)$ and $\phi_{ij}(\rho)$ we will denote the matrices with elements

$$(17.18) \qquad \pi_{ij}(\rho) = \pi_{ij}(\sigma_i(\rho)); \quad \phi_{ij}(\rho) = \phi_{ij}(\sigma_i(\rho)).$$

Then, taking all in all, we may conclude that just as in Lecture 3 prices at competitive equilibrium may be defined uniquely by specification of a rate-of-profit parameter ρ through the equations

$$(17.19) \qquad p_i(\rho) - \sum_{j=0}^{n} \pi_{ij}(\rho) p_j(\rho) = \rho \sum_{j=1}^{n} \phi_{ij}(\rho) p_j(\rho).$$

The fixed-matrix theory of the preceding lectures now appears as that special case of the present more general theory in which the optimal matrices $\pi_{ij}(\rho)$ and $\phi_{ij}(\rho)$ vary only slightly with ρ.

We shall next establish a property of the prices $p_j(\rho)$ which tells us that the family of production schemes described by the set of parameters $\sigma_1(\rho), \cdots, \sigma_n(\rho)$ has a very strong optimum property.

LEMMA 17.1.   *For each $\sigma_1, \cdots, \sigma_n$ and ρ we have*

$$(17.20) \qquad p_j(\sigma_1, \cdots, \sigma_n; \ \rho) \geq p_j(\rho), \quad j = 1, \cdots, n.$$

Thus, the production schemes described by the "optimum" parameters $\sigma_1(\rho), \cdots, \sigma_n(\rho)$ yield lowest equilibrium prices at the rate of profit ρ among all possible production schemes. This is another striking optimum property of free competition like that remarked upon in the final paragraphs of Lecture 2.

Proof: Suppose that our lemma is false, so that on passing from the family of production schemes described by the parameters $\sigma_1(\rho), \cdots, \sigma_n(\rho)$ to the family described by the parameters $\sigma_1 \cdots \sigma_n$ the price of at least one commodity will fall. Choose a commodity whose price falls by the largest proportionate amount, and, by renumbering the commodities, suppose that this is the commodity C_1. Then plainly

$$(17.21) \quad [p_1(\rho)]/[p_1(\sigma_1 \cdots \sigma_n; \ \rho)] \geq [p_j(\rho)]/[p_j(\sigma_1 \cdots \sigma_n; \ \rho)],$$
$$j = 0, 2, 3, \cdots, n.$$

Since

$$(17.22) \quad p_1(\sigma_1 \cdots \sigma_n; \ \rho) - \sum_{j=0}^{n} \pi_{1j}(\sigma_1) p_j(\sigma_1 \cdots \sigma_n; \ \rho)$$
$$- \rho \sum_{j=1}^{n} \phi_{1j}(\sigma_1) p_j(\sigma_1 \cdots \sigma_n; \ \rho) = 0,$$

it follows from (17.21) that

$$(17.23) \quad p_1(\rho) - \sum_{j=0}^{n} \pi_{ij}(\sigma_1) p_j(\rho) - \rho \sum_{j=1}^{n} \phi_{ij}(\sigma_1) p_j(\rho) \geq 0.$$

It follows from this statement, just in the same way as formula (17.13) followed from formula (17.12), that

$$(17.24) \quad \mathbf{p}(\sigma_1, \sigma_2(\rho), \cdots, \sigma_n(\rho); \ \rho) \geq \mathbf{p}(\sigma_1(\rho), \cdots, \sigma_n(\rho); \ \rho).$$

But then, contrary to assumption, the equilibrium point of the game $\Gamma(\rho)$ is not stable. The contradiction proves our lemma. Q.E.D.

At the end of the first section of Lecture 3 we established a fact of which we made essential use in analyzing the form of the schedules of labor supply and labor demand: with $p_0 \equiv 1$ as a normalization, all the prices $p_j(\rho)$ are increasing functions of ρ. It is now quite easy to establish the same fact for the present more general model. Indeed, by the result given in Lecture 3 for the case in which the scheme of production is fixed, we have

$$(17.25) \quad p_j(\sigma_1(\rho), \cdots, \sigma_n(\rho); \ \rho') < p_j(\sigma_1(\rho), \cdots, \sigma_n(\rho); \ \rho),$$
$$j = 1, \cdots, n,$$

if $\rho' < \rho$. By the preceding lemma we have

$$(17.26) \quad p_j(\sigma_1(\rho'), \cdots, \sigma_n(\rho'); \ \rho') \leq p_j(\sigma_1(\rho), \cdots, \sigma_n(\rho); \ \rho'),$$
$$j = 1, \cdots, n.$$

Thus each price $p_j(\rho)$ is a strictly increasing function of the parameter ρ. We may conclude just as in Section 7 of Lecture 3 that any measure of real wages may be taken as a parameter determining the whole set of prices, and that any such measure varies inversely with the parameter ρ.

It follows just as in Lecture 3 that ρ has a range of variation bounded below by zero and bounded above by the largest rate of profit attainable under the condition $p_0 = 0$. This upper bound for the rate of profit, which just as in Lecture 3 we will denote by the symbol $\rho_{\max}$, may be defined as follows. Let $\overset{\circ}{\Pi}(\sigma_1 \cdots \sigma_n)$ and $\overset{\circ}{\Phi}(\sigma_1 \cdots \sigma_n)$ be the $n \times n$ matrices whose entries are $\pi_{ij}(\sigma_i)$ and $\phi_{ij}(\sigma_i)$ respectively, and let $\rho(\sigma_1 \cdots \sigma_n)$ be determined by the condition

$$(17.27) \quad \mathrm{dom}\ (\overset{\circ}{\Pi}(\sigma_1 \cdots \sigma_n) + \rho(\sigma_1 \cdots \sigma_n)\overset{\circ}{\Phi}(\sigma_1 \cdots \sigma_n)) = 1.$$

Then $\rho_{\max} = \max_{\sigma_1, \cdots \sigma_n} \rho(\sigma_1 \cdots \sigma_n)$.

We may at this point remark once more that our analysis of prices shows that even in the framework of the present general model price ratios are determined up to a single parameter from the conditions of production. As we have emphasized in the final paragraph of Section 1, Lecture 3, this conclusion constitutes strong presumptive evidence against theories which attempt to tie prices to consumer demand. More generally, we see that by allowing variation in the scheme of production, we in fact introduce no changes in the fixed-matrix Leontief model other than to make the Leontief matrices dependent on the single parameter ρ.

3. Embedding the Price Theory in an Equilibrium Theory

We may now embed the price theory of the preceding section into a more complete model of economic equilibrium constructed in a fashion entirely analogous to that of the model of the preceding lecture. We shall include autonomous investment in our model, in the manner explained in the final section of the preceding lecture. Our model of equilibrium has again n "firms," and a single homogeneous labor commodity; we have a collection of possible production schemes for the ith commodity C_i described by a parameter family $\pi_{ij}(\sigma_i)$ and $\phi_{ij}(\sigma_i)$ of Leontief matrices as in the preceding sections of the present lecture. We will again have f consumption units; each firm will be required to have given fixed fraction ψ_k of total wealth, and each family will own a fixed share $h_{\nu k}$ of the kth firm. As before we put $\psi_\nu = \Sigma_k \psi_k h_{\nu k}$. Each firm will be assumed to account for a given portion $I_i^{(k)}$ of the total investment

$$(17.28) \qquad I_i - \sum_{k=1}^{m} I_i^{(k)}$$

in commodity C_i. We have family utility functions which are the same as those of Section 2 of the preceding lecture. The kth firm will have an inventory $q_j^{(k)}$ of the jth commodity; these inventories are to come into an equilibrium described by our model.

In this framework, an equilibrium is given by a set of prices $p_0, \cdots, p_n$, production figures $a_i^{(k)}, \cdots, a_n^{(k)}$ for the kth firm, consumption figures $s_0^{(\nu)}, \cdots, s_n^{(\nu)}$ for the νth family, inventory levels $q_j^{(k)}$ for the kth firm, and production-scheme parameters $\sigma_1, \cdots, \sigma_n$ for each commodity, satisfying the following conditions.

Condition (a). The prices are all nonnegative and at least one is different from zero.

Condition (b). For each firm $k = 1 \cdots m$ the profit

$$(17.29) \qquad \sum_{i=1}^{n} \sum_{j=0}^{n} a_i^{(k)}(\delta_{ij} - \pi_{ij}(\sigma_i))p_j$$

is a maximum over all $\sigma_1, \cdots, \sigma_n$ and over all the sets $\tilde{a}_i$ which satisfy

$$(17.30) \qquad \sum_{i=1}^{n} \tilde{a}_i \phi_{ij}(\sigma_i) \leq \sum_{j=1}^{n} q_j^{(k)} p_j.$$

Condition (c). For each consumer unit $\nu = 1 \cdots f$, the number

$$(17.31) \qquad u_\nu(s_0^{(\nu)}, \cdots, s_n^{(\nu)}; \quad q_{1\nu}, \cdots, q_{n\nu}; \quad p_0, \cdots, p_n)$$

is a maximum over all $\bar{s}_0, \cdots, \bar{s}_n$ which satisfy

$$(17.32) \qquad \sum_{j=0}^{n} \bar{s}_j p_j - \sum_{j=0}^{n} \sum_{i=1}^{n} \sum_{k=1}^{m} a_i^{(k)}(\delta_{ij} - \pi_{ij}(\sigma_i))p_j h_{\nu k}$$

$$+ \sum_{k=1}^{m} \sum_{j=1}^{n} I_j^{(k)} p_j h_{\nu k} \leq \sum_{k=1}^{n} q_{k\nu} p_k;$$

here $q_{k\nu}$ is defined by (16.2).

Condition (d). Everything that is consumed or invested must be produced and vice-versa, i.e.,

$$(17.33) \qquad \sum_{i,k} a_i^{(k)}(\delta_{ij} - \pi_{ij}(\sigma_i)) - \sum_{\nu} s_j^{(\nu)} - I_j = 0, \quad j = 0, \cdots, n.$$

Condition (e). No item of capital can be in short supply, i.e.,

$$(17.34) \qquad \sum_{k,i} a_i^{(k)} \phi_{ij}(\sigma_i) \leq \sum_{k} q_j^{(k)}, \quad j = 1, \cdots, n.$$

Condition (f). Firms' relative wealth must remain in specified proportions, i.e.,

$$(17.35) \qquad \psi_k \left\{ \sum_{k=1}^{m} \sum_{j=1}^{n} q_j^{(k)} p_j \right\} = \sum_{j=1}^{n} q_j^{(k)} p_j.$$

These conditions define a model of equilibrium resembling the model presented in Section 6 of the preceding lecture in all respects, save that where the previous model involved a fixed scheme of production the present model allows the scheme of production to vary. Our next task is to analyze the equilibria of our model.

4. Existence and Properties of Equilibrium

Section 6 of the preceding lecture gives us a model for our analysis which may be followed with only the slightest of changes. As we have seen in Section 2, above (cf. formula (17.18) and the discussion which comes before it), the prices and the optimum production scheme are both uniquely defined as functions of a rate of profit parameter ρ. Thus any differences which may exist between the present equilibrium model and the model of Section 6 of the preceding lecture must originate in the fact that whereas the matrices Π and Φ of the previous model were constant, here they depend on the rate of profit ρ. To the extent that this variation is moderate, we must expect our present equilibria to resemble those of the preceding chapter. Conversely, in order for our preceding conclusions to undergo modification, it is necessary that the optimal scheme of production should vary substantially with the parameter ρ.

Once it is agreed that prices are to be determined as in Section 2 above, Condition (b) becomes equivalent to the conjunction of the conditions $p_j = p_j(\rho)$ and the condition

$$(17.36) \qquad \sum_{i=0}^{n} \sum_{j=1}^{n} a_j{}^{(k)} \phi_{ji}(\rho) p_i = \sum_{i=1}^{n} q_i{}^{(k)} p_i.$$

These conditions and Condition (c) require the νth family's consumption plan to be described by the numbers maximizing the utility function (16.3) subject to the condition

$$(17.37) \qquad \sum_{j=0}^{n} \hat{s}_j p_j \le (1 + \rho) \sum_{k=1}^{n} q_{k\nu} p_k - \sum_{i=1}^{m} \sum_{j=1}^{n} I_j{}^{(k)} p_j h_{k\nu};$$

we may assume as in the preceding chapter that this determines a set of maximizing values $s_j{}^{(\nu)}(q_1 \cdots q_n; p_0 \cdots p_n)$. We may then determine total production $a_i(q_{11}, \cdots, q_{nf}; \rho)$ as a function of the savings levels and the rate of profit ρ as in (16.14)–(16.16), modifying the equation (16.15) however to

$$(17.38) \qquad \sum_{i} a_i(\delta_{ij} - \pi_{ij}(\rho)) = s_j(q_{11}, \cdots, q_{nf}; \rho) + I_j$$

(cf. Equation (16.35)). Next, we may show as in Section 6 of the preceding lecture that an equilibrium can be found by satisfying the relations

$$(17.39) \qquad \sum_{i=0}^{n} \sum_{j=1}^{n} a_j \phi_{ji}(\rho) p_i(\rho) = \sum_{i=1}^{n} q_i p_i(\rho)$$

(where we have written $q_i = \Sigma_k q_i{}^{(k)}$ for the total inventory of C_i);

$$(17.40) \qquad \sum_{i=1}^{n} a_i \phi_{ij}(\rho) \le q_j, \quad j = 1, \cdots, n;$$

$$(17.41) \qquad -s_0(q_{11}, \cdots, q_{nf}; \rho) = \sum_{i=1}^{n} a_i(q_{11}, \cdots, q_{nf}; \rho) \pi_{io}(\rho);$$

and the equations (17.35) and (16.37). At this point, we may proceed just as in Section 4 of the preceding lecture and on the basis of the assumption used there to find functions $q_{j\nu}(\eta_1, \cdots, \eta_n; \rho)$ $= q(\eta_1, \cdots, \eta_n; \rho)\eta_j\psi_\nu$, depending continuously on a set of nonnegative parameters $\eta_1, \cdots, \eta_n$ satisfying $\Sigma_i\eta_i = 1$, which satisfy the equations (17.35) and (16.37). These functions $q_{j\nu}(\eta_1, \cdots, \eta_n; \rho)$ will be defined, as in Section 4 of the preceding lecture, for all ρ in a range $\rho_0 \leq \rho \leq \rho_{max}$, ρ_0 being the rate of profit which corresponds to that real wage rate at which families with a pure wage income would begin to save at a total annual rate exceeding the specified total amount $\Sigma_j I_j p_j(\rho)$ of annual investment.

Next it follows, just as in Sections 4 and 6 of the preceding lecture, that we find an equilibrium at any points $\eta_1 \cdots \eta_n$ and ρ at which the supply and demand for labor as defined by the formulae

$$(17.42) \quad -s_0(\eta_1, \cdots, \eta_n; \rho)$$
$$= -s_0(q_{11}(\eta_1, \cdots, \eta_n; \rho), \cdots, q_{nf}(\eta_1, \cdots, \eta_n; \rho); \rho)$$

and

$$(17.43) \quad d_0(\eta_1, \cdots, \eta_n; \rho)$$
$$= \sum_{i=1}^{n} \pi_{io}(\rho)a_i(q_{11}(\eta_1, \cdots, \eta_n; \rho), \cdots, q_{nf}(\eta_1, \cdots, \eta_n; \rho); \rho)$$

are equal and at which all the inequalities

$$(17.44) \quad \sum_{i=1}^{n} a_i(\eta_1, \cdots, \eta_n; \rho)\phi_{ij}(\rho) \leq q_j(\eta_1, \cdots, \eta_n; \rho)$$

are satisfied. Such points may now be found by using the Brouwer fixed-point theorem and the form of the supply-demand schedules for labor, as in Sections 4 and 6 of the preceding lecture. Thus the mathematical treatment of the present model hardly differs from the treatment of the models of the preceding lecture.

For our analytical purposes, however, it is essential that we examine the form of the labor supply and demand schedules more closely. The schedule of labor supply should not look very different in the present case than in the cases studied in Lectures 14 and 16. This assertion may be justified by the reflection that, as we have shown, the present case shares with the earlier cases the feature that all components of real wages move inversely to the rate of profit ρ, sinking to zero at $\rho = \rho_{max}$. There is then no apparent reason why moderate variations in relative prices occasioned by shifts in the production scheme should change the general form of the labor-supply schedule from the form depicted in Fig. 24.

This being the case, Fig. 24 (cf. also Fig. 25) shows plainly that almost independently of the precise shape of the schedule of labor demand, equilibrium will be struck at a rate of profit lying in the small range in which labor supply falls off most sharply. This fact is, of course, not in dispute between neoclassicists and Keynesians. Rather, the neoclassical argument aims at showing that if by removing certain union-centered forces the acceptable wage was lowered, so that in Figs. 24 and 25 the steepest portions of the labor-supply schedule were shifted to the right, then other desirable economic consequences would follow, as, for instance, increased production and decreased unemployment. The correctness or incorrectness of such assertions relate, of course, not to the schedule of labor supply but to the schedule of labor demand. Let us next try to examine the form of this schedule.

The shape of the labor-demand schedule depends on the size of the savings of other factors of production which an entrepreneur can achieve by using labor more lavishly. As the price of labor falls, an entrepreneur may decide to use more labor in turning out a unit of his product, but only, of course, to the extent that hiring more labor makes it possible to attain other savings coming to a larger total than the wages of the last laborer employed. These hypothetical savings are to be achieved in one of two possible ways: through systematic scrimping of raw materials and other input factors, which effort the entrepreneur might have found to be unprofitable at higher wage rates; and through the use in production of less elaborate capital equipment by an increased number of laborers. Little quantitative evidence on these possibilities seems to be available, though perhaps some information might be elucidated through comparative studies of industrial practice in the United States and in nations where the real wage rate is considerably lower, as, e.g., Japan. It is hard to imagine, however, that savings in either of these two forms could be very substantial. Raw material wastage would ordinarily require such small quantities of labor for its correction that it seems doubtful that present management can be neglecting much in this direction. Use of advanced capital equipment, on the other hand, is, where profitable, often so decisively superior to preceding methods of production that only an extreme fall in the wage rate could make the use of such equipment nonoptimal. Unless so considerably increased an amount of labor can be obtained at such a slight increase in total wages as to make possible very extensive raw material and capital savings, the wage bill per unit of production will surely fall with the wage rate, though perhaps somewhat less than proportionately. In this case, we may expect demand for commodities as a function of ρ to behave as in Lectures 14 and 16. As in those lectures, aggregate demand may be divided approximately into the sum of wage-generated demand and dividend-generated demand. The first contribution to demand depends upon the wage bill per unit of production: if this falls off with a falling wage rate, so will wage-generated demand. Dividend-generated demand, on the other hand, will rise with increasing ρ, but since as ρ rises the equilibrium amount q_ν of savings which will give the νth family an income at which it will not add to savings must fall, dividend-generated demand should rise only moderately with ρ. Thus, taking all in all, aggregate demand, and hence aggregate production, may be expected to fall with increasing ρ. Correspondingly, national income will fall with increasing ρ.

If in such a case total labor demand falls less sharply than commodity demand, or even, as neoclassicists have sometimes contended, rises, it can only mean that a larger number of persons are working for a smaller total of wages. Labor unions would surely regard even this possibility as being inferior to the alternative of a higher level of wages and a shorter work-week. For the reasons explained above, however, we may expect that the scheme of production shifts only moderately with a falling pay rate, so that as in the preceding lecture the labor-demand schedule ought to fall with increasing ρ. Thus, just as in the preceding lecture, equilibrium unemployment may be expected to rise with increasing ρ.

Additional General Reflections
on Keynesian Economics.
The Propensity to Consume

1. The Propensity to Consume and the Utility Functions. A Simplified Equilibrium Model

Our analysis of the general equilibrium models developed in Lecture 16 led us to the conclusion (cf. Figs. 24 and 25) that price-production equilibrium might well tend to be struck in a wage range in which labor supply varied very rapidly with prices. To the extent that this conclusion is justified, it would follow that the level of economic activity might vary widely (say, in response to autonomous changes in the rate of investment parameters I_j of the final section of Lecture 16) without this variation leading to much of a shift in the equilibrium price ratios. In Fig. 24 of Lecture 16, an increased rate of investment would correspond to an upward shift of the labor-demand schedule. As is obvious from Fig. 24, and even more obvious from Fig. 25, this might correspond to small price changes, but to considerable changes in the employment and unemployment levels.

To the extent that the above conclusions are correct, we may say that price levels can tend to be rigid while employment levels are variable. In such a situation, it is evident that the most useful scheme of theoretical simplification consists in eliminating the price aspect of the model of Lecture 16 entirely, and merely retaining, in some appropriately simplified form, the production-level aspects of the model. To do this is to abandon the neoclassical features of the model of Lecture 16, thereby obtaining a purely Keynesian equilibrium model. Similarly, we may say that the model of Lectures 13–15 is obtained from the general model of Lecture 16 by abandoning its Keynesian features, thereby obtaining a purely neoclassical model. Our analysis suggests, however, that the Keynesian simplification is appropriate while the neoclassical simplification is scientifically inappropriate in a typical way: to wit, the neoclassical simplification ignores the most significantly variable quantities in the general model of Lecture 16 in order to concentrate on certain rather doubtful small effects.

In the present lecture we shall construct, from the general model of Lecture 16, a purely Keynesian simplified equilibrium model of the sort suggested above, and apply this simplified model to the analysis of various economic problems, especially to analyze the shift of equilibrium occasioned by shifts in various of the underlying parameters determining equilibrium. We shall also attempt to indicate the relation between the neoclassical utility functions of Lectures 13–16 and the Keynesian consumption functions.

Let us first comment on the notion of a "consumption function." In Lecture 16, we assumed a family's consumption and labor-output preferences to be described by a utility function

$$(18.1) \qquad u(s_0, s_1, \cdots, s_n; \; q_1, \cdots, q_n; \; p_0, \cdots, p_n)$$

of labor expended $-s_0$, commodities consumed $s_1, \cdots, s_n$, savings q and prices p. (In the simpler model of Lectures 13–15, we assumed similarly but more specifically that consumer preferences could be described by a utility function u independent of savings and prices.) In any case, if we maximize the function (18.1) over all $s_0, \cdots, s_n$ satisfying the condition

$$(18.2) \qquad s_0 p_0 + s_1 p_1 + \cdots + s_n p_n \leq q_1 p_1 + \cdots + q_n p_n + \Delta$$

(Δ denoting the family dividend income) we find that the maximum lies at a point $\bar{s}_0, \cdots, \bar{s}_n$ depending on the parameters Δ, q and p. In this way we introduce functions

$$(18.3) \qquad \bar{s}_j(q_1, \cdots, q_n, p_0, \cdots, p_n, \Delta), \quad j = 0, \cdots, n$$

quite equivalent for our analytic purposes (as we saw in Lecture 16) to the utility function (18.1). The first of the functions (18.3) describes the labor-offerings of a family in dependence on its savings and on market prices; the functions $s_1 \cdots s_n$ describe the commodity-by-commodity consumption budget of the same family, and may be called the *consumption functions*.

It has been customary since Keynes to write these consumption functions in a modified way. As we have emphasized in the preceding paragraphs, the range of prices in which we are apt to be most interested is apt to be one in which (for an economically significant group of families) s_0 varies very rapidly, almost discontinuously, with p_0 (cf. Figs. 24 and 25). Hence this range will also, as we see from (18.2), be a range in which the quantities s_j, $j = 1, \cdots, n$, vary quite rapidly with p_0. If we are to have functions which can be useful as a basis for arguments of a conventional sort, we need continuous rather than discontinuous functions describing the point at which the utility function (18.1) attains its maximum. How can such continuous functions be obtained? To see the answer to this question most simply, let us consider the slightly idealized limiting case in which s_0 varies discontinuously with p_0, as in Fig. 25. In such a case, the point at which the utility function (18.1) is maximized is not uniquely defined by $\mathbf{p}$; any point on the vertical portion of the labor-supply schedule of Fig. 25, i.e., any labor-supply figure in an entire range, would correspond to a maximum of the utility function (18.1). The form (18.2) of the condition defining the desired maximum then makes it evident that we can take $w = -s_0 p_0 + \Delta$ as a parameter describing this range, and, instead of proceeding as above, maximize (18.1) over $s_1, \cdots, s_n$ subject to the condition

$$(18.4) \qquad s_1 p_1 + \cdots + s_n p_n \leq q_1 p_1 + \cdots + q_n p_n - s_0 p_0 + \Delta,$$

letting p_0 be that wage rate at which the discontinuity of the labor supply occurs, thereby obtaining consumption functions

$$(18.5) \qquad s_j(w; \; q_1 \cdots q_n; \; p_1 \cdots p_n), \quad j = 1, \cdots, n.$$

In the less idealized case in which s_0 is not *sharply* discontinuous in p_0, but merely varies very rapidly with p_0 in a certain range, the functions (18.5) may equivalently be obtained by solving the equation

$$(18.6) \qquad w = -p_0 s_0(q_1, \cdots, q_n; \; p_0, p_1, \cdots, p_n) + \Delta$$

for p_0 in terms of w, and substituting the resulting expression for p_0 in the functions (18.3).

The functions (18.5) then give the dependence of consumption (by individual commodities) on income w, savings $q_1, \cdots, q_n$, and prices $\mathbf{p}$; it is heuristically evident that these functions ought to be continuous. The functions (18.5) may be called the *consumption functions in Keynesian form*. It is reasonable to simplify these functions by assuming given prices (for the reasons explained in the earlier paragraphs of the present section) and by assuming that the functions s_j depend on savings only through the total cash value of savings; with these assumptions, the Keynesian consumption functions (18.5) simplify to functions

$$(18.7) \qquad\qquad s_j(w, q), \quad j = 1, \cdots, n$$

giving the dependence of commodity-by-commodity consumption for a given family on the family's income and savings. In a slightly more general model, in which we had several labor sectors producing labor commodities $C_0, \cdots, C_{-L}$, and in which consumption of services as well as consumption of commodities was allowed, we would have in the same way a set of Keynesian consumption functions

$$(18.8) \qquad\qquad s_j(w, q), \quad j = -L, \cdots, n,$$

giving the dependence of all forms of commodity consumption and service output on income and savings.

In terms of the consumption functions (18.8), the *propensity to consume* may be defined as

$$(18.9) \qquad\qquad K(w, q) = \sum_{j=0}^{n} p_j s_j(w, q)/w;$$

K is the fraction of income expended on consumption, in dependence on income and savings. Similarly,

$$(18.10) \qquad\qquad \sum_{j=0}^{n} p_j s_j(w, q) = s(w, q)$$

defines the schedule of family consumption expenditures in dependence upon income and savings.

An appropriate reduction of the equilibrium model developed in the final section of Lecture 16 now leads to a Keynesian equilibrium model involving the consumption functions (18.8). To make this reduction, note that since, as we have explained in the early paragraphs of the present section, prices are to be taken as fixed, condition (a) of the final section of Lecture 16, which merely requires prices to be positive, is evanescent. Moreover, Condition (b), which in Lecture 16 defined prices through a condition of maximum profitability, reduces in the present situation to the condition that the whole mass of capital in the model economy is used in production. We may give a definite mathematical form to this requirement, as follows. Let our model include f families, the νth family having savings q_ν. Let the total "daily" production of commodity i be a_i; and let the amount of fixed capital necessarily tied up (for one "day") in the production of a unit of the ith commodity be ϕ_i. Then we require that

$$(18.11) \qquad \sum_{\nu=1}^{f} q_\nu = \sum_{i=1}^{n} \phi_i a_i.$$

(In what follows, we shall avoid inessential complications by assuming a single labor sector, and restricting consumption to material commodities. We also assume $\phi_0 = 0$.) Condition (c) of the final section of Lecture 16 requires that each family's utility function be maximized; this condition is automatically satisfied in virtue of our having passed from utility to consumption functions as described above, and hence Condition (c) leaves no additional trace. Condition (d) of Lecture 16 requires that production just support consumption plus investment and that supply of labor just balance demand for labor. We may write the first of these requirements in analogy with (11.34) as

$$(18.12) \quad a_j - \sum_{i=1}^{n} a_i \pi_{ij} = \sum_{r=1}^{f} s_j{}^{(\nu)}(w_\nu, q_\nu) + I_j, \quad j = 1, \cdots, n.$$

Here, w_ν denotes the income of the νth family, q_ν the savings of the νth family, and I_j denotes investment plus autonomous government expenditure, which, in the sense explained in the final section of the preceding lecture, we take to be autonomous and given.

The additional condition that supply of labor balance demand for labor then takes a somewhat different form, which may be explained as follows. The total income w_ν of the νth family is the sum of its dividend income Δ_ν and its wage income Ω_ν. Dividend income is the product of savings q_ν by the (fixed) rate of profit ρ which corresponds to the (given) prices $p_0 \cdots p_n$. Similarly, wage income Ω_ν is the product of labor price times labor supplied by the νth family. Thus the condition that labor supply balance labor demand may be written as

$$(18.13) \qquad \sum_{\nu=1}^{f} \Omega_\nu = p_0 \sum_{i=1}^{n} a_i \pi_{io}.$$

This condition evidently defines only the total of wage payments, not the distribution of wage payments to individual families. This deficiency is, of course, an unavoidable consequence of the fact that the labor-supply schedule has a near-discontinuity at the equilibrium price level p_0, so that the ordinary competitive mechanism by which "cheaper suppliers" are infallibly selected to the exclusion of "more expensive suppliers" does not function with sufficient force so that its effects may be distinguished from the effects of pure chance. This being the case, it is appropriate for us to assume that beyond what is given by (18.13) Ω_ν is determined homogeneously as by chance, i.e., that

$$(18.14) \qquad \Omega_\nu = p_0 N_\nu \sum_{i=1}^{n} a_i \pi_{io},$$

N_ν being the proportionate share of the νth family in the labor market, so that, heuristically, N_ν is a measure of the number of members of the νth family who seek work at the given price levels of our model. Instead of the parameter N_ν we may make use of the parameter $\lambda_\nu = p_0 N_\nu$ which describes both rate of wages and share in the labor market of the νth family. Thus, in our present model, the condition that supply and demand of labor are in balance appears in the rather different form

$$(18.15) \qquad w_\nu = \lambda_\nu \sum_{i=1}^{n} a_i \pi_{io} + \rho q_\nu.$$

It should be remarked that in not subtracting from the income expression (18.15) a figure representing corporate income withheld for investment from dividends we are implicitly assuming that such retained profits appear immediately as stock appreciation (capital gains), and that income in this form is valued exactly as dividend income by a family in making consumption decisions.

Condition (e) of Lecture 16 which, in going beyond the requirement (18.10), refers to the details of the physical composition of the total available capital, we abandon as beside the point for the present discussion. Finally, Condition (f) of the final section of Lecture 16, which states that each family's wealth remains in a certain given proportion to total wealth, we take over without change.

In summary, then, an equilibrium in our Keynesian model is a set $a_i \cdots a_b$ and $q_i \cdots q_f$ of activity and savings levels such that

$$(18.16) \quad a_j - \sum_{i=1}^{n} a_i \pi_{ij} = I_j + \sum_{\nu=1}^{f} s_j^{(\nu)}(\rho q_\nu + \lambda_\nu \sum_{i=1}^{n} \pi_{io} a_i; \ q_\nu)$$

$$(18.17) \qquad q_\nu = \psi_\nu \sum_{i=1}^{n} a_i \phi_i, \quad \nu = 1, \cdots, f.$$

Here, I_j are the (given) rates of investment and government expenditure; ρ the (given) average rate of profit; ϕ_i are (given) fixed capital coefficients; λ_ν are fixed coefficients whose significance we have explained above, and ψ_ν are parameters satisfying

$$(18.18) \qquad\qquad \sum_{\nu=1}^{f} \psi_\nu = 1,$$

the parameter ψ_ν describing the distribution by families of fractions of industrial ownership.

2. Existence of Equilibria for the System of Section 1

It is not hard to show that under a suitable assumption the system of equations (18.16)–(18.17) must have a solution. Put

$$(18.19) \quad S_j(a_1 \cdots a_n) = \sum_{\nu=1}^{f} s_j^{(\nu)} \left(\rho \psi_\nu \sum_{i=1}^{n} a_i \phi_i + \lambda_\nu \sum_{i=1}^{n} \pi_{io} a_i; \right.$$

$$\left. \psi_\nu \sum_{i=1}^{n} a_i \phi_i \right).$$

Then it is obvious that, ψ_ν being arbitrarily specified, the equations (18.16)–(18.17) reduce to the system

$$(18.20) \quad a_j - \sum_{i=1}^{n} a_i \pi_{ij} = I_j + S_j(a_1 \cdots a_n), \quad j = 1, \cdots, n.$$

If we assume that

$$(18.21) \qquad (w+q)^{-1} s_j^{(\nu)} (w,q) \to 0 \quad \text{as } w + q \to \infty,$$

i.e., that consumption drops to an arbitrarily small fraction of income + savings at extremely large income-savings values, then the equations (18.20) must have a solution. This assertion follows readily from the Brouwer fixed-point theorem. However, since the details of the proof would add little to our economic understanding, we omit them. Note however the conclusion that our model determines equilibrium production levels from consumption functions, prices and the rate of profit, and from the parameters ψ_ν describing the distribution by families of industrial ownership.

3. Consumption Functions in Our Earlier Models

In the cycle-theory models of Lectures 5–10, and also in our attempt to estimate the Keynes multiplier, Section 4 of Lecture 8, we assumed that a substantial part of consumption might be reasonably well approximated as being linearly dependent on employment. In our cycle theory we also found it convenient to assume that an additional part of consumption was autonomous and constant. It is appropriate at this point for us to indicate in somewhat more detail the manner in which approximation to the general consumption functions of the present lecture might lead to such conveniently simple models.

If q_ν are the savings of the νth family, ρ the average rate of profit, and Ω_ν the wage income of the νth family, while $s_j^{(\nu)}(w, q)$ are the consumption functions for the νth family, then total personal consumption of the jth commodity is

$$(18.22) \qquad \sum_\nu s_j^{(\nu)}(\Omega_\nu + \rho q_\nu, q_\nu).$$

Use of the differential calculus allows us to approximate this to first order as

$$(18.23) \qquad \sum_\nu s_j^{(\nu)}(\rho q_\nu, q_\nu) + \sum_\nu \frac{\partial s_j^{(\nu)}}{\partial w}(\rho q_\nu, q_\nu)\Omega_\nu.$$

The averages

$$(18.24) \qquad \left[\sum_\nu \frac{\partial s_j^{(\nu)}}{\partial w}(\rho q_\nu, q_\nu)\Omega_\nu\right] \Big/ \left[p_0^{-1}\sum_\nu \Omega_\nu\right] = \pi_{oj}$$

would then define the elements π_{oj} for use in Lectures 5–10. Our earlier simplifying assumption that these elements π_{oj} are constant is to be justified by the reflection that the great bulk of wage income flows to ranges of the income-savings spectrum where q_ν is small, and that there is little reason why either secular or cyclical shifts of wage income should be other than randomly related to individual-family consumption peculiarities. Of course, π_{oj} will depend linearly on the real wage rate. With this assumption we may write (18.23) as

$$(18.25) \qquad \sum_\nu s_j^{(\nu)}(\rho q_\nu, q_\nu) + \pi_{oj} \sum_{i=1}^n a_i \pi_{io}.$$

The autonomous-consumption terms in the cycle-theory models of Lectures 7–10 are now to be identified with the sum of autonomously determined government expenditures and the personal consumption terms

$$(18.26) \qquad \sum_\nu s_j^{(\nu)}(\rho q_\nu, q_\nu).$$

To the extent that $s_j^{(\nu)}(\rho q_\nu, q_\nu)$ tends to level off at high values of q_ν, the substantial concentration of savings found empirically will allow us to treat even the modest addendum (18.26) to total personal and government consumption as a constant.

4. Some Statistics of Savings

Comparison of the definition of the elements π_{oj} given by equation (18.24) with the definition (1.8) of the matrix $\bar{\pi}_{ij}$ and with the multiplier equation (7.11) makes evident the fact that equilibrium GNP decreases as the propensity to save out of given income increases; this same conclusion might be deduced on a more general basis by examining either the Keynesian model of the earlier sections of the present lecture or the general models of Lecture 16.

This circumstance has led economists to a decided interest in the actual empirical form of the schedule of consumption vs. income at various income levels. There have been many studies of this point, the facts, however, remaining somewhat unclear. Perhaps the easiest way to uncover the gross features of the statistical picture is to study savings summed over time, i.e., to study the distribution of families by net worth. In this attempt, we are assisted greatly by a recent study of Lampman.

Table XIX shows the breakdown of ownership of tangibles and intangibles as given by Lampman in the *Review of Economics and Statistics*. The figures describe the year 1953.

TABLE XIX

Noncorporate Ownership (billions of $) [a, b]

	Owned by families with total worth above $60,000	Owned by families with total worth below $60,000	Total ownership by families
Real estate	72	372	444
*U. S. bonds	23	37	60
*State bonds	17	0	17
*Corp. bonds	6	0	6
*Stocks	128	27	155
*Mortgages	11	20	31
*Life insurance	10	68	78
*Pension and retirement funds	4	59	63
Farm and nonfarm equities	20	167	187
Consumer durables	10	118	128
*Miscellaneous	43	43	86
*Bank deposits	46	114	160
Total	390	1025	1415
Less debt	29	102	131
Adjusted total	361	923	1284

[a] After Lampman.

[b] Headings marked * to be assigned as savings.

Table XIX gives value totals for individual ownership. In distinguishing savings from consumption, e.g., in distinguishing the purchase of a refrigerator as consumption from the purchase of a bond as savings, we mean to distinguish title to objects principally and normally used for the direct satisfaction of individual wants, from title to objects principally and normally used for production or exchange. Since this is not exactly the basis of any of Lampman's headings, we are as usual forced to make somewhat arbitrary assignments of his headings to one of these two categories. The headings which seem most appropriately assigned to the savings category have been marked with an asterisk in Table XIX. Examining these items as they apply for the families with net worth less than $60,000, we obtain for total savings exclusive of life insurance and pension and retirement funds a value of 241 billion. After debt is subtracted this becomes 139 billion. Compared to this the totals for life insurance, pensions and annuities come to 127 billion. Clearly, then, a substantial part of savings in this total-wealth range is in the form of emergency and old age protection. The propensity to save in this way would be measured by the normal excess of insurance and pension contributions by the living and young over receipts of insurance and pensions by survivors and the elderly. Whatever the relevant figure, it will surely be only a fraction of the total of 127 billion. Thus, for instance, 48 billion of the 59 billion sum for pension and retirement funds represent government social security reserves. We see that total accumulated savings, including all pension and insurance reserves in the group of under $60,000 families, must be rather less than 1 year's total wages and salaries. If an average working life is 30 years, we might then regard 4% as an upper estimate of the long-term propensity to save in this group of families. This then *indicates a propensity to spend near to 1* in the class of families with less than $60,000 net worth, somewhat masked of course by the movement of a given individual upon retirement from the category medium-income pension-contributor (with positive savings) to the category of the low-income pension-supported (with negative savings). We remark that these families include 97% of the population. The assumption of an 100% propensity to consume wages which we have made in our simplified cycle-theory models is at any rate not impossibly unrealistic.

If we compare these figures with the figures for families in the over $60,000 category, where net savings exclusive of pension and insurance reserves amount to $245 billion, plus $14 billion for pension and insurance reserves, the difference is plain. Making no pension-insurance correction, we would have (for the group of families over $60,000): savings $259 billion out of possessions of $361 billion. For families of under $60,000 net worth the corresponding figures are: savings $266 billion out of possessions of $858 billion. Any sizeable correction for pension and insurance would make the difference even more striking. Additional evidence pointing in this direction comes from figures given by Kuznets for annual savings (as compared to income) for those with annual incomes above and below the 90% percentile of the income spectrum, as shown in Table XX.

TABLE XX

Savings and Income in Lower 90% of Income Spectrum [a]

Year	Income, % of total income	Savings, % of total savings
1945	71	54
46	68	37
47	67	23
48	69	22
49	70	−5
50	71	27

[a] After Kuznets.

The drastic effect of the mild recession of '49 is plain.

5. Perturbation Theory of Keynesian Equilibria

Write

$$(18.27) \qquad w_\nu(\mathbf{a}) = \rho \psi_\nu \sum_{i=1}^{n} a_i \phi_i + \lambda_\nu \sum_{i=1}^{n} \pi_{io} a_i$$

and

$$(18.28) \qquad q_\nu(\mathbf{a}) = \psi_\nu \sum_{i=1}^{f} a_i \phi_i$$

for the income and savings of the νth family.   Then the equations (18.19) determining the Keynesian equilibrium may be written

$$(18.29) \qquad a_i - \sum_{i=1}^{n} a_i \pi_{ij} = I_j + \sum_{\nu=1}^{n} s_j^{(\nu)}(w_\nu(\mathbf{a}), q_\nu(\mathbf{a})).$$

In the present section, we wish to study the variation of the Keynesian equilibrium with shifts in the underlying conditions of our model, as, for instance, the shifts which might follow from changes in the investment rate, tax rates, and rate of government expenditure.   In such an investigation of gross effects it is appropriate, in the first place, to abstract from family-to-family variations in consumption preferences, and hence to identify all the consumption-functions $s_j{}^{(\nu)}(w, q)$ which occur in (18.29) with an average consumption-function $s_j(w, q)$; $s_j(w, q)$ describes the consumption habits of the average family with income w and savings q. If there are to be taxes, then income in this function should, of course, be taken as income after taxes, i.e., disposable income. Thus, if τ is a parameter (or parameters) describing the tax rates and the rate of government expenditure and private investment expenditure, then as τ varies after-tax income will vary; thus the income-function (18.27) should be replaced by an income-function $w_\nu(\mathbf{a}, \tau)$ depending on the tax and expenditure parameter τ (and reducing to (18.27) when the tax rate is zero). Similarly, the equilibrium equations go over in the presence of income taxes and government expenditures to

$$(18.30) \quad a_j(\tau) - \sum_{i=1}^{n} a_i(\tau)\pi_{ij} = I_j(\tau) + \sum_{\nu=1}^{f} s_j(w_\nu(\mathbf{a}(\tau); \ \tau); \ q_\nu(\mathbf{a}(\tau))).$$

The specific form of the functions $w_\nu(\mathbf{a}, \tau)$ depends on the details of tax policy. We shall not give any explicit form to these functions, since, as we shall see, the conclusions which we will be able to draw will be independent of the details of income tax policy.

We wish to study the effect on the position of equilibrium of a variation in τ; familiarity with the differential calculus puts us in possession of the fact that the effect of a small variation in τ is much easier to study quantitatively than the effect of a sizeable variation, and that the effect of small and moderate variations should be in close proportion. Thus, we need only consider small variations about a given value of τ; to do this, we differentiate (18.30) with respect to τ. It is convenient in manipulating the resulting expressions to introduce the following notations.

If a function f depends explicitly on τ and on certain other variables, then its partial derivative with respect to τ, the other variables being held fixed, will be written ∂f. If f depends explicitly on τ but also implicitly on τ through its other variables, then the "total" derivative of f with respect to τ will be written δf; here in taking the derivative we mean to let all the variables in f which depend on τ vary with τ. Thus, for instance, since $w_\nu = w_\nu(\mathbf{a}(\tau), \tau)$,

$$(18.31) \qquad\qquad \delta w_\nu = \partial w_\nu + \sum_{i=1}^{n} \frac{\partial w_\nu}{\partial a_i} \partial a_i.$$

The first term of this sum might represent a diminution of income arising from an increased tax rate, while the additional terms represent a compensatory rise following indirectly from increased government spending. Of course, if f depends only on τ and on no other variable, $\delta f = \partial f$.

Differentiating (18.30) we have

$$(18.32) \quad \delta a_j - \sum_{i=1}^{n} (\delta a_i)\pi_{ij} = \delta I_j + \sum_{i=1}^{n} \sum_{\nu=1}^{f} \frac{\partial s_j}{\partial a_i} (w_\nu(\mathbf{a}, \tau), q_\nu(\mathbf{a}))\delta a_i$$

$$+ \sum_{\nu=1}^{f} \frac{\partial s_j}{\partial w} (w_\nu(\mathbf{a}, \tau), q_\nu(\mathbf{a}))\partial w_\nu(\mathbf{a}, \tau).$$

If we introduce the abbreviation

$$(18.33) \qquad \hat{\pi}_{ij} = \pi_{ij} + \frac{\partial}{\partial a_i} \left\{ \sum_{\nu=1}^{f} s_j(w_\nu(\mathbf{a}, \tau), q_\nu(\mathbf{a})) \right\},$$

then equation (18.32) may be written as

$$(18.34) \quad \delta a_j - \sum_{i=1}^{n} (\delta a_i)\hat{\pi}_{ij} = \delta I_j + \sum_{\nu=1}^{f} \frac{\partial s_j}{\partial w} (w_\nu(\mathbf{a}, \tau), q_\nu(\mathbf{a}))\partial w_\nu(\mathbf{a}, \tau).$$

This disaggregated "multiplier" equation gives the variation of total production in each commodity line with government tax and spending policy and with private investment policy. To obtain an over-all view of the effect of such policies, however, it is more useful to look at the corresponding aggregate equation for national income. As we remarked in Lecture 3, Section 3, national income NI is given by the expression

$$(18.35) \qquad\qquad \text{NI} = \sum_{i,j=1}^{n} a_i(\delta_{ij} - \pi_{ij})p_j.$$

Thus, to obtain an expression for $\delta(\text{NI})$, we multiply the jth of the equations (18.32) by p_j and sum. This gives the equation

$$(18.36) \quad \delta(\text{NI}) = \sum_{i=1}^{n} \frac{\partial}{\partial a_i} S(\mathbf{a})\delta a_i + \delta I + \sum_{\nu=1}^{f} \frac{\partial s}{\partial w} (w_\nu(\mathbf{a}, \tau), q_\nu(\mathbf{a}))\partial w_\nu;$$

here, $s(w, q)$ denotes the total personal consumption of a family with income w and savings q, and $S = \sum_{\nu=1}^{f} s(w_\nu, q_\nu)$ denotes the total value of personal consumption expenditures; I denotes the total of government expenditure and private investment expenditure. The heuristic force of this equation emerges more plainly if, abstracting from differences in the physical consumption of national income, we make the reasonable assumption that at a given tax rate total personal consumption expenditures S depend on the production levels a_i only through national income, so that $S = S(\text{NI}, \tau)$. Then the first term on the right of (18.36) reduces on using (18.35) to

(18.37) $(\partial S/\partial(\text{NI}))(\partial(\text{NI})/\partial a_i)\delta a_i = (\partial S/\partial(\text{NI}))\delta(\text{NI})$.

Thus we have, on separating I into the sum of total government expenditures I_G plus private investment expenditure I_P,

(18.38) $\delta(\text{NI})[1 - (\partial S/\partial(\text{NI}))] = \delta I_P + \delta I_G + \sum_{\nu=1}^{f} \dfrac{\partial s}{\partial w}(w_\nu, q_\nu)\partial w_\nu.$

We may write a corresponding expression for the variation δG of government income G. Government income is a function of the production levels a_i and the expenditure and tax rate parameter τ. If we make the reasonable approximate assumption that at a given tax rate G depends on the production levels only through national income, so that $G = G(\text{NI}, \tau)$, then

(18.39) $\delta G = (\partial G/\partial(\text{NI}))\delta(\text{NI}) + \partial G.$

On the other hand, since government income is entirely derived from taxes,

(18.40) $\partial G = -\sum_{\nu=1}^{f} \partial w_\nu.$

If D denotes the government deficit, then $D = I_G - G$; thus (18.38) may be written as

(18.41) $\delta(\text{NI})[1 - (\partial S/\partial(\text{NI})) - (\partial G/\partial(\text{NI}))]$
$$= \delta I_P + \delta D - \sum_{\nu=1}^{f} (1 - \partial s/\partial w(w_\nu, q_\nu))\partial w_\nu.$$

In this equation, δD is the anticipated change in annual deficit based upon authorized government expenditures and *anticipated* tax collections as derived from the indicated shifts in tax rates and the anticipated changes in tax collections at the former tax rate arising from an anticipated change in national income.

Let $\sigma = \sigma(w, q)$ denote the saving in a single period of a family with income w and accumulated savings q, so that $\sigma = w - s(w, q)$. Then we may write (18.41) as

$$(18.42) \quad \delta(\text{NI}) = \left\{ 1 - \frac{\partial(S+G)}{\partial(\text{NI})} \right\}^{-1} \left\{ \delta I_P + \delta D - \sum_{\nu=1}^{f} \frac{\partial \sigma}{\partial w} (w_\nu, q_\nu) \partial w_\nu \right\}.$$

It is instructive to transform the final term of the right of this expression. Let

$$(18.43) \qquad\qquad w_\nu r(\nu) = - \partial w_\nu,$$

so that $r(\nu)$ denotes the equivalent tax rate on formerly untaxed income corresponding to a shift in the tax-expenditure parameter τ. Let

$$(18.44) \qquad u(\nu) = \left[\frac{\partial \sigma}{\partial w} (w_\nu, q_\nu) w_\nu \right] \bigg/ \left[\sum_{\mu=1}^{f} \frac{\partial \sigma}{\partial w} (w_\mu, q_\mu) w_\mu \right],$$

while

$$(18.45) \quad \mathcal{K} = \frac{1}{(\text{NI})} \left\{ 1 - \frac{\partial(S+G)}{\partial(\text{NI})} \right\}^{-1} \left\{ \sum_{\mu=1}^{f} \frac{\partial \sigma}{\partial w} (w_\mu, q_\mu) w_\mu \right\}.$$

Then (18.42) may be written as

$$(18.46) \quad \delta(\text{NI}) = \left(1 - \frac{\partial(S+G)}{\partial(\text{NI})} \right)^{-1} \{ \delta I_P + \delta D \} + (\text{NI}) \, \mathcal{K} \sum_{\nu=1}^{f} u(\nu) r(\nu).$$

It is clear from (18.44) that the coefficients $u(\nu)$ satisfy the equation

$$(18.47) \qquad\qquad \sum_{\nu=1}^{f} u(\nu) = 1,$$

and, again from (18.44), that the coefficients $u(\nu)$ should be positive. By (18.44), the coefficients $u(\nu)$ have the form of a product: propensity to save times income. Thus, $u(\nu)$ should be distributed through the population approximately in proportion to total savings, and therefore, by (18.47), should be approximately equal for each family to the family's fraction ψ_ν of total wealth. The coefficient $u(\nu)$ may be called the *Keynesian coefficient of tax utility*.

Next, let us attempt to estimate the coefficient $\mathcal{K}$ in (18.45). We first note that if the government incurs a deficit, it does so by issuing bonds to individuals, which bonds are treated by them as increments to income. Thus

(18.48) $\quad \sum_{\nu=1}^{f} w_\nu =$ privately appropriated portion of goods and

$$\text{services} + D.$$

On the other hand, I_G, the government-appropriated portion of goods and services, is $G + D$. Thus $\sum_{\nu=1}^{f} w_\nu + G$ is the total of all goods and services, i.e., is NI. Thus, introducing

(18.49) $$S = \sum_{\nu=1}^{f} \delta(w_\nu, q_\nu)$$

for the total of private savings (including government bonds) we may write

(18.50) $$\text{NI} = s + S + G.$$

Thus

(18.51) $\quad 1 - \partial(S + G)/\partial(\text{NI}) = \partial s/\partial(\text{NI})$

$$= \sum_{\mu=1}^{f} \frac{\partial \delta}{\partial w}(w_\mu, q_\mu) \frac{\partial w_\mu}{\partial(\text{NI})} + \sum_{\mu=1}^{f} \frac{\partial \delta}{\partial q}(w_\mu, q_\mu) \frac{\partial q_\mu}{\partial(\text{NI})}.$$

Now, individual-family income at a given tax rate depends upon the production levels. It is convenient here to use an approximation based upon the assumption that family income (at a given tax rate) depends upon the production levels only through national income, and that a rise in national income would by and large benefit all families proportionately, so that $w_\nu = c_\nu(\tau)(\text{NI})$ gives the approximate dependence of family income on national income, and thus

(18.52) $$\partial w_\nu / \partial(\text{NI}) = w_\nu / \text{NI}.$$

Then, by (18.51)

(18.53) $$\sum_{\mu=1}^{f} \frac{\partial s}{\partial w}(w_\mu, q_\mu) w_\mu = (\text{NI}) \left[\frac{\partial S}{\partial(\text{NI})} - \sum_{\mu=1}^{f} \frac{\partial \delta}{\partial q}(w_\mu, q_\mu) \frac{\partial q_\mu}{\partial(\text{NI})} \right],$$

so that using (18.45) and (18.51) we find the approximate expression

(18.54) $$\mathcal{K} = \left[\frac{\partial S}{\partial(\text{NI})} - \sum_{\mu=1}^{f} \frac{\partial \delta}{\partial q}(w_\mu, q_\mu) \frac{\partial q_\mu}{\partial(\text{NI})} \right] \bigg/ \left[\frac{\partial S}{\partial(\text{NI})} \right].$$

Since as NI increases total family savings ought to increase, by and large in the same proportion, while annual savings at a given income rate ought to decrease with total wealth, the second term in the numerator of (18.54) is positive. Thus

$$(18.55) \qquad\qquad \mathcal{K} > 1.$$

Since the effect of accumulated savings on current savings at fixed income is probably small, $\mathcal{K}$ is likely to be only slightly larger than 1.

If we write

$$(18.56) \qquad\qquad M = \partial s / \partial(\mathrm{NI})$$

and estimate $\mathcal{K} \sim 1$, then (18.46) gives the estimate

$$(18.57) \quad \delta(\mathrm{NI}) \sim M(\delta(\text{private investment}) + \delta(\text{anticipated deficit}))$$
$$+ (\mathrm{NI}) \sum_{\nu=1}^{f} u(\nu) r(\nu).$$

The coefficient M is evidently a version of the aggregate Keynes multiplier; the first two terms of the above equation show the effect on equilibrium national income of private investment programs and anticipated government deficits. The final term of the above equation shows the effect of an increase of tax rates coupled with an increase in government expenditure, assuming a zero change in anticipated annual deficit as well as a zero change in anticipated private investment.

It is instructive to make an estimate of the variation of individual-family equilibrium income with tax, expenditure, and investment policy, corresponding to the aggregate estimate (18.46). Assuming as above that at given tax rates individual-family income ought generally to depend on the levels of production only through national income, we have

$$(18.58) \qquad\qquad \delta w_\nu = \partial w_\nu + (\partial w_\nu / \partial(\mathrm{NI})) \delta(\mathrm{NI}).$$

If the tax rate and the rate of government expenditure are simultaneously increased, private investment and anticipated deficit remaining constant, then equation (18.46) tells us that a certain increase in national income is to be expected. Thus, while the first term on the right of the above equation, representing the direct effect of increased tax payments, is negative, the second term, representing the indirect effect on income of tax-expenditure generated expansion, is positive. The net effect will depend on the relative size of these two contributions, and may be positive or negative. To estimate this effect, we shall suppose, as above, that at a given tax rate a rise in national income would benefit all families in proportion to their incomes, so that (18.52) holds. Then using (18.58), (18.43), (18.52) and (18.46), putting $\delta I_P = \delta D = 0$ in (18.46), we have

$$(18.59) \qquad \delta w_\nu = w_\nu \left(\mathcal{K} \sum_{\mu=1}^{f} u(\mu) r(\mu) - r(\nu) \right).$$

Since the tax-utility coefficients $u(\mu)$ satisfy (18.47), the expression $\sum_{\mu=1}^{f} u(\mu) r(\mu)$ may be regarded as a (weighted) average of the tax rates $r(\mu)$. Thus the income of the νth family will rise or fall with τ in proportion to the original size of this income and to the difference between $\mathcal{K}$ times the average tax rate and the rate $r(\nu)$ newly imposed on the νth family. Since $\mathcal{K} > 1$, we see that imposition of a uniform tax rate r on formerly untaxed income will actually lead at the new equilibrium to a rise of all after-tax incomes by the (presumably small) fraction $\mathcal{K} - 1$; a conclusion which is, of course, decidedly Keynesian.

Even if some of the incremental rates $r(\mu)$ are positive while others are negative, (18.59) and (18.46) still apply; thus these formulae also describe the effect of *transfer payments*. Since the economic effects of a wage-rate shift are much the same as those of a corresponding system of transfer payments, (18.59) and (18.46) also describe the effect of a *shift in the real wage rate*.

Let us make a rough computation illustrating the significance of formula (18.59). Kuznets' savings and income estimates, as presented above, suggest that 25 per cent of income and 75 per cent of savings lie above the ninetieth percentile of the income spectrum. A rise in the wage rate whose ostensible effect is to transfer \$1 billion from the top 10 per cent to the lower 90 per cent of the population therefore corresponds, if its positive and negative incidence are both uniform, to a differential tax rate $r(\nu) = r$ for families above the ninetieth percentile, and to the differential rate $r(\nu) = -r/3$ for families below the ninetieth percentile. Estimating $\mathcal{K} = 1$ and estimating the coefficients $u(\nu)$ by the corresponding family fractions of total savings, it follows that $\frac{3}{4}$ of the total $u(\nu)$ lies above and

$\frac{1}{4}$ lies below the ninetieth percentile of the income spectrum. Thus we estimate

$$\mathcal{K} \sum_{\nu} u(\nu)r(\nu) = -\tfrac{1}{4}(\tfrac{1}{3}r) + \tfrac{3}{4}r = \tfrac{8}{12}r = \tfrac{2}{3}r.$$

For families above the ninetieth percentile then,

$$\mathcal{K} \sum_{\nu} u(\nu)r(\nu) = \tfrac{2}{3}r - r = -\tfrac{1}{3}r;$$

for families below the ninetieth percentile

$$\mathcal{K} \sum_{\nu} u(\nu)r(\nu) = \frac{2}{3}r - \left(-\frac{r}{3}\right) = r.$$

This means that the rise in national income occasioned by the wage rise can be expected to cut losses in the upper 10 per cent of the income spectrum by something more than $\frac{2}{3}$, to something less than \$$\frac{1}{3}$ billion, and to raise benefits in the lower 90 per cent of the income spectrum by a factor of 3, to a total of \$3 billion; national income then rising by \$$2\frac{2}{3}$ billion, plus the increase in government expenditures, which should be in the rough proportion to \$$2\frac{2}{3}$ billion as government expenditures to NI, roughly $\frac{1}{5}$ or \$$\frac{1}{2}$ billion. Thus the estimated net increase in national income is \$$3\frac{1}{6}$ billion, and the relevant "multiplier" for this effect is 3.2.

The common opinion among businessmen that firms can collectively benefit from opposition to a general wage rise is hence an illusion. Money "saved" in this way is merely retained to be lost in the next recession; or, at any rate, to dissipate itself silently by retarding the rate of economic growth.

6. The Keynes Point and the Business Cycle

In the present lecture we have, of course, been concerned with the location of the Keynes equilibrium point, and not with the dynamic oscillation of the economy about the Keynes point. Since the distinction between these two aspects of Keynesian theory is important for an understanding of the long-term necessities of economic policy, we shall make some additional comments emphasizing this distinction. As equation (8.1) and its derivation from cycle theory in Lecture 7 shows, the production levels at the Keynesian equilibrium are also the long-term averages of dynamically varying production levels; the business cycle is a dynamic mechanism adjusting production to this average level.   A truly and purely contracyclical policy will reduce the amplitude of the dynamic oscillations, but, almost by definition, leave the Keynes point unshifted (we have examined a mathematical model of such a policy in Lecture 10). A hypothetical ideal contracyclical policy might eliminate the cycle altogether, stabilizing production at the Keynes-point level.   Now, this level of production may be satisfactory or unsatisfactory, depending upon, say, the level of unemployment to which it corresponds.   If the Keynes-point production levels are too low, or, more realistically, if the secular rise of the Keynes-point is too slow, the over-all result, which will emerge as the secular tendency of a succession of cycles, will be a "sluggish" or "disappointing" period of growth.   Contracyclical policy may relieve the acute discomfort of a sharp recession by shoring up the dynamic low point, but will not directly effect this more "secular" phenomenon.   The problem of shifting the Keynes-point upward is then separate from that of stabilizing the production level.   Our analysis shows that to shift the Keynes equilibrium, it is necessary that either

(1) the volume of investment increase substantially and for long periods; or

(2) long periods of substantial government deficits occur; or

(3) the tax rate be substantially increased; or

(4) the level of autonomous personal spending rise secularly (perhaps through the division of estates attendant on the proliferation of wealthy families); or

(5) the real wage rate be advanced with sufficient rapidity.

7. The General Significance of Keynesian Economics from the Point of View of Consumption

Equation (18.20) is merely another form of our central tautology: total production (of each commodity), minus the amount consumed industrially, must be equal to the sum of government consumption, net increase in stock (including the difference between exports and imports), i.e., investment in equipment and inventories, intended and unintended, and individual consumption.   (This statement is a tautology in the sense that it does not depend on any very detailed assumptions about the economy. We can, if we like, call it a "conservation law.") The difference between the classical and the Keynesian economics is fundamentally a difference in attitude to the various terms in the identity (18.20). Classical economics considers that there is no obstacle to high rates I_j of increase of the material inventories (of course, services cannot be stored) and, indeed, tends to regard the increase of these inventories ("thrift"; "economic progress") as a principal end of the economic process. The Keynesian point of view begins with the theoretical-empirical fact which was the starting point for our cycle models: when (depending upon the state of the remainder of the economy) the possessor of inventory finds this inventory to be too large, he may aim to reduce it (in order to attain a more "liquid" economic position); this circumstance, general for the whole economy, makes the unrestricted increase of inventory impossible. Classical economics regards the activity levels a_i in (18.20) as given (by the maximum potentialities of the economy, i.e., by a restriction like $\Sigma_i a_i\phi_{ij} \leq b_j$, b_j being the total social inventory of the commodity C_j); regards the consumption functions s as given; and regards (18.20) as *determining the residue terms* I_j. The Keynesian view, however, is that s is given, but that I_j is determined in a largely autonomous way by legislative action and by the attempt of each producer to adjust inventory and capital levels to the demands of all the others, so that (18.20) is to be *regarded as determining the activity levels* a_j. In terms of the cycle model of Lectures 6 and 7 we may say that classical economics is descriptive only of the *scarcity line*, while Keynesian economics is concerned with the other regions of the production-inventory diagram as well. From this basic difference spring the different policy recommendations of the classicists and the Keynesians. According to the classicists, the sum I_j is restricted by the restrictions $\Sigma_i a_i\phi_{ij} \leq b_j$ on the activity levels a_i, so that government spending must lead to a corresponding reduction in I_j; according to the Keynesians, a_i is determined by I_j and is an increasing function of I_j; thus an increase in government spending may *increase I_j and a_i both*. According to the classicists, $S_j + I_j$ is fixed; thus an increase of S_j (coming, say, from a wage increase) must decrease the sum $S_j + I_j$; according to the Keynesians, a wage increase may increase I_j by increasing S_j. We have summarized this difference in Lecture 8 by calling classical economics, scarcity economics ("consumption adjusts to production"); and Keynesian economics, affluence economics ("production adjusts to consumption").

A general conclusion from the foregoing points is worth emphasizing. That surplus is production net of consumption, all must agree: whatever is produced and not consumed, remains somewhere in the economy. Classical economics assumes that the implied growth of stocks is always desired: "whoever saves, spends at the same time; what he does not use for consumption he intends to use for investment." This basic opinion describes a situation of scarcity, in accord with the basic principle of classical economics: *"economics deals with the allocation of scarce resources."* Quite differently, in considering the growth of stocks implied by their production in the absence of consumption, Keynesian economics emphasizes that this growth of stocks may be desired or undesired (as in our cycle-theory models, cf. Lectures 6–10, 11, and 12). Stock increase, it tells us, will be desired only if increased stock advances other economic ends (e.g. optimal sales). If stocks exceed optimal size, a manufacturer will prefer not to increase his stocks, but to decrease his stocks, thereby *increasing the debt which others owe him* (liquidity preference); he finds debt a safer form than stock in which to hold his assets, since the exchangeability of assets held as debt is guaranteed, under severe economic penalties, by the debtor. Keynesian economics would then assert that "whoever saves, spends only to the extent that he accepts the implied growth of stock as more desirable than an equivalent amount of credit; what he does not use for consumption or investment, he tries to liquidate." At the cost of a slight exaggeration we may then counterpose to the basic principle of classical economics a corresponding capsule formulation of Keynesian economics: *"economics deals with the manner in which the removal of certain obstacles to production can lead to the unlimited growth of income and capital."*

It has often been remarked by intellectual historians that the appearance of one or another theoretical view signaled some basic change in underlying material conditions. In this sense we may venture to assert that the rise of the Keynesian theories signals the historical maturity of the world economy; that is, the capacity of the economy to produce general plenty. In 19th century conditions, the weakness of the productive machine meant that the sum $S_j + I_j$ on the right of equation (18.20) was severely limited; held

I_j at a level generally below the level at which it would begin to exert continued downward pressure on activity; and made the existence of an economic upper limit on I_j appear visionary, for which reasons such strictures as those of Malthus were almost completely forgotten. Now, however, the economic process has run up against the bounds for I_j. Pressure to hold up the activity levels a_i, coming from the insupportable social pressures generated at high levels of unemployment, has consequently made maintenance of the levels I_j into a matter of grave public concern; the consumption levels S_j have also been able to rise. The tautology (18.20), regarded in the manner of Keynes, thus reveals a great deal about the most salient features of modern American society.

Index